SUMMON THE TIGER

Wendy Sura Thomson

FOR KEVIN: who inspired me; and

FOR CHRIS; who always has my back

TABLE OF CONTENTS

ACKNOWLEDGMENTS

I want to thank the people that motivated, helped and cheered me on throughout this little project: to my son Kevin, for suggesting it in the first place; to my son Chris, who says he can't wait to buy it; to Ron Cunningham, Lorri Biamonte and Alvina Vaughan for their strong encouragement and kind words; and to my BFF, Dana Layman, who spent untold hours editing. I can only hope that this final version lives up to your expectations.

PROLOGUE

I was born in the Year of the Tiger. While I have never been comfortable going on the offense, I have so frequently been called fearless that I accept that attribute as true. When faced with conflict I prefer to walk away, but when I can't – when I must defend - I can and will. It is then that I summon the tiger.

WALK WITH ME A WAYS

The first thing I remember was the television set. It was a rectangular blond wood box, as tall as I was but maybe only a couple of feet or so wide. The tube-powered screen bulged out grey in the top center. It was a small screen, only maybe 8 or 10 inches wide. There were a couple of dark, round knobs underneath the screen. The set was in our living room. My first memory was standing before it, holding something – probably my ever-present Susie doll. The room seemed dim, and I was watching Queen Elizabeth proceed down the aisle of Westminster Abbey to very big and important music. I only saw her back, and I only remember her royal cape. It was long and wide, trimmed in what I learned later was ermine. It seemed to almost reach from pew to pew. Just a snippet of a memory, but I was totally transfixed. That was June 3, 1953… I was 2 and a half.

I think at that time we were living in a small house on Kirkshire, down the street from my aunt and uncle. We lived in four houses by the time I went to kindergarten, so it's a bit difficult to remember which house was which. We had a part-time maid-nanny, Beulah. I remember her, too. I think we shared her with my aunt and uncle. She was a big, warm woman with a broad smile and lots of hugs in her. She was very kind to me. She wasn't with us very long – only as long as we lived in that house. I also remember there was a family across the street that was moving out of state – California, I think. She was a nice lady too. She had children with whom I sometimes played. I think my mother was a little jealous of that family – California seemed much more glamorous than Michigan.

1

That house was on a paved street. I seem to remember that our house was painted a dark color. It was on the north side of the street. I knew that we had to turn left just past the big city water tower, and then turn right at the first street. Our house was on the right, about half way down the block. There were neat rows of little bungalows on either side of the straight street, with saplings standing in for trees. My older brother was riding on that street when he fell off his tricycle and hit his head hard on a curb. My father had our one-and-only car and was at work, so we borrowed a car and a driver and headed to the hospital, my mother in the passenger seat holding my by-now-vomiting brother. I mostly remember the tension in that car. There was something really wrong – my brother was unconscious. We had to leave him at the hospital. I was later told that he had been scheduled for surgery to relieve the pressure build-up in his brain. He awoke in the nick of time. I am not totally sure he ever fully recovered. Either that, or he was burdened by his difficult birth. He was two months premature, weighing only a couple of pounds. As a result, he was slight and frail, with gorgeous pale sea-green eyes, fringed in dark lashes, that were horribly, horribly near-sighted. I was told that was because of the incubator he was in for weeks and weeks.

I turned three in that house. My mother threw a 3-year-old birthday party for me. I remember that party. My mother's post-war "everybody's-having-babies" friends brought their daughters. There must have been a half-dozen or so. I remember Kit being there. Kit was six months older than me, and at 3, someone 3-1/2 was someone to respect. I seem to remember the moms more than the girls, probably because I saw the mothers over the years, even though their children ended up in different school districts. Not Kit. Kit and I ended up in the same district in opposing high schools. I was really happy that day, until I heard my mother say she would never do that again. She seemed irritated. That was my first and only birthday party. Someone asked me why it was my one and only... I guess my mother would be the only one able to answer that. Was it too much work? To stressful? Who knows. As a child, I knew only that my mother kept her word – she never threw me a birthday party again.

I turned four in a different house. I remember that house, too. It was a small contemporary house with a vaulted ceiling, on a dirt road named Shallowbrook. The kitchen cabinets didn't go all the way up to the ceiling – they just sort of stopped, making a room divider between the galley kitchen and the living room. There was a sunroom off the back that my dad built. I remember that we had a problem with mice. We had a very big yard, and my swing set was off to the side. One day I was swinging, watching my shirtless father mow the lawn. I got stung by a bee and must have screamed, because I remember my father racing over to me.

Out back, on the other side of the property line, was a large stand of trees. My mother said there was a creek back there, and a Fruehauf estate. I never ventured into the woods – those trees were very big, and it was dark and foreboding in their shadows. My sister was born when we lived in that house.

This house had a one-car garage, but I can't remember the car ever being in it. My brother got into our Studebaker one day and somehow managed to disengage the brake, or clutch, or whatever was keeping the car from rolling into the garage door. That was memorable – the car rolled into that new garage door, damaging it. There was quite a bit of yelling going on after the fact.

Cathy Wild lived next door. We were the same age, and I considered her my very best friend. I can't remember whether her family moved first or we did: her father was a salesman and landed the pencil account at Ford Motor Company. They left for the footlights, in a manner of speaking, joining High Society. She ended up going to Vassar or Wellesley or somewhere equally prestigious after attending Kingswood, the most prestigious local private school for Young Ladies. Last I read about the family they were hosting President Johnson at some event. There was apparently a lot of money to be made in pencils back in the day.

These houses were in a new subdivision, with no telephone service. My father made the subdivision entrance signs – Devon Hills, cut out of some sort of wood in old English script and painted white, mounted on black backboards. Those signs were there for decades. My dad was very popular with the neighbors because he had an important position with the City of Detroit. He had been appointed to sit on the commission that was charged with coming up with an evacuation plan in the event the city was bombed by Russia. This was during prime Cold War times. The telephone company ran a line to our house so the City could contact my dad if need be – thanks to that, the subdivision had telephones before anyone else around. Later, my father revealed that the commission had concluded that it would be impossible to evacuate everybody living south of Eight Mile Road... the plan was to barricade them in and let them die in place. My father told us that everyone would be blind from the nuclear blast, even with our eyes closed, and we would all die anyway. From that, I knew those drills where we would climb under our wooden school desks were meaningless.

My grandparents came up from Grosse Ile for Easter that year – actually Hickory Island, off the tip of Grosse Ile. I have pictures of my brother and me standing in front of my grandfather's big sedan. It was two-tone, a late model, and had little fake air intake holes on each side. Four of them. Four meant it was a premium car, I was told. It was sometime between Christmas 1951 and then that I had my right leg amputated at the knee – I know that because in a picture the inverted leather "Y" over my right knee – part of my artificial leg - is quite visible. I think that leg must have been too short, because in that picture I am standing lop-sided.

I was born with congenital abnormalities… I was missing both the ulna and the tibia on my right side. My radius and fibula were bowed inward, and my right hand's middle and index finger were webbed together, the index finger a mere stub. I have no right thumb and my wrist is noticeably clubbed. That arm from the elbow down is quite unattractive and is now a good nine inches shorter than my left. I vaguely remember being told that for a time I was in a leg brace to try and straighten and support my right leg, but I do not remember. I was told that at two months old my mother shipped me off to my grandmother in Cleveland while she investigated facilities that took in disabled children. I don't know how long I was with my grandmother, but after visiting several institutions my mother decided that perhaps I didn't need to be shuttled off to one of them. She saw severely disabled children and decided maybe I wasn't so bad after all. That fact haunted me – I would not be surprised if it still does. My mother didn't want me. I was so far from perfect.

I remember being in the hospital for that operation – mainly I remember having a bed near a window and watching my Aunt Jean walk up the sidewalk with my mother. My aunt was carrying the biggest, most beautiful curly-red-haired doll ever – nearly as big as I was. The doll was clothed in a turquoise dress and Mary Jane shoes. I was so excited! My mother told me later that the nurses loved me – I always had a smile on my face for them. They brought me a goldfish in a bowl, and red roses for my table. My mother told me the nurses cried for me. I don't remember much more than that, except that I was not happy when they moved me away from the window.

My first artificial leg was made of willow and it strapped around my waist with a wide leather belt. Because of that, my mother tried to find dresses that would hang from my shoulders. I grew so fast that the artificial legs were very quickly too short. I would end up with different sized shoes, so I ended up nearly always wearing the same style - navy blue oxfords with navy and white laces. I came to hate them. I have scoliosis now because of those improperly-sized legs. I understand nowadays children have adjustable "shins" and visit the prosthetics shop frequently to make sure the leg length accommodates growth spurts. Not back in the day... not back then.

I never liked going there – to those prosthetics shops. They were dirty and small and bare-bones utilitarian. I do remember having a walker that was long gone by the time that picture was taken in the spring of 1954. It was aluminum and the top came up chest-high. It wrapped around me and had wheels. I remember walking with it wearing pastel corduroy overalls with a white blouse with short, gathered sleeves. I apparently fell at pretty much every tarred concrete expansion joint on the sidewalk, falling and hitting my forehead. I almost always had bumps on the corners of my forehead from that. My mother used to scream crossly at me for falling so frequently.

It was about then that my dad's assistant Karen got married. My father gave her away, and I got to be the flower girl. I was thrilled because the dress I wore was so very pretty. My mother never dressed me in "girly" clothes: everything – absolutely everything – I owned was some sort of tailored blue. I was normally dressed in blue jean jackets and sailor hats. Absolutely no lace on anything except the gorgeous baby clothes my grandmother bought at Moseley's. No big ribbons tied in back, no shiny fabric, no lace-trimmed anklets. No pink. Then came the wedding – a beautiful wedding in the equally beautiful Shrine of the Little Flower. The dress I wore was an Alice in Wonderland dress. It was powder blue organza with a full skirt and puffy petticoat, and it had a white organza pinafore over it. I had a big picture hat that was powder blue and woven so you could kind of see through it, with ribbons trailing down my back, white lace-trimmed anklets and white patent leather Mary Jane shoes. I never felt so pretty. I can still see Karen's face, smiling in her beautiful lacy wedding gown, throwing the bouquet over her shoulder.

I started kindergarten in 1955. We moved to house #4 by then... a small ranch on Brooklawn that backed up to the Pembroke Elementary School playground. I could hop the fence to play on the equipment and get to school much more easily than having to walk down to the street corner, turn left, and walk another block to the school entrance. This house had a carport with plywood doors on storage cabinets. The yard was certainly much smaller than the prior house. However, it did have the schoolyard right there, the ice cream man drove by the house, and in the summer the school district had a little summer craft/activity program a couple of blocks away that I attended. I think I liked the sense of community and activity better than living out in exurbia. I really liked being able to walk down to the summer day program – that was fun.

Even though I was not yet five, my brother had been telling me what he had been learning in school. I started kindergarten, only four, already reading. One of the first books I received was about a little disabled girl who needed leg braces. She wanted to be a ballerina so very desperately. She would practice and practice – first position, second position, third position, fourth position, plié... I wanted so much to be her. She got stronger and did end up being a ballerina. I memorized those positions and practiced them and practiced them... I don't think I ever really adjusted to my amputation until I was thirteen. It was then I had my first dream where I saw myself with my artificial leg. Up until that time I was just like everyone else in my dreams. I so remember waking up at thirteen, remembering that dream, and automatically thinking that I must have finally gotten to the point of accepting myself.

~

It didn't take the kindergarten teacher long to figure out I could already read, so she used to sit me atop the piano bench and have me read to the other children when she needed a little time to tend to something else. We didn't have para-professionals or parent volunteers back then. While I ended up generally loving school, my first day was positively terrifying. I was late because my mother and I walked down the block and around the corner. The classroom was by far the biggest room I had ever seen. The class had already started, and everyone was on the far side of the room. They seemed so far away – they looked small to me. The floor was freshly waxed and polished, and it was so, so shiny. My mother didn't walk me over to the teacher, she kind of shooed me across the room. There I was, walking towards total strangers, all alone in between the class and my mother, in my brand-new leather-soled navy-blue oxfords, on that shiny, slippery floor. Half way across the room I slipped and fell. Not a very auspicious entrance.

In kindergarten, I remember getting into a heated argument with Billy Thompson. You see, I was very insistent that he was spelling his last name wrong – as insistent as he was that I was the one confused. I think we were both near tears, so very proud that we knew how to spell our respective names and so shaken that someone was telling us we were wrong. I remember someone separating us and telling us were both right… at the time I don't think either of us believed that.

I have other memories of kindergarten. My teacher was Mrs. Wirey – she appeared old to me, but she seemed to simply accept me without qualification. I loved music time – we played little instruments like wood blocks and cymbals and sang songs. And the older children were very kind to me – they would lift me up and place me on the top of the merry-go-round. I remember sitting in the center of the merry-go-round while the older kids spun around and around. I would sit up there in the middle and sing my heart out. The merry-go-round was close to my backyard... I think it was the closest piece of playground equipment. The fence between the schoolyard and the house was also a sort of retaining wall: the house yard was higher by some distance – perhaps two feet or so. My feet were so small that they slipped right into the chain links, so climbing was a breeze. That was my very-much-preferred way to get to and from school.

I remember more about the summer between kindergarten and first grade. That was the summer that my brother got mad at me and smashed all my dollhouse furniture on the floor of the carport. That was the summer I went down to the craft camp and made beaded bracelets and loop-woven potholders. The summer I chased after the ice cream truck. My mother didn't have a nickel, so she gave me a quarter instead. I bought five ice creams because I didn't understand the concept of change. By the time I got home I was a melted ice cream mess – I wasn't a very good chaser and I wasn't a good carrier, either. I was very sad, both because my mother was mad at me, and I didn't even get much of any ice cream.

Betty Lippard lived next door. She was my mother's friend and was over for coffee after the men went off to work. I think I remember my mother's friends better than I remember mine: Fran Baird, Doris Patee, Bonnie Graham, Betty White, Ruth Cotter, Marge Goodwin, Marnie Bergman. There were others in that group that I can see but whose names escape me in the fog of time. The beautiful redhead that got multiple sclerosis – the one that was a perfect size so that nothing needed to be tailored. The other redhead with lots of freckles, with whom we went to the

Detroit Historical Museum. Most of these women met after the War, when they all bought starter houses on the same street and started families (that was our house #1). These married couples also started partying together. Back then, parents would leave their sleeping babies and toddlers at home and gather at someone's house to drink and smoke, all house doors up and down the block unlocked. Every once in a while, an appointed mother would make the rounds of the various houses, checking in on the sleeping babes. All but Ruth and Marnie. Ruth was my mother's childhood friend – Ruth didn't drink and didn't live on the same street. My dear Auntie Rudy was very saintly - I never heard a cross word from her. And my Aunt Marnie was my mother's college friend. She was a fantastic woman – she was my godmother - and she was very wise and sparkly. Marnie and her husband Ed never had children.

My father had a dental office in Royal Oak when I was little. It was a small brick building with room for only one practitioner. Across the street, set back and to the right, was a large Robert Hall men's clothing store. It seems to me that my dad's office was in a triangle made from bisecting streets. It's long gone now, having been claimed by eminent domain for the expressway and the widening of Woodward. I clearly remember my father, wearing his military brush cut until after I left for college, putting on his tie to go to work. I liked to watch him tie his tie… he's the one that taught me the difference between a Windsor knot and an ordinary, every-day knot. After his breakfast, that usually consisted of eggs, sliced peaches, toast and coffee, he would put on his glengarry and go off to work in his MG TD convertible.

I mention "his" breakfast because it was never "our" breakfast. Many foods were reserved for the adults… eggs, peaches and bacon were reserved for my father – children got cold cereal with milk, toast and orange juice laced with cod liver oil. My father would occasionally give us a small piece of bacon – such a treat! Food was a big issue in our house, and looking back, I cannot understand why. It's not as if my mother had suffered as a child during the Depression: her father was as attorney, and the worst that happened to that family was that they put the Packard in the garage and drove a Chevrolet to downplay their relative wealth. My mother had a chinchilla hat and matching coat at age five. It was my father, if anyone, that should have been food-frugal. Being immigrants, his family scratched out an existence. They raised their own chickens, grew their own vegetables... built their own house. Somewhere along the way my mother's view became warped. We were not allowed to open the refrigerator. We were not allowed more than one juice-sized glass of milk per meal. We rarely had desserts, rarely had fresh fruit besides apples, rarely had fresh vegetables. Sunday dinner was either a roast chicken, a beef roast, or spaghetti. My portion of the chicken was a wing. My mother murdered fish, so I hated it. Occasionally she made liver and onions – the only other main dishes I remember besides those were hamburger "guck," which was hamburger, onions and a can of cream of mushroom soup, and the ever-present can of tuna/can of peas/can of cream of mushroom soup combination. We must have gone through many cans of cream of mushroom soup. I learned later that my mother was skimming food money and stashing it on the top shelf over the sink. By the time I was in high school she had a wad of money - $700 or so.

We were not allowed to open the refrigerator, so of course we would sneak down and raid it. My brother came up with the Mouse Club. He would crawl into my room on his hands and knees "eeking". That was the signal. He had very, very strict rules. We could only crawl on our hands and knees. We could only use the word "eek". He would bring a ruler and measure exactly where everything in the refrigerator was placed, making sure that he would put back whatever was eaten in the Very. Same. Exact.

Location. As if my mother wouldn't realize that the hotdogs were half gone. He had a voracious appetite. When food was passed around the table we got just one shot. The serving dishes ended with him – both in terms of the seating order and in terms of nothing left. He would heap his plate inches high, finishing off absolutely everything.

My father didn't graduate from dental school until after I was born. He was drafted at the tender age of 19 while a physics major at Wayne State. When he came back from the War he transferred right into University of Detroit School of Dentistry and graduated with his D.D.S. Probably the only person to have as his one and only degree a Doctorate. I was instrumental in his attaining that degree – his dissertation was on the oral manifestations of pregnancy.

My father never liked dentistry - he made a pragmatic decision. He was a brilliant engineer... should have been an engineer. He had been invited to attend the Edison Institute while in high school, however my grandfather would not let him go. My grandfather said that they couldn't afford the suits that would need to be bought – my dad's station in life was not to dine with Henry Ford every Friday night. My father regretted that until the day he died.

I am not sure why we moved so frequently when I was very young, but house #5 was a winner... house #5 was the home I lived in the longest as a child. It was on a lake, it was an old ramshackle cottage when we bought it, and it was our home for seven years. I remember our phone number and address still. We moved during the last week of school – the last week of my kindergarten. My first day of school at Walnut Lake Elementary was the very day the students were throwing a going-away party for the kindergarten teacher. This was a very, very bad day to transfer into a new school... I crashed the party and was made to feel it. I was very glad that I only needed to endure one week of extreme outsider-ness.

My father promptly started remodeling that old cottage on Putnam - 5430 Putnam. Phone Mayfair 6-5343. No area codes back then: just a name, like Mayfair or Midwest, and then five numbers. My dad added space between the house and the street... an entrance, a bathroom and a garage. The property was only 40 feet wide, and even smaller because the Cochran's house encroached on the south side. There was only room for a narrow bed of flowers and a sidewalk between the house and the Cochran's stone retaining wall, and no space whatsoever on the north side. We had a small courtyard with a privacy fence on the north side. There was a gate facing the street, and the "front door" was accessed from the courtyard. I can't remember many people using it, though. The courtyard was concrete with small areas for plants in front of the privacy fence. My dad laid 2x4s in a diamond pattern, intending to leave the wood for both decorative and expansion purposes. The concrete truck came and poured the entire load on an over-90° day. My dad was very concerned that the concrete would set in that heat before it could be spread around, so all of us, except my younger sister, were working on it. I had a 2x4 and was screeding the concrete: laying my 2x4 over the 2x4 grid and jiggling it back and forth in front of a pile of concrete to pull the concrete flat. I liked doing that.

One Fourth of July my father was installing a large plate glass picture window overlooking the lake. A breeze caught it, it came crashing down, and it gashed his arm badly. I remember him suturing himself up, right there in the living room. He was so matter-of-fact about it that I wasn't even frightened or horrified. He was like that... no gnashing of teeth, no high drama. Just taking care of business.

My sister and I shared a bedroom across the hall from my parent's room. My brother's room was next to my parent's room. There was a short hall leading to the three bedrooms, to the left and around the corner from the steep, narrow wooden staircase. The bathroom was at the top of the stairs to the right. It had old metal tiles, not ceramic. One summer night lightning struck in that bathroom and was bouncing back and forth across the room, tile to tile. My mother was up and nearly wandered into it... my father snatched her arm before she electrocuted herself. The next day we could see the little black burn marks where the lightning bounced back and forth.

The room I shared with my sister was larger than my brother's. It had built-in bookcases and shelves on one wall which were painted white. I think we didn't have much more than a couple of twin beds in that room, maybe a small dresser, and one of those 3'x3' closets. My mother decorated the room in black and white: white walls with black curtains on the wall behind the beds, pulled back on either side. There was a hole in the wall where the doorknob crashed into it too many times. My parent's room was very much off limits. I remember it smelled differently than any other room. My parents had a long dresser that matched the headboard. Their furniture was very angular: the headboard was a simple 1.5" deep slab of wood. The dresser was equally unadorned. It all originally had a blond finish, but my mother redid everything in a mid-tone stain. I don't know what she used as a finish, but everything turned out really, really shiny. My brother's room was dark... his walls were always painted dark charcoal or black.

The staircase originated in the living room, which faced the lake. It had a closet underneath it – and at the back of the closet was a small door that enclosed a second space underneath the bottom two or three stairs. I remember hiding in there, where my mother could never find me.

The living room had plate glass windows across the entire room. The furniture in there was mid-century modern – low and sleek. We had a circular white Formica Knoll pedestal dining table, the pedestal being a graceful swoop of line. We had one of those famous mid-century Eames plywood chairs, back separated from the seat, distorted ovals. That was the most uncomfortable chair ever – so very slippery it was impossible to sit still without sort of sliding down into a slump. We had a very low-slung circular walnut coffee table with a travertine top. The living/dining room stretched the width of the house, and between it and the street were a galley kitchen, a narrow black slate-floored hallway, and a small study. There was a hallway behind that trio of spaces, leading to the front door, the garage door, and the new half bath. That front door.... oh, my, that front door. My mother got the idea that it should make a Statement, so she made a big X with masking tape corner to corner and painted the resulting triangles white, turquoise and orange – Harlequin-style. It reminded me of a clown suit. My mother papered the study in a dark tortoise-shell wallpaper. The study couldn't have been much larger than 8-foot square. I remember being in there watching Packers football games with my father, he in his wood-backed pedestal black leather chair with ottoman.

The black slate hallway held an antique chest that had on it a carved Koran holder supporting an antique, padded orange-velvet-bound thick tome of some sort. There also was a 5' tall suit of armor standing next to it. The kitchen was quite small and held an old metal-edged table with tubular metal legs that was pushed up against a wall. My toddler sister would crawl under that table and eat dog food. My sister – a little flame-headed roly-poly child with a temper to match. My mother called her uncontrollable, pretty much from the day she was born. Her hair was very, very red and very, very curly; but around her face it was lighter - brassy-gold light-up-the-sky red. My father called her Carrot Top. All three of us children were freckled, to varying degrees: my sister the most, then me, then my brother. We did not resemble one another at all, either in coloring or bone structure. We knew for sure my brother resembled people in my mother's family, I was the spitting image of my paternal grandmother... but my sister? She looked so different that we had convinced her she actually was an alien from Uranus. Thanks to connections made through genealogy, we now know that she very much favors our great-grandmother – my father's paternal grandmother, Elizabeth Sharp.

My parents each had half of a two-car garage. My father's side contained metal storage cabinets, boxes and boxes of dentist give-away Crest toothpaste stacked on the floor, and a disassembled Czechoslovakian Arrow. It was vintage 1930's, there were only two in the entire United States, and it looked like an old Duesenberg. It was cream-colored, had widely exaggerated, flared fenders, a long prow and running boards. My mother always yelled at him to get rid of it – I don't know why, because she had her own, un-encroached side. Anyway, he did sell it, unfinished. And about that toothpaste: we were still grabbing tubes out of that box when I went to college.

My dad kept his work-related papers in those metal cabinets. I was bored one day and went out to see what was in there. I found a box of official-looking blank forms that looked very interesting. I grabbed a handful and "filled them out." What I didn't know was that they were sequentially numbered DEA forms for the narcotics my father was authorized to prescribe, of which he was required to submit a carbon copy of every completed prescription to the government for control purposes. He had a devil of a time explaining exactly why his young daughter had access to them.

The house had a lower level under part of the house that faced the lake. Metal posts supported the living room above, forming a covered porch. We played in that lower level. We had a wicker basket full of slips and other old finery of my mother's, and my sister and I used to play dress-up with them. There was one dress my mother never let us have: it was an ankle-length dancing dress with a full crinoline petticoat. It had huge pink flowers printed on the fabric – my mother said they were cabbage roses. I thought it was beautiful. It was the only feminine-fancy dress my mother had – she had thrown away her wedding dress. She didn't like it, she said. She had to buy it in a rush during the War, when not much was available. I only saw it in a picture.

We used to put on plays and such in that lower area. We would hang a sheet from the ceiling and shine a light from the back, behind the "operating table." We performed "operations" on each other using my father's tools: a hand drill, a hammer, a screw driver… the "audience" only saw the silhouette through the hung sheet. We thought it very cool that we would place the drill behind the "patient" and have it look as if we were operating.

The lower level had a green linoleum floor, and over in the corner there was an unfinished access to an area that was probably a half-basement. It was always wet in there.

There was a steep hill down to the lake that my father terraced with railroad ties. Down the north side he built stairs from the ties, hugging the weeping willow trees. We had a small yard and a smaller-still patch of sand next to the dock. My father built a raft from four 55-gallon drums lashed under a wooden platform he built over them, with a wooden ladder. The raft was anchored at the drop-off, with maybe five feet of water shore-side and nothing but black water on the other. I lived in the water all summer long –

it was difficult to pull me out to even eat lunch. My dad called me an otter. Between our house and the neighborhood beach and clubhouse (for those not lucky enough to have their own waterfront) were the Hoffmans, the Smiths and the Thomases. Then there was an empty lot, then the beach and clubhouse. I learned to swim at the Thomases. They had a T-shaped dock, and one day I just jumped in and swam to shore. I was very proud of myself. I clambered back up on the dock and looked back into the water and saw a water snake pop its head up where I had been only minutes before.

I was unsupervised in the water – my mother told me she would look out the window to check on me, but that couldn't have been very often. I would often swim down to the clubhouse beach or swim under the raft playing hide-and-go-seek with either my brother or some of the children that lived on our street. She never noticed I wasn't in view, or if she did, she didn't say anything.

The railroad ties became home to yellow jackets, and my father would cover every inch of himself in heavy clothing and a welding helmet and take a blowtorch to them every year. He coated the ties every couple of years with creosote, which turned hot in the sun. I remember one day a storm brewed very suddenly when my brother, sister and I were down by the dock. The wind was howling – my father yelled to us to stay put, and he ran down and brought us up in his arms, one by one. He was concerned that one of the willow trees might crack and fall on one of us. There was some precedent for that: old Mr. Cochran, who my mother said was an alcoholic, had a tree fall on the flat part of his yard, by the water. We pretended it was a horse, and we sat astride it "riding". We "rode" until Mr. Cochran, face flushed startling crimson red, came flying down, yelling with arms flailing, to shoo us off. He didn't like children very much.

We lived on the east side of the lake, and when the wind blew hard all sorts of leaves and seaweed and yuck ended up on our little beach. We had to take rakes and bring the stinky mess up on shore to dry and subsequently throw away once or twice a year. We hated that. On top of that, the sand became home to sand fleas left by the many dogs that wandered loose in the neighborhood. All the dogs wandered, I think – ours included. My father taught our dachshund mix Madchen to walk to the empty lot about four doors down and across the street to relieve herself. We never had dog mess to clean up in the yard. My copper-headed, freckle-faced toddler sister's legs were quite flea-bitten, looking as if she had a rash or the measles or some other disease. Once when we were in the grocery store she was sitting in the grocery cart, her chubby legs protruding in all their inflamed glory. A concerned woman asked her what was wrong with her, to which she loudly proclaimed, "I have fleas!" I thought my mother was going to die right there on the spot.

There were lots of children in the neighborhood close to our ages. Starting from the empty lot next to the neighborhood beach, there were three Thomas children, two girls and a boy. The Smiths were elderly, the Hoffmans had a boy and a girl, both in high school, then my brother, sister and me. The Cochrans were elderly, but next to them were the Speichers, with two boys and a girl, then the Croreys, two boys and a girl. The mob of us would gather in front of the Speicher and Crorey houses and play Red Rover until the sun went down. We played Cowboys and Indians, we played Hide and Seek, we played Mother May I… we played and played. We also climbed trees and built sand castles and took our sleds and toboggans over to the Croreys in the winter. Their hill wasn't terraced, and we would start up by the side of the house and fly down the hill, soaring onto the iced-over lake. Mr. Crorey built a mogul near the edge of the lake, and the older kids launched off it to see who could go the furthest. We took our snow shovels and made rinks so we could ice skate. That was a dicey proposition, though – if the lake froze while there was any wind the surface of the ice was rippled. Ditto if the snow partially melted and refroze. I had white figure skates with red plaid lining. I tried to skate – I really did. However, I can only put weight on my artificial leg when it's in a full upright position. I could only shuffle along a little bit, and if – correction: *when* - I fell, I had to pull myself to the edge of the rink to push myself up. Ice was tricky for me.

I may not have been able to skate, but I certainly loved my sled. It had wooden slats over red metal blades. I would sled and sled over at the Croreys. Normally that was uneventful, except for the time Cindy Thomas was walking back up the hill and stepped too close to my path as I was heading down. I yanked on the steering handles to miss her and ended up smashing my coccyx into a pipe that was sticking out of the ground. I think I might have cracked my bone – I absolutely could not move. The kids got me back up on the sled and pulled me back to my house.

Running and skating were not easy for me, but swimming and hopping certainly were. The neighborhood beach held a Fourth of July party every year. They had hot dogs and Kool-Aid and games and races. One of the races was a hopsack race. The first year I entered two-legged and didn't do well at all. That night at dinner, as I was telling about my day and poor showing, my father asked me why I didn't hop with my leg off? I remembered that advice, and the next year I entered one-legged. I was down the course and back before anyone else even got down. I won – the prize was a crafty make-a-stuffed-animal kit. I also was disqualified from that race for ever more.

We also had boats. We had a row boat that my dad covered in pretty turquoise fiberglass. It had three wooden seats, and after a few years my dad put a small outboard on it. We also had a snipe, a sailfish and a canoe. The snipe was too much boat for me, but my brother and I could sail it together. My father bought it from the adult son of the Smiths, two doors down. The two of us once took my sister out sailing with us – a little sausage of a thing in her bright orange life jacket. I was fore, my brother aft on the tiller, my sister fore of me. She fell in and I managed to grab her life jacket as we passed her bobbing in the water. We hauled her in and did our best to dry her off. I liked the sailfish much better. I could take that out by myself… however, I can't tell you how many times I would be ¾ across the lake when the dinnertime lull hit, leaving me to use the little craft as a kickboard, sail useless as a wet rag. That, or learning the hard way (more than once) that it's proper to come about *into* the wind. I capsized more times that I want to remember.

The rowboat was heavy, with all that fiberglass over wood. It was definitely a two-man show. My fondest memory of that boat was when my grandfather rowed me all the way across the lake and back, during which time he taught me "Roamin' in the Gloamin."

> *Roamin' in the Gloamin' by the bonny banks of Clyde,*
> *Roamin' in the gloamin' wi' my lassie by my side.*
> *When the sun has gone to rest,*
> *That's the time that we love best.*
> *Oh it's lovely roamin' in the gloamin'*

That's an old Scottish folk song… my father immigrated with his parents from Scotland. I can still see my grandfather with those oars, me sitting across from him repeating the song over and over.

I adored my grandparents. They were wonderful to us, not so much with hugs and kisses, but with huge effort and constant thought of what we might like. We would spend several weeks every summer with them. My grandfather would get up early every day and leave clues and treasure maps leading to some surprise from Dead Eye Dick, the Dirty One. Clues and notes nailed to trees… scavenger hunts. It was magical. My grandmother would tut-tut over us, making sure we were absolutely spotless and properly fed. They had a small house, so we had to camp out on the living room floor. Maggie brought out a silver satin down comforter for us. That was my very, very favorite part. The satin was so cool and slippery, and the down so light and warm. My grandfather would sit me on his lap, facing him. I would snuggle against his chest while he rubbed my back. I remember thinking to myself, "If I don't move at all − if I don't move an inch, maybe he won't stop." Years later I was reading a book that had an exercise in it: go back and think about your most comforting experience. It was sitting on my grandfather's lap. Why was it so comforting? I came to the sudden and frankly shocking conclusion: it was the only time I felt safe.

My grandmother ran a typical Scottish household… porridge and tea with milk for breakfast, up when the sun rose and down to bed when it set. Everything needed to be so squeaky clean that she thought tans made us look dirty. She would take our white Keds and wash them at night − and then paint them with white shoe polish. She would regale me with tales of Scotland: the tinkers and the gypsies that stole, so everything had to be put away when they showed up. She told me about the Scottish sword dance, and I would take a couple of sticks, lay them down across each other and try to imitate the dancers. She told me of the dances in Kirkcaldy where she met my grandfather: she led the Grand March. She told me we had a sailor in our background − we had some German in our background. She told me of having to take care of her younger siblings, saying that it seemed there was a new baby every payday. Her favorite sibling's nickname was

Daisy. She said John Forsyth was Scottish and was the most handsome actor, that Andrew Carnegie was Scottish, too. She was quite proud that she knew how to "cipher" – that was adding and subtracting in her head. She would have a grin on her face, and she had a way of lifting up her hand, index finger out but crooked a bit, twisting her wrist when she made a point. She told of how my father, as a toddler, wandered out of the row-house and took himself down to the village streetlight, where the men of the hamlet would gather under its glow to converse. She left out the hard parts: that unless your family was wealthy, you left school at twelve and started working. That families of ten and eleven – up to fifteen, even – lived in 3-room row-houses. That she worked as a domestic: that my grandfather worked in the coal mine until it ran out of coal, that he made golf clubs, that he raced whippets. That he didn't have a proper pair of shoes until he enlisted in the 42nd Blackwatch in World War I by lying about his age. That their first child died in infancy, left in Scotland never to be mentioned again.

My dad and his family came to Detroit in October 5, 1929, just weeks before the huge Depression-inducing stock market crash. The entire Thomson clan – my father's grandparents, seven aunts and uncles and several cousins, had left Scotland, at various times, during the 1920's. My father and his parents came next to last in those waves of Thomson family emigrants. They all came through Montreal, and the first set of immigrants headed to Winnipeg. That lasted only one winter: they headed to Chicago. My grandfather was still in Scotland, as was his older brother James. My grandfather waited until my father was born and was healthy, then he left for the States. He tried to join his family, which by then had moved from Chicago to Detroit for jobs in the auto industry, but was stopped at the border. The Immigration Act of 1924 had passed after the rest of his family immigrated but before he tried to enter, and he did not have a quota number. He ended up in Windsor, and after he landed a job at Ford Windsor he sent for his family. My grandmother, son in arms, headed to Montreal, escorted by her brother Alec, on the Athenia - the Athenia was that first ship sunk by a German submarine in World War II. The family stayed in Windsor for five years, until they were granted US entry. My grandfather's entire family, cousins included, lived by Clark Park in Detroit. My father and his parents would take the ferry across the river on Sundays to visit with the family. My father remembered playing with all sorts of cousins and other Scottish tots when he was small.

The extended family did not do well during the Depression: my great-grandfather went back to Winnipeg with his daughter Margaret and passed away within a few years. James and his family went back to Scotland, along with my dad's uncle Alec and his aunt Jean. John, Robert the first, and Andrew died between 1930-1931, as did my father's younger brother, who died in infancy in Windsor. The only relatives left in Detroit by the mid-1930's were my dad's grandmother and his aunt Elizabeth.

Regarding Robert the first: my grandfather Robert had an older brother, also named Robert. My great-grandfather apparently quite liked that name, and when he went to register the birth of his fourth son he conveniently forgot he already had a son named Robert. My grandfather was therefore known as Frank in Scotland, and once Robert the first passed away, my grandfather assumed his given name. People that knew him from Scotland would call him Frank, while people that met him after Robert the first passed called him Robert – or Scotty. Most everyone called him Scotty.

Speaking of names, there is something called the Scottish Naming Convention: first born son named after the paternal grandfather, first born daughter after the maternal grandmother, then the next boy and girl were named after the remaining grandparents. So my father was named John Paton Thomson, the name of his paternal grandfather. That was all well and fine, however there ended up being a gaggle of living John Paton Thomson's: patriarch, uncle John Paton Thomson, cousin John Paton Thomson, and my dad. A total of four!

We didn't socialize much with my mother's family. She had two older brothers who between them had five boys: two older than me and three younger. My mother's relationship with her parents was odd: I think she lived in mortal fear of her father's potential displeasure until the day she died. My grandmother was institutionalized on and off for some rather significant mental health issue during my first ten or fifteen years. Because of the hushed whispers I never knew a lot about it, except that she once burned my mother's dress in the basement. I remember having to sit in the car outside a large brick building named Eloise as my mother stopped in to visit. It was the local mental hospital - children not allowed. I only remember doing that once, though. By the time I was in high school my grandmother was medicated to the extent she could come home. She was adorable: giggling like a school girl and sneaking chocolates. She was as wide as she was tall, but she had a very charming personality. I only ate that grandmother's food once – it was at their lake cottage, and we had my grandmother's home-made borscht, topped with a dollop of sour cream. Incredibly delicious! I don't think I ever stepped foot in their permanent home.

My mother's ancestors were Rusyn, although they did not know it. Rusyn is a Slavic minority in several Eastern European countries - Subcarpathian Rus was a country in its own right for exactly one day, in March of 1939. Between belonging to the Russian Orthodox church, which was intent on convincing its SubCarpathian followers they were actually Russian, and the

26

similarity to the word "Russian," the family believed they were Russian. Not at all - the Rusyn's are not found in Russia – they are mostly found in Ukraine. My grandfather's family came from Zemplin county in what is now in the most easterly part of Slovakia, pushing up to Ukraine. My grandmother's family came from Lesko county, in what is now southernmost Poland.

My mother wanted to be Russian, though – she wanted to be Russian royalty. Princess Anastasia. My grandfather was an attorney by trade and a Russian Orthodox priest on weekends. He was born in Wisconsin, attended seminary in Minneapolis, and met my grandmother when he was sent to his first parish in Yonkers, New York. My grandmother was a sixteen-year-old choir girl. They subsequently moved to Pennsylvania, did a stint in Ohio, and ended up in Detroit, where my mother was born. In the 1920's, when there was a large fear of Eastern European immigrants – large enough that the Immigration Act of 1924 was passed – my grandfather did not want his children to be subjected to any discrimination. The house language was changed from what would be generally recognized as a Ukrainian dialect – Rusyn - to English, and the children were sent to Methodist church while my grandfather went to his weekend job. My mother told me stories about how the church sponsored fleeing Russian nobility after the uprising in 1917. How the Russian Orthodox community would hold formal balls in their honor, the men wearing broad red sashes across their chests. I have a dress from one of those balls, quite Russian in appearance. It is made of a dusty pink moiré, fitted princess-seamed waist with a very full, flared skirt. It has a band of embroidered ribbon braid around the neck and all the way down the front, decorated with plastic buttons that seem to have been a poor imitation of banded topaz. The sleeves are very full lace, with deep moiré cuffs. The headpiece is astounding: a 5" or 6" moiré scalloped-edged crown with maybe an inch of seed pearls strung closely together encircling the forehead. There is a full lace train attached. It's about six inches too short for me and about six inches too wide. I also inherited a hand-embroidered Ukrainian peasant blouse and apron, resplendent in huge cross-stitch red and black roses on the sleeves, collar, placket and apron.

My mother told me that the escaped royalty had no money and no employable skills. My mother had a Baroness as a music teacher and a Duchess as a dance teacher. But besides those stories of foregone glory, we did not embrace the culture – my mother did not embrace the culture. I have a cousin that calls me up on my birthday every year and sings to me Mno Hyaleta (the Ukrainian birthday song). We never sang it at home: I had never even heard of it. We did go to Russian Easter one year when I was in high school. It's an all-night affair, with no sitting, and several treks around the perimeter. Lots of chanting and gorgeous, resonantly heavy Russian music. Russian music is unmistakable, if only for its distinctive harmonies. And there was my grandfather, all decked out in his clerical robes, all brocade and heavy embroidery, walking down the center aisle swinging the incense holder, three times this way, three times that, as he intoned the orthodox liturgy. The smoke nearly choked me. It was all very exotic and foreign to me – we were raised stereotypically WASP.

I never spent much time with my maternal grandparents, but I did spend those summer weeks with my Scottish grandparents. By the time I was regularly visiting them they had become a success story. My grandparent's house was narrow – entrance doors were on either side, but it was also lakefront property, very near where the Detroit River spills into Lake Erie. The entrance door to the right entered into the kitchen from a small landing that also led to the basement. There were two doors in the kitchen: one led to the living room overlooking the lake, and the other the hall to the bedrooms and the sun porch, which held the formal entry to the house. My grandparents did not share a bedroom – his was on the left and hers was on the right. His was full of books – books on the war, books on marine craft… manly books, they were, bound in dark and serious colors. Her room was soft pale green with a big mirror over the dresser and a little porcelain open bible figurine on her nightstand. The seal on the living room double-pane picture window had broken, so the view out was always cloudy. There was a brick fireplace in that room, across from the window.

My grandfather had finished the basement. At the foot of the stairs to the left was his wood-working shop. It had lathes and table saws and tools I had never seen before. Behind that was my grandfather's darkroom – again, fully equipped. To the right of those two rooms was a full bar: full bar, as in; go behind the counter, turn on the bar lights and be a bartender kind of bar. There was even trim hanging from the ceiling defining the space. My grandfather had a hand-carved whistling hobo leaning up against a light-post sitting on the bar. The light-post had a flashlight bulb in it that could be turned on, and there was a music box inside the man. The man's head turned left and right, whistling "Show Me the Way to Go Home" when the music box was wound up. Past the bar, to the left, was a TV room. On the wall was a stuffed mahi-mahi that my grandfather had caught in Florida. There was a laundry/utility room, too – my grandmother had a wringer washer. Wringer washers had no spin cycle – instead they had two wooden rollers side by side, attached to a crank handle. That was the wringer. I remember helping her with the sheets. She would start them in the wringer, feeding a corner between the rollers, and then she would turn the crank while I gathered the fabric coming out the other end. The wringer was so tight that the sheets came out at me straight, like boards. I would put my arms out to gather them, and then we would put them in a basket and take them out to hang to dry.

My grandparent's house was across the water from a military base that had aircraft taking off and landing on a runway that ran parallel to the water's edge. Their driveway was the longest I had ever seen. Dori lived next door to the left with her widowed mother and sister. Dori's house was cool – it looked like a stone castle. It had a stone wall between the houses that was tall enough that there was an arched opening in it. Dori was more than a decade older than me – college age - but she was wonderful to me. She taught me how to play badminton.

My grandparents also owned the home to the right. We lived there for an entire summer once, while my dad was doing the most severe remodeling of our house #5. That's where my mother recoiled in horror after she discovered that the bag of potato chips she was absent-mindedly nibbling was crawling with red ants. After we left that summer, my grandparents rented that house to the Wyzbinski's. We played with the Wyzbinski children all the time – Patricia was about my age. There was a screened in porch that faced the lake, and we played Canasta in that porch hour upon hour. Patricia had a brother and a sister, and the three of them adored my grandmother – but why not? My grandmother always loved her "wee bairns" (small children in Scots English), and she always had some treat for them. They fondly called her Mrs. T.

Next to that house lived the Peeples... there were two children in that house. My grandmother disapproved of the Peeples, so we couldn't play with them, even though Doreen was about my age. The disapproval was never explained to us children – it was whispered between adults with turned backs. Whispers notwithstanding, I believe that the disapproval stemmed from no Mr. Peeples in situ.

One door down from them were the Johnsons, who had boys. Past that was the yacht club. We would take the row boat and go up the small stream until we got to the low pink bridge owned by the yacht club. We would fish off my grandfather's dock, too. We would catch nightcrawlers by putting mustard down the earthworm holes in the grass. What we didn't know was that there were no fish to be had... Lake Erie had died. There are pictures of me in a life jacket, in the water, when I was very young. The lake had become so polluted by the time I was in elementary school that we couldn't go in it anymore.

My grandfather had built a large concrete seawall that spanned both of his properties. He built a covered boat well and had big winches installed so he could lift his Chris Craft cruiser out of the water in winter, and he built a large brick grill on a wider concrete pad near the seawall. The Chris Craft was a beautifully maintained, shiny-shellacked wooden cruiser that could sleep all seven of us. My grandfather christened it "The Seven T's". It was such a treat to go out on it. One summer he took us over to some city on Georgian Bay in Canada – I don't remember how many nights we slept on board. I remember docking in a river next to some men that were lawn bowling in a riverside park. No one there was speaking English. My brother and I went exploring and found an alley that must have been behind a glass factory. We found glass pieces in the most beautiful colors: ruby red, cobalt blue, emerald green. We thought they were jewels and brought several back with us.

Past Dori's house, many doors down, was a very small island – probably more aptly called a sand bar - that we could walk to through shallow water, if the tide was just right. My brother,

Patricia and I would go "exploring" on that little island… we were castaways, we were pirates – were heading into safe harbor from a terrible storm. Next to it, on the shore, was a small, fake lighthouse decoration that led us back to "safe harbor."

My grandparents had two dogs: Kay, a trained German Shepherd guard dog, was my grandfather's. Tammy, a white toy poodle, was my grandmother's. Kay went to work with my grandfather. Kay was decidedly a man's dog, but little Tammy was so, so spoiled. My grandmother never fed her dog food – she would cook up some ground beef, or chicken, or liver. If Tammy wasn't in the mood for whatever my grandmother fixed her, my grandmother would cook up something else. Maggie was a great cook, and she loved her little Tammy.

Tammy wasn't a dog with whom any child could play. My toddler sister terrorized that little dog to such a degree that when my sister showed up, the dog would back under a low shelf of an end table, crouch down, growl, and bare her teeth. That was as much Tammy as my sister, though. One Fourth of July, after we had finished our steaks on the grill, my grandfather gave each of the dogs a bone. Kay was content to sit down and gnaw on hers, but little Tammy wanted both bones. She was running around Kay, yapping and snapping. After a bit, Kay quietly stood up, picked Tammy up by the scruff of the neck like a mother carries her pup, carried her back to her own bone, and unceremoniously dropped her. Tammy was in a state of shock. She never tried that again.

During the school year my grandmother would often drive up on Wednesdays. I loved her visits. She would bring homemade soup or Scottish meat pies from Windsor. Nothing like coming in to a steaming hot bowl of homemade soup, ready right after school. My very favorite was cock-a-leekie… that's kind of like the

Scottish version of chicken noodle soup. My mother and her friends were much more enamored of the cans of soup and boxes of cake mix that became available than in cooking from scratch like their mothers did. My grandmother's cooking was special, and it was delicious.

My father wasn't home for dinner a couple of nights a week - he was working two jobs: dentistry during the day and medical professor at night. He taught gross anatomy at the University of Detroit School of Medicine. When he came home he smelled of formaldehyde. He named the cadavers... the one I remember was George. These were unclaimed bodies from the morgue. My father told me fascinating but yucky things, like the difference in lungs between a non-smoker (pink and firm) and a smoker (gray and dissolved so they needed to be spooned out). He also mentioned that he always let his students drop their worst test grade. He said that it made no difference to those students that were going to flunk out anyway, but if there was a good student that happened to be sick on test day or was just having a bad day, it would help. I never forgot that.

We had a couple of stand-out neighbors. The Hoffmans were a very handsome and glamorous couple – he tall with dark hair, she a tall, beautiful blond. They would throw very sophisticated parties. He was in media or marketing or advertising – he knew local celebrities and would entertain them. The Hoffmans had a beautiful wood Chris Craft speedboat. Had as in past tense: before Bill Bixby went to Hollywood and became the original Hulk, he did local television ads and shows. He took that Chris Craft out drunk during a party one night and ended up smashing it right through the Hoffman's dock.

The Hoffman's teenage children were my idols. Bob and Dana were so grown up... Bob so tall and trim and handsome... a varsity swimmer … and Dana so very pretty. I used to watch her walk home from the bus stop in her saddle shoes and poodle skirt. They were a good ten years my senior, so we hardly ever spoke. I had never lived by high schoolers before, though, and I was fascinated by them.

The Cochrans moved away after a few years, selling their house to the Schwaries. The Schwaries were Lebanese, and he was a country club manager. Mrs. Schwarie was a beautiful, very exotic-looking woman who wore fuchsia-purple lipstick. She had a thick accent and would call for her children out the front door, "Rrrroy!! Lau-o-rah!! Jo-eye-cee!" It became an inside joke. My mother thought that Mrs. Schwarie was so very glamorous and gorgeous that she went out and bought fuchsia-purple lipstick for herself.

I had never met spoiled children before meeting Rrrroy, Lau-o-rah and Jo-eye-cee. Roy was the worst – not only spoiled, but a braggart and a tease. One day he got a brand-new red two-wheel bicycle. It was beautiful! As he was bragging about his brand-spanking-new bike, he sneered that he would let me take a ride, but gee, I didn't know how to ride. Too bad – such a smirk-smirk shame. My father used to tell me that if he wanted me to do anything, all he needed to say was I couldn't… I grabbed those handle bars, hopped on and rode down the dirt road. Not too good at turning, I ended up in a culvert instead. No matter – I had ridden Roy's bike. It was the talk of the dinner table that night… it never occurred to my parents that I would ever be able to ride a bike. The very next day I saw a used girl's bike, a light blue with a white basket, perched in the driveway. My dad had gone out and gotten me a bike, just like that. Wonderful surprises like that were very, very rare in our household. That was a very special day.

My public school days can best be characterized as crowded. Very crowded. New building had not kept up with the post-war baby boom. My first grade was held in half of the cafeteria/gymnasium/auditorium, with the second graders on the other side. The lunch tables were mounted in the walls Murphy-bed style, so we had to break half an hour early so the lunch tables could be brought down. They must have been eight or ten feet long, with attached benches that tucked behind the tables when they were up. They were on the west wall, across from the wooden stage. There was no hot lunch program – all anyone could buy was a 2-cent, 8-ounce carton of milk. My mother made the same lunches for my brother and me for six years: he got peanut butter and jelly, two sandwich cookies, an apple and two cents. I got a cheese and mustard sandwich, two sandwich cookies, an apple and two cents. My mother was not exactly a morning person, and more than once I bit into my sandwich only to find that the plastic film separating the Velveeta cheese slices was still on the cheese. We only had to hold class in that common room for one year – by the time second grade rolled around, the new addition had been completed.

There were two classes for each grade in my elementary school. I found out that Cathy Wild was in the other second grade, and I was thrilled that my friend was in the same school. That excitement was very short-lived, because Cathy had no interest in being my friend with other children around. I can't remember having any friends at all in second grade. Backing up to the school play yard was Knollwood Country Club. There were large, old trees that screened the golf course from the playground. One tree had a very low crook in it – just the right height and width for a second grader. I remember sitting in that tree and crying during recess – it was my Crying Tree. I wasn't welcome in the games the other children were playing. That didn't change until wall ball, and once I was permitted to play jump rope everything changed. I was really, really good at jump rope – and not too bad at wall ball, either. No running required.

The schoolhouse was a one-story brick building, very symmetrical, except for the new addition, for which there was absolutely no attempt whatsoever to match architecture, building materials, roof line, or anything else. I liked the old building. It had pretty, dark wood doors in the office and big paned windows in all of the classrooms. The office was to the immediate left of the main entrance, which was dead center in the middle of the original building. The front doors were painted dark green. Across from the office was a hallway leading to the auditorium et al, and beyond that the new addition. Next to that hallway and to the left was the third grade classroom of Mrs. MacDonald. Past the office to the left was the main schoolroom hallway, with the classrooms of Mrs. Hilty and Mrs. Fremont, plus the bathrooms. The original building had the most interesting contraption for hand-washing… it was a stone, or maybe terrazzo, half-moon extending out from the wall, large enough for maybe six, eight… perhaps even ten children that could gather around it. It had a fountain in the center, mounted to the wall, a trough encircling that, and a stainless steel half circle foot pedal. Step on the pedal and the fountain turned on.

At the end of that hall was a very large classroom that had its own door to the playground, and past that was the nurse's station. We had a fulltime, white-uniformed nurse on staff. She was the one that would put mercurochrome (ouch) or merthiolate (yes!) on scrapes and scratches. Mercurochrome really stung, but merthiolate was not only a pretty fluorescent pink color, it didn't sting at all. My second grade was in the new addition (which held kindergarten through 2nd grade), but the rest of my classes were in the original building.

Most of the teachers were women, but my fourth grade teacher was Mr. Faust. He was a tall man, dark-haired, on the slender side. He always wore a dark suit, white shirt and tie. He would buy his two-cent milk carton at the milk table and shake it all the way back to the lunch table he chaperoned – each table had a teacher sitting on the end. Mr. Faust's class was in that big classroom at the end with its own playground door. When recess was over we lined up along the side of the brick wall on the concrete slab that was used for jump rope, waiting for permission to re-enter the classroom.

~

I was a few days late starting fourth grade. Early in the summer I had gone to a Girl Scouts day camp. I remember it raining and raining one day… we had to take shelter in a large tent. I somehow ended up with walking pneumonia. I don't remember feeling particularly bad, but I do remember coughing a lot. I coughed enough to go to the doctor. That doesn't sound like much, but we hardly ever went to a doctor. We didn't even have a family physician – when we needed a school physical, my dad would call on one of his friends to do the favor. So going to the doctor was one very big deal. My bout with walking pneumonia was pivotal in my childhood. The prescription was total bed rest. I was allowed to walk down to the porch overlooking the lake once a day and walk back up at night – and except for bathroom breaks, that's the only exercise I was allowed. For the entire rest of the summer I reclined on an old wooden outdoor chaise wistfully watching everyone else play. And I read. I read Gone with The Wind, I read a book about Shirley Temple, I even started The Fountainhead. Pretty heavy reading for between third and fourth grades. The day before school started, I rebelled, got on my bike, rode down to the schoolyard, and played on every piece of playground equipment there. I had a relapse and missed the first couple of days. I must have felt awful: we kids were not motivated to stay home when sick. Even with a fever, come about ten or eleven in the morning my mother would come up, roust us out of bed, and make us do chores. It was easier to suffer through a school day.

That year I couldn't go out for recess until after Christmas. I was sent to visit the nurse twice a day, for morning and afternoon recess. She was busy giving fluoride treatments to the children whose parents paid the extra money. The nurse gave me the fluoride treatments for free (being the daughter of a dentist, this was not something my parents would ever think of paying someone else to do.) And I read. Mr. Faust had a series of books on a shelf below the huge paned windows that faced north. The books were designed to be a self-paced set, with each subsequent book more difficult that the preceding. There were tests that needed to be passed before you could graduate to the next. I seem to remember there were 21 or 22 books in the series. I finished them all. I believe I was the first student to plow through all of them.

Neither our homes nor school were air-conditioned, and Mr. Faust would open the door to the playground in the afternoons when it got hot, near the end of the school year. Madchen knew when school let out, and she would walk the mile to school to come to that back door, waiting for me. Mr. Faust would let her come and sit by my desk for the last ten minutes or so of class. She was perfectly behaved. Then she would walk my brother and me back home. Across the street from the school were several little stores: there was Jean's candy shop – a favorite of the children in the neighborhood. Many children stopped in there after school to buy candy, but since my brother and I never had any money, we almost never did. Jean was a heavy-set, tall, raven-haired woman with a slow way about her. Her store had wooden floors, and the glass display was to the right after walking in. Jean sold candy buttons on paper strips and little wax bottles filled with colored sugar water and Tootsie Rolls and Mary Janes and root beer barrels. I don't remember a lot of chocolate.

There also was a little grocer's store, and there was Ed's pharmacy. Ed was a mustached man who always wore a white pharmacy jacket. He always smiled at me.

The rule in the school district was that anyone within one mile had to walk. We were almost – almost but not quite – a mile away. I could walk to school: go down to the empty lot that Madchen used as her bathroom, down the trodden dirt path to the next street over, to the right of Rolf Week's house, across another street to Eastman, down the big, big hill with the red brick ranch on the corner, then up from the back between Jean's candy store and the grocer, across the one and only paved road to the school. Or I could double back, three blocks east past Russell Mullen's red house and one block north, to Connie Aiken's house, which was the last bus stop before school. Almost always the last bus stop, because if we were one short block south, on Appoline, the bus driver would stop anyway. All our streets were dirt. In the spring, before the creosote was laid down and before the frost was totally out of the ground, the roads were just plain mud. Deep mud. I remember my white rubber over-boots with the single elastic loop at the top that was intended to go over the button that was on the other side of the pleat, but which always seemed to break in two early on. Those boots would get stuck in mud that was a good three inches deep, and I would end up either stepping in the mud with my shoe because my foot came all the way out, or falling/dropping my schoolbooks in the mud because my foot would come only partially out and get stuck midway in the boot, making me trip. We didn't have book bags or backpacks back then. I did make grocery bag book protector covers for my books, but that didn't stop the pages from being permanently mud-stained.

~

Things definitely turned around for me in fourth grade – we put on musicals, and I could sing. In fourth grade we put on Englebert Humperdinck's Hansel and Gretel. I was the Sandman, singing the opera's Evening Prayer. I needed to be all in beige. My mother came up with old-lady support hose for me, which I thought were simply awful, and a homemade beige cotton tunic. In fifth grade our school play was Peter Pan. Little Janie Russell was Peter, since she could fearlessly swing on the suspended wire to fly, but for the life of me I can't remember what part I played. In sixth grade we tackled South Pacific. I was Bloody Mary, singing Bali H'ai. I was in a colorful mu-mu, those being all the rage at the time. The "soldiers" were supposed to form a half-circle around the back of me, and I remember that Chris Chudik, on the far left, was too far downstage. Before I started singing I motioned to him to step back, which made everybody in the audience laugh. I was always singing – or humming. I got in trouble from first grade on, humming while I would intently do my work. Disruptive, I was told. However, I never even knew I was doing it. There is a place in my brain filled with music which used to bubble to the surface.

We had some excellent assemblies in elementary school – the two standouts were watching the Harlem Globetrotters live (right there, in our elementary school!) and then, in sixth grade, watching Alan Shepard go into space on the rolled-in television. That was fascinating. Not so spectacular were the cartoonish health movies we would assemble to watch. "Go, chicken fat, go?" That, and cartoons of germs and how to outwit them. We also watched newsreels - about the iron lung and polio vaccine, about the Cold War and how to duck and cover under our desks… all in assembly, all in the multi-purpose room that had been my first grade.

~

Halloween was a big deal in our neighborhood. I was almost always a witch, and my brother almost always a hobo. My mother would paint one of my front teeth with black enamel so it looked as if it was missing. My brother would take a big wicker basket my mother had, and I would take a pillowcase. The minute dusk hit, all you could see were children running – absolutely tearing – from house to house. There were legions of us. We all had strategies: mostly the strategies entailed assigning streets to various siblings and returning home to dump the loot before heading on out again. We did not go in groups and we did not go with adults – the operative word was volume. We needed to hit all the houses between home and the parking lot in front of Ed's pharmacy by 8 pm, where the costume parade was held and the prizes given out for best costume. We never won, but no matter. I remember that there was one small cottage that was owned by an elderly single man. Most of the children never rang his bell – they were frightened of him - but once I did. He was so surprised when he came to the door. I think he gave me a dime, or a quarter… must have been a quarter. That was some sort of fortune for a grade-schooler back in the day, and no one could believe I had the nerve to ring his doorbell.

We also had a school fair at the end of each school year. It was held both in and outside. There was the spook house, which had things like cold boiled spaghetti hanging down so it hit your face while walking through the pitch-black schoolroom. There was also a cakewalk. My mother baked a cake for it that turned out lopsided – a Leaning Tower of Pisa kind of cake. I entered the cakewalk and won! I chose my mother's cake as my prize and proudly brought it home, which did not please her at all. I didn't understand why she was cross with me for that. There also were games that the dads had built: one was throwing balls into a grid… a physical version of tic-tac-toe. I remember playing that with my very last penny. I threw the first ball and it made it into a square. I threw the second into a square that could never result in a win. I became angry and threw the third ball so hard it dislodged one of the balls, moving it so the three did complete a straight line. I won a prize, and I walked away with the new-found knowledge that sometimes some well-timed and well-placed anger can be a very useful tool.

My favorite time of year was from Thanksgiving to Christmas. I was very fortunate, in that my birthday is at the end of November. I would get money from my grandparents, which meant I always could buy Christmas presents with it. Or, more accurately, buy materials so I could make presents. One year, obviously older, I made knit slippers for everyone. I must have made over a half-dozen pair. Another year I made a quilted suit for my sister – they were all the rage in the mid 1960's, calico quilted suits. Hers was pink. My brother went to the five-and-dime. He bought my mother a 12-ounce glass that had narrow rainbow stripes on it. He thought it was beautiful and was very proud of it. My mother embarrassed him by berating him… "A glass? One glass? Hahaha… one glass." Ever the sensitive one, he was crushed.

My sister's birthday was a few days after Christmas and my brother's was in February, so they were not as fortunate. We never got anything "big" for Christmas – we predominantly got clothes from my parents - but everything was wrapped separately. There were so many presents! We were not allowed to go downstairs until my parents were up and went with us… we would congregate in the hallway upstairs and wait excitedly in new nightgowns and pajamas. That was pretty much the extent of our tradition: we did not attend church, we did not gather together to put beloved ornaments on the Christmas tree while listening to Christmas carols, sipping hot chocolate or eggnog. The Christmas tree was always a decorating Statement: one year it was decorated turquoise and lime green; another year, pink and orange.

My mother's parents would come over for Christmas breakfast. We usually only saw them a few times a year, Thanksgiving and for Christmas for sure and then very infrequently, during the summer, and not every year. Grandpa always gave us $5 and a plastic candy-cane-shaped container full of Cracker Jacks. He was a small, stern man. That was one breakfast that we could also eat eggs and bacon. My mother often said she resented that her oldest brother Ted was the favorite. She was not close to her parents, so neither were we. We would leave for my beloved Scottish grandparents early afternoon. They put up a white flocked table tree that had a light behind a rotating circle with four color quadrants that would shine on the tree, making it alternately different colors.

My grandparents were the ones with the cool toys for us. My grandfather painstakingly made a doll cradle for my sister and me – it was maybe 30" long, painted pink, with teddy bear decals. We used to dress up our dog in doll clothes and lay her on her back in that cradle. We used that cradle as a bed for the black kitten we snuck up the stairs because my mom had said "no" to her. On day two, after my sister and I had fallen asleep, the kitten got out, wandered down the hall and headed down the stairs as my mother was heading up in the dark. Her scream woke everybody up – she thought it was a rat.

We met up with our aunts, uncles and cousins for sure twice a year – we had a family Thanksgivings and Christmases the Sundays before the actual holidays. My mother and her two brothers rotated the holidays – one year someone had Thanksgiving, the next year Christmas and the following year was a "bye." We would get quite dressed up… after-five wear. One year I made myself a velvet "cage" dress: the under-dress was a pale celery heavy velvet with sequin straps, and the long-sleeve "cage" over it was in a matching lace. My youngest cousin, then about two, managed to dump his plate of spaghetti all over the front of it. I should have never gone near that high chair.

There were sixteen of us all together: I have five first cousins, all boys, ranging from nine years older than me to twelve years younger. Those parties were wonderful – my uncles and their wives were all kind and fun-loving. After dinner the men would gather by the fireplace, light up cigars, and talk "man-talk" while the women cleaned up and chatted in the kitchen. We kids would hie ourselves off to whatever basement to play. My uncle Ted had a pedal-driven player piano in the basement, along with a slot machine. The player piano was loaded with Rossini's *William Tell Overture*, and we would tire ourselves out pumping hard on the pedals to make the music go as fast as we could make it. My uncle Gene lived on Indian Lake in a lovely log-cabin home he built. It had a built-in eating area in the kitchen – I liked the built-in bench that ran along two sides of it. That house had a cathedral ceiling in the living room with a gorgeous, rustic stone fireplace that had a deep hearth for sitting. They always had the biggest tree! They also used big, old-fashioned Christmas lights every year, even though my mother and my aunt Midge had graduated to the mini-lights.

We were quite home-bound as children: dinner out happened only very, very occasionally. My father loved Japanese food, so we went to a Japanese restaurant a couple of times. I remember him telling me to go easy on the hot mustard. We only had pizza once, and that was at the Goodwin's. My little sister was coming down with something and became ill – she associated pizza with being sick and wouldn't eat it for years. Once in a while we would stop at an A&W root beer stand… there was one on the way to my mother's parent's cottage. I remember that our station wagon's muffler had fallen off. My mother saw a police car on the road and coasted by him, so as to not get a ticket. The A&W had car-window service, with those trays that would hang off the windows. We were waiting for our order, and my mother was laughing so proudly at herself for outwitting the police when she noticed a police car parked right next to our car - they were listening. My mother turned red, and the rest of us giggled uncontrollably.

My parents would sometimes go to the drive-in movies at the Miracle Mile Drive-In on Telegraph, north of Square Lake. They were always double-features, from when the sun went down until well after midnight. My parents would pile the three of us into the station wagon in our jammies – we were always asleep well before the second feature, no matter how we tried to stay awake. The speaker was always perched on my father's window. We children would stand between the front and back seats to watch the movies between our parents' shoulders until we were too tired to watch any more, and then we would climb over the back seat and fall asleep. I remember intermission, when they would show cartoon ads about all the candy and popcorn available, and watch as the people would stream by our car in search of snacks. We never bought any of that. We had a red and white Ford Fairlane station wagon, which was christened "Tootie Bell." The back of the front bench seat had a metal edging around the top of it, and the back of the seat was rigid. Somehow a piece of glass got stuck between the naugahyde and the edging, and I cut my middle finger rather deeply with it while standing up in back. I still have that scar.

Sometimes on Saturdays my mother would drop my brother and me off at the matinee so she could shop, with instructions to go everywhere together. When I was about eight, the feature was "House on Haunted Hill." I had never seen a horror flick before. So there I was, sitting in the aisle seat, next to my brother, when the first shocker scene hit: a woman had gotten stuck in a closet, and when she turned around there was this hideous, scraggly-haired woman behind her. I was positively shaking. I remember getting up and stumbling to the lobby, visibly shaken. By myself.

My brother and I had one large vacation event: we went to Florida with my grandparents one Easter break… he was in sixth grade; I was in fifth. We got all dressed up for the airplane – I remember I had a short-sleeved camel and white gingham, empire-waisted, tailored dress with white piping. We flew to Miami and then got on a bus to Marathon Key. I had never been either on a plane or on a commercial bus before.

The bus's diesel smell and the rough stops and starts made me nauseous… I was very glad to finally get off. It was night when we got to our motel, so I didn't see where we were until the next morning.

I was amazed when I awoke. Marathon was like nothing I had ever seen before. Back then there were no such things as national chain stores. Every little town and burg had its own, distinct flavor and independent stores. My memories of Marathon are of everything sun-faded: low-slung stucco buildings in distinctly faded pastel colors. Bright sun and lots of sand. Sand even on the streets and sidewalks in the middle of town, if Marathon could be called that. The Key was so narrow that it seemed there was only one street – A1A – with not much but beaches behind on either side. There were little knick-knack shops, a diner – I remember it seemed that everything was seashell or seahorse-themed. I bought a seahorse pendant necklace in one of those knick-knack shops. And the palm trees… I had only seen those in pictures. I remember panhandlers, too… my grandmother was disdainful of them. To her, it was a disgrace to be "on the dole", and it was a disgrace to be dirty. She would look at some of those men and say that she knew what it was like to not have much money, but that a bar of soap didn't cost much.

My grandfather was passionate about deep sea fishing. He kept a boat in Florida, and he took the four of us out every day. We all had zinc oxide-white noses and wide-brimmed hats. I remember seeing a couple of hammerhead sharks lazily swim by the boat, but mostly I was drinking orange pop and sleeping. The sun made me constantly thirsty and the rocking of the boat put me to sleep every single day, so I would crawl up under the bow, curl up and snooze. I was a big disappointment to my grandfather, but I simply couldn't help it. When we got back to school we were quite the item, all tan and everything. Trips like that were rare back then, at least in our school. Back in the day.

A HAZE OF PAIN

We had fun times in house #5, before things started falling apart. There were fights between my parents, and sometimes my father would come home drunk. He frightened us terribly one night, chasing my sister and me around the house, grabbing us to "tickle" us. However, that "tickling" hurt. I remember grabbing my sister and locking us in the new half-bath, huddling in the corner. My dad was too drunk to stick a pin in the handle to pop the lock. We were petrified.

That being said, I was a feisty one. The number of times I was frightened can be counted on one hand. My parents did not attend church, but they would drop us off for Sunday school. We would sit on the front steps waiting to be picked up, frequently sitting there after the parking lot was emptied. Apparently one day while we were in church my parents had another argument, because when we got home we were met with my father yelling at my mother, "You want me to spank them? I'll spank them." We children were not angels, but that particular Sunday morning we had not transgressed (which basically meant not making too much noise, awakening my parents before they were ready to get up). I stood there in my hand-me-down navy and orange dress, hands on hips, and told my dad that I hadn't done anything wrong, so I was not going to get spanked. My mother, brother and sister audibly gasped. My father picked me up by the arm, but I wiggled and fought back – I mean, I *really* fought back. By the end my dress was ripped, my face was red and I was panting, but I don't think I ended up getting spanked – what my bemused father did was simply to give me a tap on the bottom, to save face with the spectators.

Waking my parents up on Sunday morning was about the worst thing we could do. One morning we kids awoke and noticed that we all had soot around our nostrils. Our oil-burning furnace was on fire, three levels down. We snuck into our parents' room, Jeff standing on my father's side, me by my mother. We were whispering hoarsely across the bed, "You tell them!" "No, you!" My father rolled over annoyed, ready to yell, but the second he saw a face he leapt out of bed and tore down the stairs, butt naked. He liked sleeping in the nude.

The fighting got worse, and then, after lots of adult whispers behind turned backs, my parents were gone for a while, replaced by a very stern and unpleasant white-uniformed-with-cap nurse. I don't think she ever smiled, and I can still see her standing there, hands clasped primly in front. Having her there was unnerving. Not knowing where my parents were, more unnerving yet. Not knowing what in the world was going on was the most unnerving of all. My parents came home after a while. Nobody ever told us where they had gone. All we knew was that we were ordered to never speak the name Marge Goodwin again. Ever. Continued adult whispers behind turned backs, but it later became clear to me that Marge and my father had been having an affair. Marge was being sued for divorce and my father was named in the divorce papers as co-respondent. I didn't even know what any of that meant at the time.

The fighting got worse and worse. I have visions of my mother, hunched over, wielding an iron skillet. She would go into total rages at the smallest of things. We didn't straighten up our room fast enough? We could hear her stomping up the stairs - Oh My God, here she comes again - and in she would swoop, taking her left arm, placing it on the far side of the built-in shelf, and walk along the shelf, smashing everything to the floor. She would scream at us that she was not a "mommy-mommy." She was college educated! She was Somebody!!! And don't ask her to pick us up after school. Don't even *think* to ask her to babysit when we had children of our own. She broke more than one white, unbreakable Fuller brush on our backsides. Her emotional governor, if she ever had one, was irreparably broken. Home became a war zone. I would come home from school and frequently go straight up to my room. I would hug my Susie doll, keeping totally to myself. I remember telling myself that nobody would see me cry. I became very withdrawn, which didn't solve a thing. I can't decide whether it was because I was seemingly unbreakable or what, but then the insults started. It was as if my parents wanted me to hurt as much as they did. "Your grandfather doesn't like you: you look too much like your grandmother." "Your father doesn't like you: you are smarter than he is." "Nobody will like you." "I don't like you." "Don't be so smart – you are the reason your brother has no self-esteem." "You are lazy." "You are fat." But I did not break. I went to my room and hugged my Susie doll. And they did not see me cry. And after I placed one of my mother's breakables on our bedroom shelf, after she came in and once again smashed everything to the floor, after she realized she had broken one of her valuables amidst ours, she never did that again.

I put most of the growing family dysfunction on my mother. My father came back from the war very sick, very changed, and apparently very emotionally damaged. He had seen and been through horrible things. My mother has always been all about her – very self-absorbed. She came across as, "Oh: now you're back. I want babies, let's play house." She cared little for my father's recurring bouts of malaria and amoebic dysentery, getting angry when his illness got in the way of her plans. She never even considered what he wanted, how he felt, or what he might need. My father was certainly not perfect, but my mother did nothing to bring out the best in him, to notice he was deeply troubled, to try and help him sort it all out.

My mother never grew up. She was a little girl playing house. She wanted to put her toys away (her children) when she got tired of playing with them. "Don't touch my walls!" "Get out of my refrigerator!" As if we didn't belong there – as if we were guests.

To say she was not nurturing is an understatement. One of the reasons I withdrew was she refused to acknowledge or validate my feelings. If I tried to tell her I was sad, she wouldn't ask why, she would reply, "No you're not!" She was fairly bereft of any sense of empathy. I remember starting seventh grade, which was in Groves High School, grades 7 through 12. My experience had been that it took several years for me to get accepted by peers that didn't know me, and here I was heading off to a huge 2,000-student school with students up to age 18. I so wanted to at least dress like the other kids, but Oh No. First day of school: while the other girls were in their Villager plaid skirts with cardigans trimmed in the same plaid and matching plaid Capezios, I was dressed in this grey pinstriped dirndl-skirted chintz cotton dress with a large white pilgrim collar, crinoline petticoat included. I was sobbing at the bus stop – not that it mattered to my mother. "That's a brand new dress!! Don't bite the hand that feeds you!" Those were my mother's only comments.

In fact, she cared little for anything that got in her way. She was a drama queen – a real Sarah Bernhardt. Even her brothers called her that. I truly believe she had a histrionic personality disorder. She was often totally outrageous. She got stopped for speeding once when I was with her. She absolutely snarled at the officer. She didn't pay the ticket – she went to court, toothbrush in hand. Toothbrush! She started waving it at the Judge, ranting that he was running a kangaroo court, and that, toothbrush in hand, she would go to jail. To her chagrin, the judge obliged. My mom called her brother, who happened to also be a judge, and he got her out. No consequences. No one had ever taken her to task for her outlandish behavior, so she never had to face appropriate consequences. She would proudly call herself a spoiled brat. She nailed it.

The environment got worse and worse, not better. My middle and high school home years were basically a haze of pain. There were some stand-out non-home moments, to be sure. My 7th grade math teacher was Ms. Piepho. I loved her: everybody loved her. She was so energetic, so no-nonsense, so fair. She made us rather govern ourselves by making everyone responsible for what happened in class, so if any of the boys, (and yes, in 7th grade it was always the boys), started acting up, we were all held responsible. The rest of the class, not wanting detention or extra work, took it upon ourselves to rein in the miscreants. There was a girl in our class named Kathy – a heavy-set, socially awkward and sometimes mean girl that had baked a cake and brought it in for Ms. Piepho. Ms. Piepho had not yet come into the classroom, and the cake was a surprise. A few of the boys got rowdy and knocked the cake on the floor. Kathy started to cry… although Kathy had been mean to me, and I didn't like her very much, I felt sympathy for her right then.

Ms. Piepho told me her father had an artificial leg, too, that he kept under the bed at night. She was the first person ever that was openly comfortable with the subject – most of the other people I met were politely and often uncomfortably silent on the subject.

After spending 7th grade at the high school, we were moved to Berkshire Junior High, a newly constructed school, for 8th grade. That was such a good move: the high school was so overcrowded that they had to schedule extra time for students to get from class to class. The halls became simply a massive, human traffic jam every time a bell rang. We would just slowly shuffle, shoulder to shoulder, to our lockers and then to our next class. They couldn't build schools fast enough.

I remember my 8th grade science teacher, the red-headed Mr. Wilson. The classroom did not have individual desks – it had several rows of long, multi-student tables. I remember he was writing something on the board, and I had a piece of paper I wanted to throw away. Every time I could, I would sit in the first seat, farthest left, facing the black board. I wadded up that paper and threw it into the waste basket next to the door – a true 3-pointer. Mr. Wilson saw the shot from the corner of his eye, turned around, and asked sarcastically who the basketball star was. When I rather sheepishly raised my hand he said, "You?", quite surprised. He kind of grinned and went back to writing on the board. I was quite fond of that class – I especially liked learning about the weather and drawing cold, warm and stationary fronts: half-circles and triangles, red and blue.

I sat in that first seat, furthest left, facing the blackboard for a couple of reasons: first of all, I was not in the direct line of sight, teachers warily watching the boys that invariably sat in the back for totally non-academic reasons; and secondly, that was the only way I could read the blackboard. The school gave eye tests back then, and I failed in 7th grade. I brought the note home to my mother, who did not act upon it. The next year I again brought home the same note – again no action. The school, thinking I wasn't passing along the information, ended up finally calling my mother. She accused me of intentionally failing the vision tests so I could wear glasses. Shamed by the school district into taking me to an ophthalmologist, my mother did come to realize I had become near-sighted. Those first glasses were tortoise-shell plastic, classic cat-eye glasses. I now could sit anywhere I wanted, but I remained in the first row, farthest left, every time I was allowed.

I was seated right next to Jenny Thomas whenever I could manage to arrange it. I remember one English class… our teacher was a tall, extremely thin, high-strung red-head. Jenny was vastly more interesting than Mrs. Cahill… but there was no talking. So we started passing notes. Then there were no notes. So Jenny and I learned to sign – not ASL, which uses large motions for entire words, but letter-by-letter, in the style of Helen Keller, of whom we had recently read. We would put our hands down by our sides, fingers flying. We drove that teacher crazy.

The school district also gave a battery of aptitude and placement tests in 8th grade. I remember the reading test – I ended up off the charts. All they knew is that I was reading somewhere north of 800 words a minute at 100% comprehension. The scale stopped at 800. That, and I was never meant to be a clerk (10% on that test) – I was best at mechanical engineering (85%). I had no idea what a mechanical engineer even was at the time. I rather naively brought home the test results, only to watch my parents go into some infinite do-loop of incomprehension: how ever could a girl's highest aptitude be in engineering? A girl??? I was always told I should be a teacher. Be a teacher, my mother would say, so if anything happens to my eventual husband I could get a job. Engineer? Out of the question.

~

We took a big family trip during the summer between 8th and 9th grades… we rented a trailer and went to California. My dad had an army buddy there in the movie business: Peter Tewksbury. He was going to get us into the studios. Wow, I was going to be "discovered!" Foolish, insecure me….

We hit several national parks on the way out to L.A. – Bryce, Zion, the petrified forest, the Grand Canyon. It was raining when we were in Bryce, and the spires were very slippery. It's at a pretty high altitude, and I remember how hard it was to breathe when we were climbing up. Zion totally took my breath away. When we got to the end and saw that huge semi-circle of stone, I was dumbstruck. It rained when we were in the painted desert, too, so the colors were not very brilliant. Those sights are much more memorable than the movie studio. I tried so hard to look my best, but thirteen is a very awkward age. I remember what I wore, and looking back I can candidly say I looked horrible.

My father cut his family time short and flew back from Denver, leaving my mother with the three of us to bring back the trailer. We had done all the sight-seeing, so this was the boring return. In the middle of Nebraska, a pheasant in the brush by the side of the road became startled and took off – right into the front trailer window. Damage claim #1. We spent the night there, and the next morning my mother got us up early and made pancakes in the trailer before piling us in the car and taking off. However, she was in too much of a hurry, and when she stowed everything in the trailer she stowed the still-hot range elements in the drawer with the potholders. By the time we hit the corn fields of Kansas, smoke was leaking out of the trailer. Cars that had been behind us kept speeding up next to us, honking their horns and pointing, but it was a while before my mother realized they were trying to warn us. She eventually pulled over and went back to the trailer. When she opened the door, the oxygen-starved smoldering immediately became a full-fledged, roaring fire. Damage claim #2 – totaled. We ended up staying in a farm house that we could see in the distance. The woman of the house was very kind – she fed us well, put us up for the night and gave me a pair of her underpants (since everything we had was gone) which were way, way too big for me, but farmhouse clean. We left that trailer there, in the middle of a Kansas corn field.

Ninth grade was back at Groves. My homeroom teacher, Mr. Carson, was a great guy. He was the basketball coach, and he always had silly socks he wore on around the major holidays. He was my homeroom teacher for 4 years – homeroom C-9. I was not a popular student. I was quiet and shy… years of being told nobody liked me had taken its toll. I was so insecure that if somebody said "Hi" to me in the hall, I would turn around first to make sure they were talking to me. I was a social mess with my peers. I was most at ease with my 9th grade history teacher, whose classes I also took in subsequent years. I had him last class period, and I would hang around to chat for a bit before the bus came. Mr. Guilmet was concerned at first, saying that hanging around wouldn't get me a better grade. I shot back with, "I don't need that," which was true: I was an "A" student. He would often walk with me towards the office, where he would go in to conduct some business while I carried on towards the waiting busses. He was smart, he was sharp, and he would just talk. I think we mostly talked about history or other classwork of mine, but for some reason it worked. He wrote in my yearbook that it is uncommon for a student to also become a friend, but we certainly were. He ended up marrying the German teacher, Judy Kent, a few years later.

I got to know the shop teacher quite well. You see, my knee hinge broke more than once, and I would go down to shop and sit on the bench while the class worked on cobbling me back together so I could get on the bus and go home. School was a good ten miles away, so it was imperative that I caught that bus.

The shop classes were across the hall from Home Economics… girls took Home Economics, boys took shop. I remember the dress I made in sewing: it was a simple shift in a pretty aqua cotton. I picked that color because it was my father's favorite. My first attempt wasn't a roaring success: the dress didn't fit me very well, and I was self-conscious at the "fashion show" where we wore what we had made for our mothers. I had been a tall and thin child – one of the tallest in my elementary school classes – until I got sick that one summer. That illness really took its toll on me, interrupting my metabolism. It left me with incredibly long legs for my ridiculously short torso, since I got sick in the middle of a growth spurt. As if I should be split at the waist: the person proportional to my legs, 5'10", the person proportional to my torso maybe 4'8". I started to get pudgy and it became very difficult to find clothing that fit well.

~

We moved when I was in middle school, to a four-acre property with 160' of lake frontage on Middle Belt Road. It was the original homestead on the lake. My father nearly doubled the size of that house – he added the parent's wing, with a master bedroom, his and hers bathrooms, my dad's study, a rec room and a sewing room. My father's bathroom was very utilitarian: a tile shower, single sink over a vanity, a toilet – standard fare. My mother's bath was at least twice as large – it had an extra-large, custom, all-tile, raised tub with a large wall mirror over her vanity. I had never seen anything like it before: it was gorgeous!

I loved that house. Years later, when I was bored and doodling, I would draw that house. My sister and I shared a large bedroom over the garage. It had been a family room or something similar – it had pine-board walls. My mother painted those walls white – that took four coats of paint because the knots would keep bleeding through. My father crafted two built-in desks along one wall, and a very large walk-in closet behind the desks. At the end of the closet, not tall because of the swooping eave on that side of the house, my sister and I built a doll-house on the shelves. There was a small window back there, so we had natural light. We made walls and furniture and decorated our little two-story shelf-house. That effort took us a very happy forever.

Our room had windows with diamond-shaped aluminum fake muntins, which I loved. We had powder blue carpeting. Our beds were across from each other, up against opposing walls, with a white dresser under the front window overlooking the long driveway. There was a long crawl space, accessed by a short door in the wall hugged by my sister's bed, and there was a door to the outside that my dad nailed shut past the foot of mine. By the feet of our respective beds were two wing-back chairs. They were upholstered in a blue patterned fabric, but each had a large orange bird of some sort right in the middle of the backs. My mother didn't see the orange in the swatch she chose for the chairs, and she wasn't very pleased with the orange birds. I loved those chairs – they were just the right size to curl up in and read. My grandmother had given us a yellow handmade quilt. I loved that quilt, too, although I think my sister used it more than me.

Between the door to the outside and the crawl space next to my sister, I had ample fodder to tease. I remember lying in bed, lights out but before we fell sleep. I would say things like, "Tracy, what if you rolled over in your sleep, and your arm fell off the bed, and your hand landed on…. a beard?" She would lie there for a few minutes contemplating the scenario, then leap out of bed and come screaming across the room, jumping on top of me and beating me with her fists, me safely under pulled up covers.

That house had a very long driveway. There was a shed – more of a small barn – half way to the road. We kept the Bolens tractor and the riding lawnmower in there. My dad hired a gardener – Bill. Bill had a brother that would sometimes help him. I can't remember the brother's name, but I do remember he was exceptionally thin, with tumors on his face, neck and chest that made his skin lumpy. Having the equipment that far from the house gave us a couple of extra snow days: we had quite a blizzard one year, in early April, when my mother's AAUW fashion show was scheduled. There was a side door off the basement, the soil on either side graded down to allow access to the door. I opened it after that blizzard and it was snow all the way up – not even a hint of light. It took us two days to shovel out to the shed to get to the tractor, with its snow blade.

The bus stop was at the top of a steep hill, in front of the where the Akers lived. The Akers had two children: a boy and a girl. Mrs. Akers was a pleasingly plump woman with big, salon-styled blond hair. She was a DAR member with roots back to one of our early presidents. That meant nothing to me, but apparently it was important to my mother. I had dinner one night at the Akers and was entranced by the rice. Yes, the rice – it was all buttery and salt-and-peppered and utterly delicious. Never knew rice could taste like that.

The hill of which I speak was a significant hill. It was a long walk down the driveway and then up the hill – along the side of a major, but only 2-lane, north-south road with narrow shoulders, no sidewalk, no lights and a 45 MPH speed limit. It was intimidating, and probably not very safe, in retrospect. Except when there was deep snow, I would more often walk out that side basement door, up across the two back lawns and up along the side of the Akers house. That was also a long walk up a steep hill, as each house had acreage, but it was away from the traffic. I would take off my ugly white rubber over-boots at the bus stop and hide them in the evergreens lining the Akers driveway. One day when I got off the bus my boots were gone. Oops! My mother was angry about that.

One non-snowy day, as I was walking down the long, steep back lawns between the Akers and our house, a little dog came running at me from the far woods, barking. He ran up and bit my leg. He, however, chose the wrong leg to bite. I'm sure his teeth rattled when he wrapped them around wood. He simply stopped, backed off confusedly, and wandered off from whence he came. Those wooden legs were very convenient for fending off biting dogs and mosquitos.

We had lots of mosquitos: they would breed in the cove we owned and live in the woods that occupied the space between our shed/barn and the road. My brother took up survival skills when we lived in that house, and he and I pitched a tent and spent a weekend in the woods. Ever the man with strict rules, he dictated what I could and could not do. We were not – NOT – to go in the house to use the bathroom, to get food, to eat... not to go in. The second or third day we were camping it got to be over 90°. I hadn't packed my swimsuit, so I went in the house to grab it and came back to the tent to change. According to Jeff, I broke the rules. He banished me from the campsite. I was unhappy, thinking he was too harsh, but that didn't last long. Pshaw on that – I went and jumped in the lake.

~

As I said, I was very shy in high school – so shy that when I tried out for Choir I opened my mouth and nothing came out. Dear Ms. Micheletti let me in anyway. Every time Ms. Micheletti wanted to have someone sing a line because she had heard a wrong note, the same thing happened – not even a croak. Ms. Micheletti was in her twenties at the time: she was a very thin and elegant woman who had our collective attention at her fingertips... literally. When directing she never waved her arms, never mouthed the words, never pointed to any section. She stood like a statue, Ferragamo-shoed feet primly together, elbows to her sides, hands mid-center. From the back she looked motionless – it was all in the hands. We always placed first in competition – everything memorized, everything motionless but for moving mouths, eyes fixated on those magic hands of hers.

I never could get a regular summer job in high school – for one thing, I was a year younger than my classmates, so I wasn't sixteen until the summer between junior and senior years. Classmates had two summers of opportunity: I had only one. That, and I did not have reliable transportation and obviously, I was disabled. Employers were put off by that. The baby boom that had surrounded and crowded me for my entire life was alive and well. I did manage to get a babysitting job when I was fifteen, for the Clouse family. They lived about a mile away, and I could walk there. They had three young children – none yet in public school, two boys and a girl. Patricia Clouse was a very unhappily married woman and a very distant parent. Those children were a handful. Mrs. Clouse was far more interested in shopping – she was a compulsive shopper and would come back from shopping with one of her friends and hide the bags of clothing under the bed. She was a terrible housekeeper. Mr. Clouse was quite a big guy, and he didn't seem very happy, either. Anyway, one night after the children were asleep I started cleaning – I just couldn't bear to sit in the mess. You couldn't even see the kitchen counter for the stacked up dirty dishes, and the pantry was a dumping ground. It was impossible to even tell what was on the shelves. Mrs. Clouse liked what I did, and I spent more and more time over there, babysitting and cleaning. They even took me on vacation with them, to some amusement park in Ohio. I spent maybe a month or two working for them... I think they decided to divorce, and that was the end of the line for me.

The summer between my junior and senior year I worked for my dad's office partner, Dr. Schultz, on Wednesdays. By then, my father had abandoned his Royal Oak office and had started working for the Teamsters. I believe my grandfather had a big hand in that: he had met the "right" people, and the five of them formed Dearborn Machinery Movers. That company was responsible for moving the huge "Spirit of Detroit" statue into place in front of the Detroit Municipal building in 1958.

There was something a bit dark about my grandfather's work, I think. Looking back, it is unlikely that a newly formed company would get a contract that big without some "assistance." There were rumors of a deal he had concerning some property in Florida and the Teamsters. Rumors of some sort of fishing-related dealings. You couldn't even get into the rigging and business without the blessing of the Teamsters – they would make you or break you. Conversations that abruptly ended when I walked in the room. My grandfather was absolutely wonderful with us, but looking back, I think I don't want to ever know any details about his business dealings.

My dad became the Hoffa family's dentist... and that's the office within which I worked in the summer of 1967. I was good at the front desk, good at mixing the amalgam for fillings, but absolutely horrible at taking X-rays. I had a difficult time figuring out the angle and line of sight through a cheek to take a centered picture.

The summer of 1967... July 23rd, that's when the Detroit riots started. The Teamsters offices were near Fenkell... Livernois: I can't remember, I had memorized the route rather by rote, since I had no mental map of the city. July 23rd was a Sunday – the riots started on Sunday. By Wednesday the National Guard was out in force. On my way to work I passed machine guns mounted on Jeeps manned by soldiers stationed at the street corners. I wish I had a better mental picture: my impression looking back is gray – simply gray, bleak, abandoned and eerie. Except for the soldiers, the streets were totally abandoned. The area was not the best anyway – I always made a sandwich for lunch in lieu of trying to find a place to eat. I was very glad for that on Wednesday, July 26th. Absolutely no one made their appointments. Nobody called to cancel, either – no one expected the office to be open. I didn't think a thing of going into work that day, and my parents said nothing.

That was also the summer my mother shattered her knee when a wheelbarrow tipped over on it. She was bed-ridden for quite some time. By then we had moved into house #7, on Comfort Street on the south side of the lake. More remodeling: we slept dormitory-style in the attic with nothing but plastic clothes storage bags between the row of beds. There wasn't a wall in the house: the bathroom "walls" were hung sheets. It was up in the attic, in front of one of the four beds lined up dormitory-style, that my mother and brother got into an argument. He was probably eighteen at the time. My mother went to hit him, but he grabbed her wrist to stop her. She flew into a rage and grabbed the closest thing she could reach – a leather belt with a big metal belt buckle. Not a buckle with a pin; a big metal buckle with a wide, rigid hook at the end. She sunk that hook into his bicep. It was horrible to watch.

This house was a split level, but instead of one level on one side/two levels on the other, it had 2 and 3, respectively. Two levels lakeside, three levels opposite. There were separate garages facing the street with a private, concrete courtyard in between. It had a fountain in it, and my father had taken a plain door and built up very intricate designs using molding. I always liked that door – it looked so very substantial. Facing the lake was the living room, and above it my parent's room and bath to the left and my brother's room and children's bath to the right. Facing the street was the basement (again, always wet), the kitchen and dining room above that, and my sister's and my room above that, with a couple of walk-in closets and an office. My grandmother had gotten my sister and me yellow chenille matching bedspreads with big daisies on them. My sister and I got to pick out our carpeting, and we picked a bronze color that went well with the bedspreads. My mother did not like either the bedspreads or the carpet.

We had a huge, old walnut writing desk in the office. We had to leave it when we moved because the walls were built around it, and we couldn't get it out of the room. Our piano was in the closet that was meant for the office. I played that piano hour upon hour. Beethoven's "Fur Elise" was my best piece, because it had very few right-hand chords. I can't do anything more than a two-note chord, no greater than a third apart. I must choose my music judiciously. That's why my mother wouldn't give me piano lessons – she reserved those lessons for my sister, who didn't want them, and who ran away from home more than once because of them. My brother took cornet lessons. I did end up with teach-yourself-piano books: John Thompson's books. They had red and white covers. The books started with the assumption that I could correlate the notes on the pages with the keyboard, but – not true. I remember playing a tune that was in the book, but I was playing it by ear: I was playing it in a different key than what was written. I had no idea. My maternal grandfather came over and tried to play an accompaniment with me, but he could read music. He stopped abruptly and told me I was wrong. It didn't go well. Nevertheless, I worked at it and worked at it, and finally figured it out.

While the house was still under construction, when we had temporary 2x4 stairs to the top level, I popped out my left knee. My patella had relocated itself to the outside of my leg. I remember the paramedics had a devil of a time with those temporary stairs and the stretcher. When I got the emergency room one doctor grabbed my ankle and pulled hard, while another doctor pushed my kneecap back into place. My leg was extremely swollen. I couldn't make it up the temporary stairs, so I took up temporary residence in my brother's bed for several days. His room was painted black; with the samurai swords my father had brought back from Japan hanging over the bed. We had a bit of a heat wave, and I couldn't believe how hot it was in that black bedroom. That knee has popped out a couple of times since.

So were in that house with four flights of stairs when my mother shattered her knee. That was the summer that suddenly I was "Mom." I was not prepared for that. I remember coming home from work one day, only to run into my mother screaming at me that the children's bathroom needed cleaning. I got down on my hands and knees and started scrubbing. I remember my father getting angry that, although the laundry was done and folded, his socks were on the washer and not in his drawer. He had big feet – we all have big feet. We had to take his cotton socks and stretch them on sock stretchers so he could get them on his size 13-with-high-insteps feet. Taking longer to dry, they had not made it up 3 flights of stairs to his dresser. What never got me in trouble was my cooking. I remember my father bragging about how I made potato salad early so the chopped-up onions properly flavored the mayonnaise. He was smiling when he said that.

I was stuck at home: my brother kept escaping to Billy Wilbur's house, my sister to Susie Bellinger's. I had nowhere else to go. I escaped into my schoolwork, where I could do well.

I took the school-offered driving class the summer between my junior and senior years. Back then all sorts of programs were offered in public school: we got vaccinations (sugar-cube polio), we took eye tests and TB tests, we took driving. At first the district wouldn't let me enroll. My mother, never to be slighted, marched down to the Superintendent's office and started yelling (yes, it was yelling. She was anything but calm and collected), repeatedly screaming that, "No one does this to MYYYY daughter!" Anyway, she cowed the man enough to get me into class. To drive, the only thing I need to do differently is use my left foot, not my right. The only restriction on my license is glasses. My dad said that I would be able to drive a manual transmission if I would listen carefully enough to hear when the gear could be shifted, but that's nothing I ever did. After I passed that class, my father took me out to practice driving early one Saturday morning in his '65 Mustang convertible. Sauterne gold with a black top – an awesome car. He had me stop at the bottom of a hill and reached over to hold on to the wheel. He told me to floor it, which of course I was too timid to do. So he yelled at me, and I punched that baby as hard as I could. The car fishtailed all over the road, tires squealing. He then told me to pull over. He very calmly told me that, as I could see, even he was having a hard time controlling the car: I obviously wasn't going to be able to. I never forgot that lesson, nor the speech he gave me about my needing to be a better driver than anyone else. He said if I ever got into an accident they would blame my handicap and try to take away my license. Words to live by.

My parents took a couple of international trips my senior year: the first one was to Spain/Portugal/Morocco, and the second was to the Far East. My brother was away, living on campus, so it was my sister and me, alone. I was 16-17, she was 12-13. I got her up, got her fed, made her lunch and got her on the bus – did the laundry, cleaned the house, cooked dinner. I liked being alone: I could drive to school in one of the five cars my parents owned. I drove a different car every day – that was fun. And no one was yelling at me, no one was fighting. It was good. Decades later Ms. Micheletti mentioned that she had never seen a more maternal older sister than me – that surprised me.

~

My school life changed dramatically my junior year on three major fronts. First, I joined the drama club. I had a bit part in "Guys and Dolls" – I was a Salvation Army lady with a single line to speak. The drama teacher, a ballerina, wasn't very keen on me. She tried to make us all into dancers, and she loved choreography. She was the one that taught us how to spin and point, as to not get dizzy. She would have us on the stage floor doing stretches, and she would breeze by, waving her arms rather dramatically, taking long, pointed-toe, graceful strides, telling us, "It is only pain... it is only pain." That was a big step for me, though. The second big thing was choir. The school soloists were always seniors: the female star of Guys and Dolls was also the choir soloist. However, seniors did not go to class the last week of school. The freshmen, sophomores and juniors were in choir, and Ms. Micheletti, ever the strict disciplinarian, passed out Schubert's Mass in G. We were going to sing. She always directed from the piano, and I was seated to her far left, first row. We started singing, but when we got to the second page there was a soprano solo. Not looking up, she threw her left arm out, finger pointed, and said, "Sing it." Well, her finger ended up on me. So I sang it. No time to choke up. Many years of swimming had given me some pretty substantial lung capacity, so sing I did. I did an entire run without needing a breath. I hit a very clear, strong and operatic high G. At the end of that solo she just stopped. Everybody stopped. And stared. She looked at me and said, "Where did that come from?" I replied, rather timidly, "I don't know." And at that moment I became the next year's school soloist. I had quite a voice – 4-octave range and plug-your-ears power in the high register.

The third thing that changed my life was taking the National Merit test. I remember thinking it was the hardest test I had ever seen. I was humbled by it. But this awkward, shy student became a Semi-Finalist. It made the local papers. Nobody knew what I was capable of - not even me. All of a sudden everybody knew me, and I was a brain. I started getting letters from universities as far away as Louisiana, promising me full scholarships. I really had no idea - I had always thought school was difficult – I had to study hard. I remember pulling all-nighters in high school, propelled by the knowledge that the grade I would be getting the next day would be forever. Yes, I took Honors classes, and no, I never got less than an occasional B (I graduated fifth in my class, with just under a 4.0 GPA), but I thought it was difficult. Renata Klass was the smartest person in school, not me.

School was hard, but I mostly figured everything out for myself. My one and only attempt at asking my dad for homework help was remarkable. The subject was math – right up his alley. So I asked him. And it was as if he had been waiting his entire life for this. This he understood! This was something he was supposed to do! He was so into it!! So he started… and I stopped understanding on like sentence number 3. I didn't have the heart to tell him – he was just so into it, so I just kept nodding and making affirmative murmurs. When he was done I thanked him very much. Then I went up to my room and figured it out by myself.

I did make the National Honor Society – the choir was on stage singing, and I saw my parents in the audience. My father was unmistakable: taller than most men and prematurely white. I knew I had been elected before the big announcement. My father proudly presented me with his NHS pin – that remains one of the most significant moments in my life.

It's not that I didn't have hints I might be a bit different: I remember taking a Civics class. Our teacher was a young, tall and gangly man with a Polish surname who walked toes-in – that's when I learned that people with that gait and physiology are normally fast runners. Anyway, I had missed a day of school, so during lecture I borrowed Jenny's notes and busied myself copying them (she also was a National Merit Semi-Finalist). Mr. O, thinking I wasn't paying attention, asked a question and then – attempted trap – asked me to answer it. I had been listening all the time... the note copying was totally automatic. I did have the presence of mind to lay down my pencil and look up to answer, but truth be told, I wouldn't have needed to at all. I could have answered his question and not missed a note-copying beat. Something told me at the time that would have been seen as too over-the-top. Mr. O never bothered me again.

~

The school district teachers went on strike my senior year. They showed up and taught, but they did not volunteer for any extracurricular activities. No after-school dances, no senior field trip... nothing but the academics. I was talking about that at dinner one night, and my father started advocating for full year school. We talked and talked, and encouraged by him, I ended up writing up a flyer. I went to work with him one weekend and ran off maybe 4,000 copies on his old mimeograph machine... one that you had to crank out the sheets one by one, spinning the barrel with the heady, make-you-dizzy purple ink. Kit – the Kit from my 3-year-old birthday party - attended the other district high school. I gave her a couple thousand copies, and one day during homeroom she and I managed to get a copy in the hands of every one of the 4,000 high school students in the district. Well, many of those mimeographed flyers got into the hands of parents, which led to it being published in the local newspaper. And THAT led to op-eds and a very heated and spirited discussion in the community. I got in trouble for that. As in: getting called into the Superintendent's office. No, not the Principal's office – the Superintendent of the School District's office. Trouble was, there was a lot of parental anger at the teacher strike, and I was a National Merit scholastic superstar, which put the Superintendent in a rather delicate position. I remember him telling me that it was against the rules to distribute anything without permission. He dejectedly sighed, told me not to do it again, and when we were walking out I remember him asking me how I managed to do what I did – logistically, that is. How did I manage to orchestrate such a seamless and complete distribution? He said even the school district had a difficult time with that. I remember walking out smiling at that.

My Honors English teacher read that flyer in class and told me it was very well-written. She was grinning. Mrs. Mandelbaum – the award-winning English teacher with excruciatingly high standards told me I had written something well. And now there wasn't anybody in town that didn't know me, or know of me.

~

School was so different back then. Girls could not wear pants. Boys could not wear jeans. Mrs. Sherrard, an Assistant Principal, would walk around school, making girls kneel on the floor if she thought the girls' skirts were too short. Skirt hems were supposed to touch the floor. We would all roll our skirts up after leaving home and pull them down if we saw Mrs. Sherrard coming. After that, up they would again go. White lipstick was popular back then, and before class girls would crowd the bathrooms, putting on forbidden makeup before homeroom and wiping it off before going back home. Boys wore short, short hair, and one scandal was that the football team grabbed some guy that had become enamored by the Beatles and who had accordingly let his hair grow a bit, yanked him into the boy's bathroom, held him down and cut his hair. The most common transgression was smoking in the bathroom.

There were the football/cheerleader popular kids, there were the Greasers, and then there were the rest of us, uncategorized. Greasers were edgy: the girls wore lots of makeup and teased their hair to the stratosphere. The guys wore tight black jeans and slicked their hair back with Brylcreem... Fonzie-style. Black leather jackets were part of their uniform. Understand that back then, "normal" kids did not wear black. They just didn't.

While school was going well, the home front was deteriorating by the hour. My brother's new name was "Shit for Brains," and my moniker went from "Peg Leg" to "Lard Ass". My parents had lots of parties, and it was our job to get up early the next morning and clean everything up. We were pretty much responsible for ourselves – do our own laundry, fix our own breakfasts and lunches, get ourselves to and from school unaided...I remember my mother yelling down the stairs one morning that I was making too much noise getting myself up, fed and off to school. I remember missing the bus a couple of times and hitchhiking the ten miles to school with my brother. Ms. Micheletti remembers my mother forgetting to pick me up, leaving me to start walking the ten miles home by myself.

I became convinced that my parents were looking for any excuse at all to kick me out – the parents that had both told me, at different times, how they didn't like me. So I became the model teenager. I never got into trouble. I got almost straight A's. I never went out. I remember telling myself, well, if they didn't like me, at least they would respect me.

The awards kept coming. I was called down to the office one day to see my counselor, who informed me I had received a full scholarship to Michigan State. Full tuition, room and board, books and supplies, four years. I hadn't applied for it, so that was a complete surprise. I remember going back to class, sitting next to mean Kathy. She asked me what was up, and I told her they had given me that scholarship. She was pretty upset about that. I went down to Ford Auditorium, downtown on the river, to receive an award from Phi Beta Kappa. None of that caused as much as a raised eyebrow from my parents… they were too lost in their own misery. I could shine in academics… but still not socially. The only way I got to the Prom was to volunteer serving punch. I wasn't invited to parties, to the movies… I wasn't invited to anything.

Senior year the drama department put on West Side Story. I was both the wardrobe mistress and the soloist for the dance sequence to "There's a Time for Us." That song became the class song. The choir traditionally put on two concerts, one near the end of each semester. The winter concert featured Brahms's Requiem – that's one challenging piece. It is so rich – I remember thinking I didn't like it very much when I first heard it, but when I was in it – inside of it – the tapestry of sound was astoundingly and almost overwhelmingly beautiful. That concert was my first solo work since elementary school… the first time after I must have realized that there were actually people out there listening. Desiring the ever-understated presentation, Ms. Micheletti dictated that the soloists were not to be dressed in formal clothes with chairs and stands in front of the chorus. We simply stood in the front row in our choir robes and took a step out to sing our solos, and then stepped back to totally blend in. I will never forget that step out. I sang the first solo – I actually pulled it off – but when I stepped back into line my knees were shaking so much I fell into the person next to me. I didn't have a friendly face in the audience upon which to fix my gaze: my parents didn't come. It wasn't important enough for them to take time off work – at least, work was the excuse they gave me.

The first time something like that happens it is devastating. After that it doesn't matter much anymore. I can't even remember the spring choral concert. I remember that I had an opportunity to go down to Atlanta and sing in a workshop with Robert Shaw. Ms. Micheletti wanted me to do that. I was so sure that it was an impossibility that I didn't even mention it to my parents... I mean, why even bother? I do remember that we had a senior concert... the concert for graduation. I made a pink formal gown... I remember needing $15 to buy the fabric. My mother took my side, and I remember my father pulling out his folded bills, peeling off $15, and grudgingly giving it to me, saying, "But I don't want to do this." The dress was beautiful – white satin overlaid with pale pink lace, empire waistline with a darker pink satin ribbon at the seam. I sang the class song and I sang the title song from "Alfie." My parents were at that concert, but my father was drunk. He was talking loudly and disturbing the people around him. He told me afterwards my pitch was a bit off on the Alfie song. It is not a happy memory.

He was desperately unhappy. One of his best friends, Dick Baird, had died of cancer. That sent my father into deep depression. I remember that he apparently had taken a cab home one night, so drunk he couldn't remember where he had parked his car. He and I took off the next day in my mother's car to try and find his Lincoln. He vaguely remembered what bar(s) he had visited, and we drove the streets until we found it. My father did not like sullen people, and I had become a sullen person at home. Ipso facto, he said he did not like me. In the car, while I was driving him to his misplaced vehicle. I will never forget that car ride.

I graduated with little ado. Graduation was June 13th, but as luck would have it, my parent's 25th wedding anniversary was June 20th. That totally overshadowed my graduation, as everyone was focused on the 25th anniversary party my aunt and uncle were throwing for my parents. My grandparents came over for dinner and gave me $100, with which I bought an industrial strength sewing machine. Then all eyes were on my parents. My father borrowed my Uncle Ted's WWII uniform for the party, and my mother bought a silvery blue silk suit to wear. I made them a seven-course gourmet French dinner as my gift – it took me two days to make.

~

I can't remember anything much more about the summer between high school and college, except that I had to go up to MSU for three days for a battery of placement tests. That summer interval was several weeks shorter, since college started weeks earlier than public school. "Off to College" shopping was minimal back then: no phones/refrigerators/televisions etc. – not allowed: not enough power available in the old dorms. I did take with me some sea shells and a turquoise fishing net, which I hung from the ceiling over one of the two desks. Crowded as always, the school jammed three girls into a two-girl room. We had a bunk bed and an extra single bed, which left room for only two desks for the three of us. We had one dresser – each of us got two drawers. There was one small closet. The bathroom was down the hall and around the corner. There was one public phone in the hall. With so little space, packing was not much of an effort – at the time the dorm passed out clean linens once a week... all I needed was a blanket. The blanket I took was medium blue, with embroidered flowers on the top satin edging. My mother took me up on a Friday and dropped me off – she didn't stay to help me organize. What I didn't know is that she dropped me off early: three days before the cafeteria opened, with no money. I didn't even have a dime to call home. The RA came on Sunday and after hearing my story gave me a pack of crackers – the only food she had. I hadn't eaten anything since Friday.

When the dorm cafeteria opened I was amazed – there was a huge stainless steel bowl of cottage cheese and trays of bananas... every night. I loved cottage cheese, and I loved bananas. Given the food frugality with which I grew up, I was acting as if I had an eating disorder. I went right to the cottage cheese and bananas straight away, every night. After a couple of weeks, I realized I was acting irrationally – the cottage cheese was going to be there, every night, as were the bananas. The freshman 15? That's what I lost that first term.

I had a difficult time finding classes to take… I placed out of every course requirement. Every requirement, that is, except English. I placed out of that class after Day One. We got the syllabus, and the textbook we would be using was the textbook I had in eleventh grade. When I approached the professor to tell him I had already used that text, he was affronted. He told me to turn in some of my high school work, and he would judge whether I could write or not. I did, he did, and I was excused from that last requirement. Bless my high-performing high school!! That left me with trying to fill my schedule with 300 and 400 level courses, since placing out of the requirements did not place me out of the required credits for graduation. I had wanted to major in French – I had dreams of being a United Nations interpreter – but I was so fluent by that time, the only thing available to me were classes in French Literature and one class in Idiomatics. There were not enough credits offered in classes advanced enough to allow me to major in French. And all at the tender age of seventeen.

That first term I took a Shakespeare class – 300 level. I felt so out of my league. The mid-term was the first blue-book I ever completed. I never knew we were going to have to buy blue-books at the Union bookstore to take tests. I thought I did not do well at all. The professor, a leering, bespectacled, balding man taken to bowties, stood up and chastised the class in general for overall poor performance. OMG, here we go – first class test and I blew it. He pulled out a blue-book and said, "Here. Here's an example of the kind of work I expect of you." He started to read, and the words were very familiar. He was reading my essay. That professor pointed out that I often threw humor into my writing - a fact I had never realized. I became very light-headed as I listened to him – I felt quite dazed. All of these juniors and seniors, and he was reading a 17-year-old first term freshman's essay.

That first semester my two roommates were both named Cathy: one was from Kalamazoo and one was from some Detroit suburb. We lived in Room 124, Phillips Hall. It was on the first floor, in the corner so we had two windows on adjoining walls. The Kalamazoo Cathy was very quiet, pigeon-toed, and very discomfited by the Very Large MSU. She was horribly, horribly messy, and she would get into huge arguments with me after I would clean things up. With so little space, we had to be tidy or all was lost. Literally. She would have her clothes hanging out of dresser drawers so I couldn't get into mine. The other Cathy was a raven-haired high school cheerleader who proudly told her mother she went to mass every week, leaving out the part that she went Saturday early evening so she could party hardy at the various frat houses and sleep in Sundays. The Kalamazoo Cathy left after her first term and was replaced by Liz Vialpando, a student from the Upper Peninsula. Raven-haired Cathy met another cheerleader, Susie, and partied with her every weekend. Cathy moved in with Susie second term, and it was just the two of us – Liz and me.

Liz was very worldly – her father had worked internationally, so she knew several languages. She was quite petite, with the shiniest hair I had ever seen, and she was very vivacious. Her high school boyfriend, Gary, also attended MSU. He was full-on smitten with Liz, but Liz, realizing the opportunity available to her with the tens of thousands of people at the school, decided that small-town Gary needed to be history. Liz told me Gary was bi-polar: he told her that if she dropped him he was going to commit suicide. She did drop him, he didn't commit suicide, but I was uncomfortable with the way Liz treated Gary, and that ended up coloring our relationship.

I had signed up to attend a college-within-the-university: Justin Morrill College. The catalog described it as follows: "Justin Morrill College, combining the traditional with the innovative, challenges each student to discover himself and who he wants to be, and to learn something of the interdependence of the modern world." We were not lost in a 40,000-student college campus: we were housed in a pair of adjoining old dorms up in the northeast corner of the campus. Our classes were almost all within the Snyder-Phillips dorm complex itself, making it seem like a small college. I had chosen MSU not only for the scholarship – I did have other offers – I chose it because my brother was there. He lived in the adjoining dorm. My mother graduated from there, also, so we had a family history. I was uncomfortable going somewhere where I knew absolutely no one. I had absolutely no faith in my social abilities.

The flower children of the late 1960's totally disdained Greek life, but my mother had been a Sigma Kappa and she was really sold on the idea. I wasn't. There was a woman from my high school, a year older, named Gwen Compson. There was also another Wendy Thompson, a tall, leggy blond. The three of us hooked up and rushed together, Gwen and I just to confuse those cute little sorority sisters with the surfeit of very similar names. I was not excited to rush – I knew that no sorority would want me, and I obviously didn't have the money to join. I was right: not one single call-back. No matter.

That other Wendy Thompson also had scholarships, and second term I got a letter telling me I owed the school money... the office had confused the two of us and had given the other Wendy all my scholarship money. I went down with my paperwork, and a while later I got a big check... they gave me all her scholarship money. I went down to the Admin building and tried to give the check back, but I was told it was mine. Come sophomore year, the school realized they had made a mistake and dunned me. I turned the entire matter over to my father. He called the school and told them that in his practice, if he made a billing mistake, and the client attempted to no avail to correct it, and a year later he realized his mistake, he would never be able to go back and demand the money. He won the argument.

That other Wendy... she caused confusion on several levels. She had taken Spanish in high school – I had taken French. Since I was searching for classes to take, I enrolled in Spanish. So close to French, I was excelling so much the teacher believed I was in too elementary a class. She went to the office, found out about the other Wendy, and accused me of sandbagging. I had to prove to her there were two of "us." And then there were the weekend phone calls from random men looking for Blond Wendy. I remember fielding a call from some guy she had met the night before. He was furious, thinking I – she – was blowing him off. I just couldn't convince him until I told him to pull out a campus phone book and look us both up.

Not everybody in the dorm was enrolled in Justin Morrill... there was Julie, a very sturdy and intimidating upper classman who lived down the hall and who was a Criminal Justice major. There was a water fight one day, and she was unabashedly watering down everyone. No one would take her on... no one except me. I got a large trash can from the utility room, filled it up with water, and leaned it against her door. When she opened her door to come out, about 30 gallons of water flooded her room. She was absolutely furious. She headed down to my room... I locked the door and climbed out the window. That was no mean feat, since there was about a ten or twelve-foot drop from the window ledge to the ground. But, Julie being who she was, I was highly motivated. There also was the fascinating woman across the hall, a beautiful black woman who was married to a serviceman. She was finishing her education while he was in Vietnam. She was so sophisticated – I was very impressed.

I entered college in 1968. It was the era of the Vietnam War protests, and the re-establishment of the draft, of Woodstock and flower children and psychedelic posters and acid rock. We decided we didn't want curfew anymore, so one night we held the dorm open. That experience was quite enlightening: I saw for the first time the effect of mob psychology. It is quite strong, and it was rather disturbing to me. There were war protests on campus, and I remember hitching a ride home one weekend right after there had been campus demonstrations. I was there, mind you, and it was so clear to me that the news media had exaggerated the protest by film editing that made the protest look a lot more violent and widespread than it was. That's when I learned that television news reports are so very easily sensationalized – I was so naïve... I was so shocked. And then my brother's friend was killed at Kent State, and I looked at both media and government in an entirely different way.

We had fun in the dorms: there were raids back and forth. Snyder was the men's dorm: Phillips was the women's. We would sneak into the Snyder bathrooms and smoothly cover the toilet bowls with Saran Wrap. They would stage panty raids. We took Vaseline and coated door handles, and then set off alarm clocks in the hallways. They must have raided every single utility closet in a two-mile radius, and they TP'd the trees around our dorm so heavily that the university had to bring in cherry-picker trucks to get it all down. The boys must have climbed up on the roof and thrown roll after roll to get it so high in the trees.

We all gathered in the basement for the first Vietnam draft lottery - December 1, 1969. The drawing was broadcast live: one by one, birthdates were drawn, and the closer your birthday was to the first number drawn, the more certain it was that you would be drafted. The guys were pretty tense – except for one black guy with a last name of Jones. He was in ROTC, and he had the lowest draft number of the guys in the room. Everyone knew he was going to 'Nam, but he had planned to serve, anyway. Most of the guys were hoping for high numbers…my brother pulled a high number – his number was 236. He had already decided he would run to Canada if he had a lower number, but probably, he would not have qualified for military duty anyway, on strictly medical grounds.

There was a lad in Snyder Hall that had been friends with Stevie Wonder in high school. One evening when Mr. Wonder was in the area visiting family, he stopped by the dorm and did a jam session. That was incredible – I wasn't in the dorm room, but I got a glimpse of him as he walked in. I heard just a bit of the music when the door opened. How cool was that?

I got a job near the end of freshman year… short order cook in the basement grill. Although I had a full ride, I didn't have money for doing my laundry or for eating on Sunday night when the dorm cafeteria was closed. My mother told me she would send me $5 a week, but she kept forgetting. Without any money, I couldn't even use the pay phone to call home. I went over to the Student Union and borrowed pocket change, waiting for my allowance so I could eat and do my laundry. I finally wrote home asking my mother about it and got a scathing "how dare you" letter back… without the money. So I got a job, paid back the loans, and started making my own money. The day I got that job was the day my GPA landed at 4.0, and that's where it stayed for the rest of my time at MSU. I needed the incentive to do the classwork, and having a work schedule fit the bill. It was just too easy to put things off without the work pressure.

The grading at Justin Morrill was different: we got two grades for every class: one for the classwork and one separate grade for our term papers. Take six classes, have six term papers to write. I discovered that if I picked topics about three weeks before the papers were due, I could forget about them until the day before they were respectively due... I could tuck those topics tidily away in what I fondly call my co-processor until the day before due date. I would go to the library and start writing: my subconscious co-processor had the paper entirely composed – all I was doing in the library was finding the cites and the quotes required. We had to type everything out on typewriters - no delete/re-enter possible - and my typing wasn't the greatest. We had some professors that marked down for white-out use, so I would correct, cut and paste if needed, and run it through a copy machine. By my sophomore year I could walk into the library and eight hours later have in hand a typed, ready-to-submit, annotated and sourced paper, footnotes and sources properly presented per professor requirements.

I got exciting news during the second half of my freshman year: how about going to Scotland with my grandmother so we could visit family and see the sights? I was thrilled at the prospect. It would be a girl's trip: my father and brother didn't go. My grandmother, my mother, my sister and me. I remember making a 3-piece wool suit that I could mix and match for the trip. We flew out of Windsor, not Detroit. My sister had her tonsils out just days before, and in the airplane, her incisions started hemorrhaging – there was blood all over, and she was choking on a blood clot. She spit up the blood clot and the stewardesses gave her ice until we landed. Our first stop upon landing was to get her medical care.

We rented a car, and the first place we went was to my grandmother's favorite sister, Bessie. Bessie had married Oliver

Howie, a very jolly man who worked for the railroad. They lived in a row-house on the outskirts of Markinch. Bessie was ten years younger than my grandmother... my grandmother was the eldest girl, and Bessie the youngest. Bessie towered over my grandmother. They were so very overjoyed to see one another again. My grandmother gave up a lot coming to the States with her husband. Grandpa's entire family emigrated, although they didn't all stay. My Gram left everyone behind.

Bessie and Oliver were great hosts, and we were quite the attraction in the hamlet – the relatives from the States! I remember going into town with Bessie to the butcher shop so she could fix a nice Sunday dinner for us all: her daughter's family would also be coming. The hamlet of Markinch looked to me to be out of some fairy tale – it was all stone, with a few narrow, gently winding streets, very little room between store fronts and the streets. All stone: roads and building and fences and everything. Really charming. I grew up going to big grocery stores: here you stopped in at the specialty shops... the green grocer, the butcher, the baker... all individual stores. I was astounded that Bessie bought a just a quarter pound of beef. The price of beef was very close to the price Stateside, but wages were maybe a tenth as much. Bessie was going to feed nine people with a quarter pound of beef.

After shopping, I went and stood on the ground where my father was born. It was simply a field... the row-houses of Greenwells, Rosie-near-Buckhaven long gone. It was across the street from the ruins of the MacDuff castle, which stood on the cliff overlooking the Firth of Forth. The beach was rocky – the rocks coal-black. It was a cold and windy day, and the weather suited the ruins, the wind, and the rough terrain.

Oliver and Bessie had no phone or car: if you had one or the other, you were doing better than average. If you had both, then la-di-dah weren't you the fortunate ones? The common payphone was down the street – you could see it from the Howie's front door. There was a bus that stopped on the road that would take you into Kirkcaldy if need be.

On Sunday Bessie's daughter and family came. Bessie had just one child, Jessie. Jessie had married and had an adorable tow-head tyke, three years old. He was just so proud he could tell us his name – loudly, chest thrust out, hand on hips: "Andrew Wilkie!!" What a cutie. Jessie's husband was very intent on impressing us, which he did by continually passing around a pack of cigarettes. That was also a gesture of wealth, since they were quite dear in Scotland. It was a perfectly gorgeous day out, but we were not allowed to go out (which would have been my strong preference). Back in 1969, in Scotland, it was not seemly to be out on the Sabbath if not coming or going to church. Not seemly at all. So there we were, shoehorned in Oliver and Bessie's little parlor, cigarette smoke so thick and the room so stuffy... and we were allowed no escape.

The conversation was interesting in its negativity... Gram and her sister talked about their siblings. There was Ben (Ebenezer), the one with "airs," the one that simply had to wear his "plus-fours," the one that ended up being a musician in London. He owned a car AND a phone!! How dare he – so uppity. Markinch was not good enough for him. And then there was Nessie – Agnes. She, the second oldest daughter, ended up with the family Bible. There was some tiff about that Bible, so Bessie was not speaking to her. How dare she! And then there were the neighbors and the families my grandmother knew growing up – this area is quite small, so everyone knew everybody. And all I heard was complaints and negative comments about all of them, in order. I came away clearly wondering was there anyone they liked at all? That was quite the Sunday.

The next day we left my grandmother to continue her visit with her sister, and my mother, sister and I headed out to explore. My mother had a terrible time with the whole driving on the "wrong" side of the road thing, and we were forced to swerve to avoid lorries more than once. We headed up to Loch Ness (of course), then further north to Inverness. The Highlands roads were single lane through the moors, glens and hills, with occasional pull-offs. If you ran into opposing traffic, one or the other vehicle would need to back up to the closest pull-off to let the other go. I remember there was a pull-off near a little white bridge that crossed over a small stream. We stopped to take a break there. On the bridge was a sign, "Beware of Adders." My sister innocently asked what an adder was. I started laughing, knowing that the answer was going to set her off… she was petrified of snakes. Absolutely, irrationally terrified of snakes. So, when I told her what an adder was (not being able to keep that little smirk off my face), I was waiting for a reaction – and boy, did I get one. She screamed bloody murder and pulled her legs up and tucked them under her, never getting out of the car. She wouldn't even put her feet down on the floorboard.

We didn't stop much in the Highlands except to spend nights at bed and breakfasts. Our hosts were uniformly warm and wonderful… and many of them were trying to angle a way to the US. Scottish breakfasts are very hearty, and these hosts did their very best for their US guests. I had never seen toast racks before, nor knew of "silver" and "gold" marmalades. We never made reservations ahead – we would simply pull in around suppertime at whichever B&B we managed to find and ask if there was room at the inn. There almost always was. One night we even managed a stay in the Farquhar castle - me with dreams of knights and fair maidens.

We did get out and walk around the old town of St. Andrews. There was an old church at the far east of town, by the water. It had an old graveyard, and I walked it. I saw so many Paton's and Thomson's... at the time I thought they were relatives. I didn't know then how common those names were in Fife. It was cold and blustery – Wuthering Heights kind of weather. Just perfectly melancholy for gravestone reading.

My mother had friends in London, so we headed down and spent an afternoon with them. I walked around a little and ended up in Piccadilly Circus, watching the men on their soapboxes discoursing their political beliefs. While I was there watching, a young man walked up to me asking directions. He was an American, and we started chatting. He said he was from Colorado Springs, and I mentioned that my mother's maid of honor lived there. He asked me her name, to which I replied, "Ginny Smith." He looked at me in total astonishment and then said, "That's my mother!" Six degrees of separation is alive and well, and in June of 1969 took up residence in Piccadilly Circus.

We decided to head for Carnarvon - we wanted to get there so we could watch the investiture of the Prince of Wales, scheduled for July 1st. Again, we had not planned on doing this, but it was a once in a lifetime event. Even though the United Kingdom is relatively quite small – the entirety of Scotland is only one third the size of Michigan – the roads were only two-lane, slow and curvy. We found ourselves on the road, headed to Carnarvon, on June 30th. It was evening, and my mother was getting tired. She told us to be on the lookout for a B&B, but my sister and I conspired to remain silent because we knew if we stopped, we would miss the royal procession the next morning.

My mother couldn't drive on the wrong side of the road and watch for B&B signs simultaneously, so we passed several possibilities. She knew that B&B's were not that rare, so she figured out what we were doing and was furious with us. Our conspiracy ended up wildly successful, though, and it got us to Carnarvon, and into a B&B, later that evening. The next morning we headed out and joined the throngs lining the streets. There were a couple of young men that offered to hoist me up on their shoulders, which they did, so I could watch the queen, the prince, and the entire entourage pass not 50 feet from me. Quite a spectacle! Afterwards my mother admitted that she was glad we were able to see history being made. The British are all about royal souvenirs, and I bought several: a little commemorative handkerchief, a plastic standard and something that has been gone for decades with the red Welsh dragon emblazoned on it – I can't even remember what it was just that it had the red dragon. I always liked that dragon.

We then headed to France for a couple of days – Paris. I had taken French since seventh grade and was totally fluent. I even dreamt in French and could speak it without translating to or from English. It just came out. I was our translator. This was the time of the Ugly American, and the Parisians were very unwelcoming. My mother gave them ample reason; she wearing a pearlized leather coat with a huge fox collar, clutching her purse in front of her and watching everybody warily, as if one of those walkers on the street was going to snatch it right from her grasping arms. She was an embarrassment. We met up somehow with a man named Jean-Luc, a black-haired minor government clerk from somewhere near the Basque country. He could not speak a word of English. He was an avowed communist and was totally sure the capitalistic French government was going to be overthrown in short order. Lord, he was right out of Sartre. He had a little blue Citroen Deux-Chevaux, and he became our personal guide around Paris for a couple of days. He drove us everywhere. And all the while, he and

I spoke of politics, religion, philosophy, and of world affairs. We chatted non-stop while my mother and sister sat silently in the back seat. My mother had smugly told me earlier that I only *thought* I could speak French. She didn't know whether to be jealous or impressed... or both. I blew her away. My French was so, well, French, that a couple of French soldiers on the street wouldn't believe I wasn't French until I pulled out my driver license. And I saw first-hand the dripping distain of Parisians to Americans. By our last night in Paris we were so cowed by the icy reception we had been getting, that instead of suffering through another restaurant dinner, we decided to get a baguette and a chunk of cheese and simply go back to our hotel room. I was ahead of my mother and sister, so I entered the patisserie alone and ordered a baguette. No problem... I was "French". Then my mother and sister entered. The entire store changed – everybody in the store changed. And they changed towards me – significantly. It was chilling. I wanted to lose my two Americans and see the friendliness, or at least dispassionate acceptance, once again.

After that we headed back to fetch Gram. The flight back was very uneventful, but the car ride back from the Windsor airport was anything but. Somebody had purchased a long walking stick or something similar. I believe it was my brother that picked us up – in one of the Lincoln Continental convertibles we owned. He had the top down, but as we were coming back he pushed the button so that the top would go up. Unfortunately, the walking stick was upright, and it tore right through that ragtop. My father was none too pleased – that turned out to be one expensive car ride.

While we were away in Scotland my father had time to day-dream. He had toyed with building a sailboat and sailing around the world for years: he even had a naval architect draw up a plan once, a few years earlier. Apparently, he decided we would be too cramped in that, so he started looking for existing vessels. He located one in Amsterdam... the Alja V, a 110-ft canal freighter. I went back to college, and he bought that freighter. It stayed in Amsterdam until my father arranged for it to be sailed across the Atlantic.

So I was back at school, second year, still working at the basement grill, and still looking for classes to take. I remember one fill-in course – Modern Turkish History. Sorry, but Ataturk was doing nothing for me. I took that thick tome and used it as a pillow, falling asleep in the grass on warm spring days. End of term, I opened the blue-book essay final exam, and out of the five possible topics upon which we were to opine, I could not address the first three. I was getting a bit concerned, because that had never happened to me before. Me, flunk a course? I answered question #4, throwing in Aristotle and whatever else I could tie in... and got a better grade than my brother did. It was then, I decided, that my true core college competency was test-taking.

I had a new roommate – Sharon Powell. She and I got along famously. She was extremely petite: I remember being asked by people if she was some kind of child prodigy. She had a broad grin and a great sense of humor. She and I started hanging out with the girls from across the hall and down one door: Suzanne and Ellen. We were quite the foursome: we looked like a staircase. Suzanne was a good six feet tall: Ellen 5'10". I came in at 5'4", and Sharon was 4'10". It's amazing we became such good friends: Suzanne was an extremely thin, anxious woman, Ellen laconic and wry, Sharon quick and peppy. I can't say how I was perceived: I was still trying to figure that out. I remember being so very shocked when Susie the cheerleader started becoming very friendly, only to find out that she had decided to become my "friend" because she wanted to be introduced to a gorgeous guy named Frank, and according to her, I knew everybody. She thought I was her best bet. What?? I knew everybody? However could that be? I was shy, "bookish," introverted and withdrawn. I had been told that my entire life. I started thinking that maybe the real "me" was not the "me" I had adopted for the war zone.

Even with those three friends, without a compelling challenge I was not a very fulfilled or happy person. There was a young man in our neighboring dorm who totally caught my attention – of course, it wasn't reciprocal. I knew that, but that didn't stop my yearning. I became so unable to deal with the flood of emotions I was feeling that I got his schedule and made sure our paths never crossed. So I decided, the weekend of my birthday, to bum a ride home. Home, where my birthday would not pass in silence. Or so I thought. When I walked in unannounced, I found my parents and sister getting ready – my parents were going to a party and my sister was going "out." My sister had commandeered our shared bedroom to such a degree there was not a lick of space for anything mine, so I moved into the office. I was greeted with something akin to, "Oh! We didn't expect you. We are going out – I'm sure you can find something in the refrigerator." I kind of lingered for a while, but with no further greeting I dejectedly went up to the office. After a while my mother came up and asked what was wrong. I said, "It's my birthday." She hesitated for a moment, and then said, "Oh! Well, then, you are coming with us." "No, I don't want to." "Of course you do!" "No." She paused, and with a harrumph, turned and left. The very last thing I wanted to do was go to an adult party, full of cigarette smoke and generous amounts of alcohol, to be introduced as Pitiful Pearl, Birthday Girl. I spent a very quiet night at home. The next morning, before I was even awake, my mother came storming up the stairs. She was quite angry. "I hope you are proud of yourself. You ruined my night!!"

Why did I even bother? I was looking forward to going back to school… my ride came early afternoon, and I was off. From one miserable setting to the other.

When I went home for Christmas break I was sick. I had quite a fever, and I just wanted to sleep. I kept on telling my parents that finals week had been rough, which was true. We would pull all-nighters the entire week. The cafeteria was open for study all night long, and an ice cream sundae truck would appear in the hallway at three in the morning. I remember Susie the cheerleader doing catapults and handless flips down the middle of the cafeteria to blow off energy. But it wasn't just finals week that was dragging me down. I was seriously ill. I lied about it, because the very *last* thing I wanted to do was to have to stay home. I went back to campus and immediately headed for the clinic. I was admitted to the hospital with a high white blood cell count – 17,000 or something ridiculous. I had a bad case of mono. The doctor said I had the worst white blood cell count in the entire ward. Funny, but while lying in bed I felt fine, unless I tried to stand up and walk. That just wasn't happening. My mother for some reason had kept buying me lingerie for Christmas… I had gorgeous stuff, albeit purchased at second-hand stores. Barbizon and other higher-end labels. They were lovely, but they were not flannel pajamas. I remember the nurse cluck-clucking about my inappropriate nightwear. She probably thought I snuck out and bought it for wild nights: when I told her my mother bought them, she was in total disbelief. I mean, what mother would send her girl-child away to college with seductive nightwear?

I had enrolled in private voice classes. They were held in the Quonset huts, over a mile away, across the Red Cedar River, across to the far corner of the campus. I didn't have a bike (I had so outgrown my old bike), and I didn't have any money to buy a campus bus pass. So I walked. I had bought a maxi-coat, a la

Doctor Zhivago. It was a heavy, very closely-woven black wool coat that needed nothing for warmth but its satin lining. It was double-breasted, had a stand-up Napoleon-type collar, went to my ankle bones, and was the very warmest coat I had ever owned, by a wide margin. I bought a pair of thickly knit black mittens, knee-high black leather boots and a fur toque. I remember going out and walking campus just because I could, without getting cold. So I would walk to and from the Quonset huts, which took a while. That was far more walking than I was used to, and I developed a seven-inch blister from wearing my artificial leg that started at the center back top of my thigh and wrapped around the inside, along the rim of the leg. I remember padding the rim with cotton and wrapping it in Saran Wrap – and I kept walking.

My bout of mono totally ruined my vocal chords – I just couldn't sing well. My range was quite limited, my breath control was limited… I had a hard time recovering, and my vocal instructor could not buy into how long my recovery was taking. I dropped voice.

The basement across from the grill where I worked was home to unending bridge games. There were a couple of upper classmen that were always there: Rick and Al. Rick was a tall, good-looking guy who loved practical jokes. He kept asking me to play bridge, but I kept on demurring. I kind of knew the game, but not well at all. My parents played bridge all the time, and my father was some sort of Master bridge player. When I got home between second and third terms, I cornered my dad and asked him to give me a crash course in the game, which he did. When I got back to the dorm, the next time I was asked, I was in.

Rick was fun. He treated me like a kid sister. He said I needed a nickname, which is difficult when I have a given name that already sounds like a nickname. He decided to call me

Breezy, "windy" being close to "Wendy". He would reach down and take out the valve that holds my leg on and play keep-away. His parents lived in Grosse Pointe, and he would give me rides home. He was graduating that term. He had broken up with his girlfriend and was sad and wounded by it, but he loved and took solace in his two Great Danes. Rick Jensen – Rick with the quirky, kind-of sideways grin. He was a really good friend. At the end of the term, when I had bummed a ride home and borrowed a car to take myself and belongings back for the summer, he played his best practical joke ever. While I was gone he got into my dorm room and had hung toilet paper from every metal grid on the suspended ceiling, making sure to wrap it around everything he could find. He had asked me if I could babysit one of his Great Danes when I got back to school. Of course I agreed. So there I was, unlocking my dorm room, Great Dane in tow, to find a Great Dane playground of TP. That dog bounded in, tearing through all that TP, managing to shatter an entire bottle of my roommate's Chantilly perfume. Whoa – did that overwhelm!

~

I didn't live at home that summer – I went to live with my grandparents and work in my grandfather's marina. He bought that marina when he was 65 and worked hard to improve it. There were gas pumps out front that needed an attendant – these were well before the days of self-serve gas pumps, and well before credit card-enabled pumps. Gas was leaded and smelled much better than it does today.

The marina building housed a small convenience store with chips and candy, a marine store with paints and cleaners and similar boat maintenance items, an office, and a back mechanical bay where my grandfather would fix engines and do other maintenance for boat owners. The boat wells were behind that, in a bay surrounded by reeds about half a mile or so inland from Lake Erie. My grandparents' house was right next door: a modest early twentieth-century two-story red brick house. I took up residence in one of the upstairs bedrooms and went to work every day. It was not the most pleasant of experiences: my grandfather's former secretary, Dorothy, worked for him too. She had been in love with my grandfather for years: I found out decades later that as early as 1958 she had listed her name on the Dearborn Machinery Movers articles of incorporation as Dorothy Thomson, Secretary. I am not sure that my grandfather ever knew that. That woman did everything in her power to make my life miserable, in part because I was a constant reminder of her love's family, in part because even my grandfather was disconcerted because I was the spitting image of the wife he brought with him from Scotland. He would be busy concentrating on something, and when he looked up he would see the lass he had married. He would shake his head and mutter about me being her spitting image – I think it made him quite uncomfortable.

I did tease him a bit: I would open my window and play one of his LP 78's – bagpipes – so loud you could hear it by the gas pumps. He was all about being American: no bagpipes, he liked Army male choruses. No haggis for St. Andrew's Day, he cooked steak on the grill the Fourth of July. No Highland Games, he went to watch the Red Wings. So the bagpipes rather drove him nuts. Bad me.

My grandfather was a perfectionist and a rather stern task-master. Dorothy was even worse. She knew how much I looked like my grandmother, and she was so jealous that she would never have the man she loved for her own. Working around her was difficult, to say the least. I remember making a mistake with the candy I was sent to buy for the convenience store. Nothing great shakes, mind you... a minor quantity error. I can still hear her saying, "The road to Hell is paved with good intentions."

There was one very big benefit to living there that summer: I got over my hatred of spiders. I had to, or perish. Spiders love water, and the house was crawling with them. They were on the windows, in the corners, or the floor – the defining moment was when one started descending from the ceiling as I was sitting on my bed writing a letter. I watched it as it headed for me, and right then I came to the conclusion that; (1) I was much larger, (2) it had much better reason to be afraid of me than I had being afraid of it, and (3) as long as it was not running at me at a high rate of speed, I could let it out or get out of the way. Peaceful coexistence.

I would borrow my grandmother's light blue Ford sedan to visit my parents or visit the freighter, which had made it across the ocean manned by a hired captain, my brother and one or two of my brother's friends, with my cousin Tom joining in Montreal. That sedan had hokey brakes – they took to locking at the slightest provocation. I remember heading back to the marina one afternoon and coming up over the huge bridge just south of Detroit, on I-75, where at the crest you leave behind a city and view industry: refineries and iron works and whatever else is in that area, numerous large smokestacks spewing forth, factories and huge, squat, cylindrical gas and oil tanks. There had been some sort of accident, and the traffic had ground to a halt. I was in the left lane by the concrete median wall. The driver of the car in front of me panicked, lost control of his car, slammed into the median wall and bounced back towards me, turning in the process so the driver's door was directly in my path. He was looking at me, and I was fixed on him as I was pumping those brakes madly, knowing I couldn't slam them on. I think he thought he was going to die, and I thought I was going to kill him. I can still see that face – and it's true about everything slowing down in times like that. I managed to stop inches from his door. I was quite shaken, but probably not as much as he was.

It was interesting watching a different couple manage their marriage. My grandparents were not happy, either, but neither of them took it out on me. My grandmother was the most generous woman you could ever want to meet, but her sense of humor could easily move to being humor at the expense of others. My grandfather, not wanting her to insult any potential customers of his fledgling new business, forbid her to go visit neighbors. She was heart-broken, but she obeyed. I never understood why she didn't just go out anyway, just like I never understood why my father didn't attend the Edison Institute anyway. I just must be that much more self-directed, I guess. Anyway, she was stuck in that house, friendless. I have never met a more selfless woman, and that was just not right. She would look out the window at my grandfather and Dorothy. I don't know if those two ever did have an affair, but my grandmother believed that they were having one right there, next door. She was tormented by it – but still she stayed.

Anyway, I dropped out of college at the end of the summer and walked away from that amazing scholarship. By the time I got to the ship, my parents and sister were already there, my dad having sold his practice and the house on the lake. I boarded the boat in November 1970 with all my meager belongings in tow and left the Motor City for parts unknown.

LIFE ON A FREIGHTER

I never considered staying back like my brother did. I could not conceive how I would stay in school, how I would get back and forth to my grandparents; if they would even have had me. I could not imagine being happy at school anymore, though. Rick and Al were gone, Sharon dropped out to get married to her high school sweetheart, and after Susie's admission of outright using me I became a bit gun-shy of friendly people. I should have known... there was no logical reason why Susie would try and take up with me – we were so different. I had exactly two dates in two years, and I never got invited to a party. Academics were not a challenge... I just thought that while I didn't know what I was getting into boarding the ship, I knew that MSU was not doing it for me anymore, on any level. Besides, now that my dad was pursuing a dream he seemed to be in a much, much better mood. He was chatty and sang to himself – it was wonderful. That was such a huge relief.

The boat was moored at Miller Marina in St. Clair Shores. While I was living in LaSalle my dad took to a major ship renovation. He had a metal bulwark built over the aft hold, so that it was a two-story space inside for our new home. There was also some engine work that was needed: my cousin Tom told me that on the trip from Montreal to Detroit, someone would have to go down to the engine room and sprinkle gritty cleanser on a brake belt so that it would stop slipping. The ship was re-christened the Brigadoon, and we painted the hull bright red. The pilot house and the trim were painted black and white. I remember hanging over the side and scrubbing off rust with a very stiff metal brush.

The ship had a three-cycle Brons engine that would totally permeate a body with its slow, rhythmic "CHUG-chug-chug-CHUG-chug-chug" day and night. The engine room door was accessed on the port side, aft of the pilot house door. It was very stereotypical, rounded edges and a very large handle square in the middle, maybe a foot long, that swung up a quarter turn to unlock the lever. When you swung open the door you could see that someone had painted a crying Donald Duck, hat in hand, on the inside of the door. My sister became the mechanic, scampering down the gangway ladder when required. I became the navigator, learning both Loran C and celestial navigation. We had on board three young men, Warren, the son of the man from whom we procured all our electronics, Jimmy, a young man that worked with my mother at the furniture store, and Charlie Brown, the welder that would be finishing up some work and getting off in Welland. Charlie tried to teach me how to weld – now that's a craft with which I could never make a living.

The Thomsons' 110-foot family freighter at its Miller Marina berth

Jimmy and I had the graveyard shift in the wheelhouse. We had a cassette tape player, and while we were chugging along, in the dead of night, he and I would listen, and sing along to, James Taylor... Sweet Baby James. Jimmy announced the day before we set sail that he was red-green color blind. Oh boy... not anything you want on a ship.

My dad had run out of outfitting time, so when we cast off we were pretty much the last ship to leave the Detroit River. The great plans for a two-story house in the rear hatch were quite incomplete: there was an open stairway, the beginnings of a full kitchen, and not a whole lot else. We stowed a Rolls Royce and the Mustang convertible in the front hold, along with all the furniture. We were left using the original crew quarters far aft. This craft, built in the 1930's, was very much a ship that could have been used in a King Kong movie. The crew quarters were all varnished wood, with the bunks very narrow and protected with a raised edge so it would be difficult to be dumped out in heavy seas. My mother and sister had glued colorful fabric on some of the walls, and the stateroom Jimmy and I shared was decorated in an orange and pink paisley fabric. Jimmy took the top bunk. There was only standing room between the bunks and the door – I became quite able to slip a long flannel nightgown over my head and get completed dressed within it.

The pilot house had a huge oak wheel – it was nearly as tall as I was. There was a three or four-foot-tall brass cylindrical gear shift sticking out of the floor on the side, but it only had three gears: forward, neutral and reverse. We only had a single prop, but that engine had tremendous torque. The gangways aft were very narrow, circling the arced aft deck. You couldn't go fore from the pilot house directly: you had to go down the gangway first. The pilot house sat a good seventy feet from the bow and was fifteen feet above the main deck.

The Brigadoon had two cargo holds, and the superstructure only went over the one mid-section of the ship. The forward cargo hold was flush with the deck, and fore of that were the anchor and chain lockers.

Our send-off from Detroit was well-publicized: all the local papers covered this great adventure. So we took off one cold November morning and headed east, out of Lake St. Clair and into the channel. The Detroit River is not particularly wide – at its narrowest it's only a half mile across. It takes a significant amount of freighter traffic, and it has islands that dot the middle. Every one of us were in the wheel house that November morning as my dad piloted the ship. We sailed around Belle Isle, under the Ambassador Bridge, and headed towards Lake Erie. And then trouble began. We were downriver, and foreign freighter "Manchester City" was headed west (Detroit is actually north of Windsor: the river runs east and west at that point). At 9:26 PM the Manchester City, having missed the entrance to the East Outer Channel, corrected course – right across our bow. We ended up with a 12" hole in the starboard chain locker. I ducked under the chart table, Warren took off his glasses and sat on the floor, Tracy grabbed on to the wheel. It's the strangest thing seeing a monstrous ship running into you. You simply seem to accept the fact calmly at the time and act accordingly – afterwards, my mother started picking up things. Warren and Jimmy went fore to assess the damage. And I went to the radio-telephone and hailed the nameless ship: "This is the Brigadoon WZR2964 calling the ship we just hit."

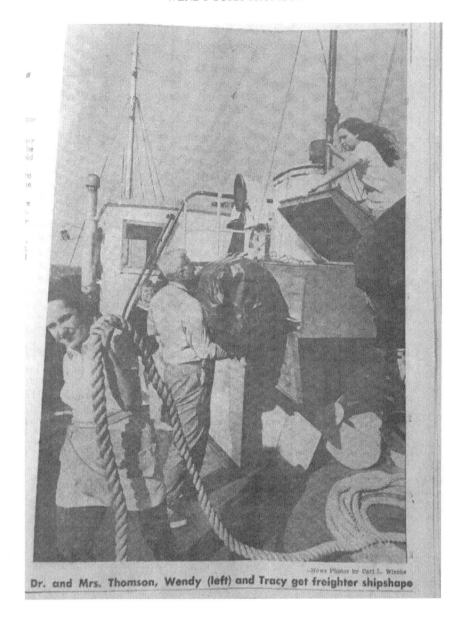

News Photos by Carl L. Wienke

Dr. and Mrs. Thomson, Wendy (left) and Tracy get freighter shipshape

So there we were, Day One of our Great Adventure, heading out to Lake Erie with a very crumpled bow. We should have stayed in port, though: we ran right into a huge gale. Lake Erie is relatively shallow, and so waves can't get huge and rolling – they get very choppy and angry. Thousand-foot long lake freighters have been known to crack in two - riding up and down large swells is easier than surviving significant short chop. We lost communication – lots of ships lost communication. We could occasionally hear the Coast Guard calling for us, but they couldn't hear us answer. We ended up taking shelter in Long Point Bay as best we could and bedded down for the night – and stayed there for two days. The next morning there was an entire string of lake freighters across the entrance of the bay – thirteen of them, getting in as close as they could. We only drew ten feet – I am sure those huge lake freighters drew much more. We found out later that one of those ships called in that we had not sunk.

I have never been so sick. It takes a lot for me to get seasick, but it was over two days of sick. Had to work: we only had ourselves. You excused yourself to go vomit over the side – one hand to the ship ALWAYS - then you came back to station. Everybody was sick, all except my dad. People have it wrong about being that seasick… it's not at all the case that you can't stand the sight or smell of food. Not at all. Food tasted delicious, even if it came right back up. I will never forget the moment I got my sea legs: the acid test was a corned beef sandwich. That was by far the very best sandwich I have ever tasted.

It was still rough after we hoisted anchor and left the bay, but we got our ship-to-shore back. We found out that the collision and the subsequent gale had made nationwide news: both the Free Press and the Detroit News were waiting for us in Port Colborne, as were TV reporters and the Wall Street Journal. The WSJ reporter, Norm Pearlstein, took a white fishing trawler out to meet us and clambered on board. He stayed a couple of days with us, getting off at Welland – and we made the center column, Page One.

The weather calmed by the time we hit the Welland Canal. I don't know how many locks we went through, but it was probably dozens over the course of our trip. We had it down in no time: wrap a hawser around a bollard a couple of times, pull it in going up, feed it out going down. We had a person on each bollard, easing and/or tightening synchronously. Except once: we were going down, and I was letting out line. However, somehow my hand got stuck between the hawser and the bollard. Charlie the welder came running over, and he pulled on that hawser enough that I got my hand out. That must have been an amazing, adrenaline-induced feat: he was pulling against hundreds of tons of steel. I will never forget that courageous act.

So through the locks of the Welland Canal, and into Lake Ontario - right into a fierce blizzard. We were going to get to New York City via inland rivers: into the Oswego River, through Lake Oneida to the Erie Canal, to the Mohawk River, then to the Hudson into New York City. We were in nearly a white-out coming into Oswego – and the weather had blown one of the entrance buoys off point. We made it, but by the skin of our teeth. Lesson #1: sea charts are inaccurate the minute they are published. Buoys and channel markers move, lights go out, sandbars move all the time, depths are approximate.

It was good to get into calm river waters again. We spent five days in Oswego – we had the ship documented instead of state-licensed, and we had to finish the process before heading on. When a ship is documented the number is etched or carved permanently, somewhere mid-ship. Documentation is national and it lasts forever: no re-ups at all. I spent my 20th birthday in Oswego, quietly knitting a sweater for Warren. Somewhere between Oswego and NYC, my sister and I got off ship and found a hardware store. We bought a roll of pinkish contact paper and went up to our crumpled bow. We used Magic Markers to polka dot that long strip of plastic, fashioning a large Band-Aid to tape across the bow. And so decorated, we ended up at NYC's 79th Street Boat Basin.

We spent several days there, re-provisioning and getting off ship. We went to Greenwich Village and went to the movies: we saw "2001, a Space Odyssey." The lot of us felt as if we were walking drunk: after being through all that weather we were used to the deck moving under us. With our sea legs, the concrete beneath our feet felt as if it were being tossed at sea. We were laughing at ourselves walking down the sidewalk.

While we were in New York, my mother's cousin Walter came to visit, bringing his wife and three children. Walter was a psychologist, and Walter's children were the least well-behaved, oddest children I had ever met, by a long shot. When they left we were all dumb-founded. I don't know what school of child-rearing Walter liked, but as far as everybody on that ship was concerned, it was an unmitigated disaster. Those children became an inside joke.

We were again ready to sail away – into the Northern Atlantic. In December. This is something I would not recommend. Nothing like December in the Northern Atlantic. We hit a storm like I have never seen. Sure, we were chopped up in Lake Erie. But the ship had weight in the Great Lakes. In the Atlantic it tossed about like a plastic bobber when a perch takes the bait. I will never, never forget one night. There I was, in the dead of night on the wheel, in that terrible storm. I looked to the left: water at eye-level. I looked to the right: water at eye-level. I looked out past the seventy feet of deck to the bow, which was pointed down a trough at some significant angle: water at eye-level, seventy feet out, from bow to eye level. We must have been in 30 or 40-foot seas. Our ship was quite sea-worthy, we were in huge swells and not in crashing waves… the ship took it well. That being said, it was awe-inspiring, and it gave me a respect for the power of the sea that will never leave. Let's just say I will never be the one to take off for the Polynesian Islands in a 40-foot sailboat.

Once again the seas calmed themselves. Off the coast of Maryland, I went aft one night and saw phosphorescent algae churned up from the prop off the stern. It was magical – mesmerizing. However, even though the weather calmed, my dad decided that we had had quite enough of the winter Atlantic. The salt had coated the entire ship as if it were frost, and it needed a good cleaning. We headed into the Chesapeake Bay and re-routed ourselves via the Inland Waterway.

All along the inland route, Tracy, Jimmy, Warren and I would go ashore together. We were a perfect foursome, by all accounts. We had so much fun! Warren had perfect pitch: on a bet we tested ourselves, singing a "C" and then walking into a music store to see who was right. Warren was. We would joke, shop, eat lunch… just great buddies. Warren taught all of us how to jump off the ship, even if we were quite a bit higher than the ground and/or dock: feet, knees, hips, back, shoulders and then up, to distribute the impact. He was wiry and quick, broad-shouldered and with an absolutely remarkable amount of energy. I gained Warren's respect with my navigating: he said the only two that could navigate were the two of us, and that we could use another on board. I guess I earned my stripes.

My sister was just sixteen, and she was infatuated with Jimmy. I had the same relationship with both Jimmy and Warren that I had always had with men-boys: we were friends. They liked me… like Rick liked me and Al liked me. Good friends… nothing more. It made me sad, hate to admit it. I wanted more, but could never figure out how to make it work. My penchant for totally ignoring my disabilities – that drive and perseverance that had gotten me as far as it had - was useless in the romantic arena. It was a sad time for me on an emotional level, even as the adventure was fascinating.

After spending a week at Christmas in Charleston, we headed to Albemarle Sound via the InterCoastal Waterway (ICW). We had to spend time in port periodically so we could restock food, buy local charts, and clean ourselves. Hair-washing was the most complicated. We had to wait until we found a marina with a shower, and we all had simultaneously clean hair. Both my sister and I had waist-long, curly hair. We would wash it and then either braid it or put it in a bun – the only other alternative was to walk around for hours in curlers. We had a marine toilet on board that also had to be taken and emptied. We all contributed to that rather nasty chore.

With the tides and the shifting sandbars, we seemed to have made a habit of getting grounded on a daily basis. We took advantage of the forced respites to lower either the canoe or the ski boat and either go exploring ashore or go skiing. We didn't run much at night – sometimes, but not every night. That was good for all of us, because when we were at sea we each had two shifts a day: a 4-hour shift during the day and a 2-hour shift at night. I had noon to four in the afternoon and 2AM to 4AM every morning.

My father tried very hard to do everything right, but I think he needed night glasses. My dad made one more attempt at heading out to the ocean to save time. We were leaving port to try and head back out to sea, through a pair of long jetties. There were a series of seven or so navigational lights on them, but my father miscounted them. I thought he was wrong, but he was not one to be easily corrected. He turned us directly into the jetty, thinking he had cleared the entire length. The Coast Guard had to pull us off that time. Back to the ICW: we were definitely amateurs.

The flats from South Carolina into Georgia were vast – and flat-boring. There were highlights: we stopped at a wonderful marina and went to dinner at a very Southern, bench-seated crawdad restaurant that was like nothing I had ever experienced. There we were, passing down biscuits and baskets and bowls of food, chatting with total strangers as if they were family. It was so warm and inviting.

Warren started talking about heading back. I so wanted him to stay on, but he was subject to the draft and believed he couldn't be gone for two years. He had a best friend – Ken – that was going to join us in Miami. They were planning on bumming around Europe, doing the youth-hostel "thing" for a summer with Warren's girlfriend Jan. I loved having the four of us on board, and I didn't want anything to take that away. It became clear that was not to be.

Besides the daily groundings, there was only two other incidents of import between Georgia and Miami. There were many bridges crossing the ICW, some high enough for us to pass under, some not. I remember one bridge that said on the chart we had clearance. Of course, everything depends on the water level. It was close – really close. I remember Warren running back and forth, climbing up on top of the pilot house trying to figure out whether he needed to emergency drop some of the electronics and antennae… he was frantic. All his nervous energy. We made that one by a hair. Thought Warren was going to have a stroke.

The second incident happened in Fort Lauderdale. We were chugging away in the dead of night, Jimmy and me in the wheelhouse. The procedure for bridge raising was for the vessel requiring clearance to sound the horn well upstream to alert the Bridge Master to raise the bridge. Dutifully, I sounded the horn about ¾ of a mile upstream… but the bridge did not start to raise. I sounded the horn again – still no movement. By the third try I jammed the gear into reverse and put everything that three-stroke had to the task. My father came bounding up the gangway at the sound of the engine, saw what was happening, jammed the gear into forward and moved the throttle to full speed ahead, turning the bow as sharply as he could to port. He didn't know if he had enough clearance in the canal, didn't know whether there was enough depth, but he definitely knew that we could not stop in time to avoid hitting the bridge – it took a good mile or two to do that. Luckily the canal was widely dredged, and we managed to avert disaster. He hailed the Bridge Master on the ship-to-shore and gave him bloody hell. There was some sort of government review of the incident – the Bridge Master had fallen asleep.

Except for that drama, the trip down the ICW from Ft. Lauderdale to Miami was beautiful – the mansions lining the ICW were gorgeous, many having incredible yachts docked out front. It was especially beautiful at night, with the lights bouncing off the water, lighting up the homes and illuminating the palm trees and other shrubbery. Quite the gracious life. And then daylight hit, and we were pulling into North Bay Village – our next dockage, and our next base.

JOURNEY TO A CAREER

We were berthed in a smallish marina, along the south edge of the concrete break-wall, just east of an old, 1920's vintage yacht that had been turned into a restaurant and bar. The concrete break-wall was quite wide and was only long enough to accommodate the two ships... it must have been 250'-300' feet long. Across from us, on the other side of the break-wall, were houseboats. These were homes, not vessels... they were not motorized. If they needed to be moved, a tug had to be called in. There were perhaps a half dozen or so, mostly two-story homes on small barges. All the self-propelled boats were in slips along three or four docks north of the break-wall.

The houseboats were owned by a most remarkable cast of characters. The one most easterly was the home of a plastic surgeon, Dr. Sachs, who lived there with his Cuban houseboy, Osmar Castro Vega – known simply as Castro. Rumor had it that the doctor, originally from California, was hiding out in order to dodge some hefty alimony payments to his ex-wife. Rumor also had it that he was using his houseboy to hide assets and whereabouts. West of his home was the houseboat of a couple of commercial airline pilots. They were obviously only sporadically home, but they were renowned for the parties (and stewardesses that dallied there with them) that they threw when they were in town. The next houseboat was occupied by a man and wife psychologist couple who spent 95% of their conversations on sex. We had walked into a sitcom, populated by stereotypes. I had never met such characters.

The marina caregiver was a gnarled, walnut-tanned man named Gene. Not sure if he ever had been married – I think he had been a sailor once upon a time. He lived in the marina, had a deep knowledge of fishing, and spent his days cleaning the pool, tending to repairs and keeping the docks clean. The only other people with whom any of us had any consistent relationship was a man that lived on a boat two docks down – Matthew Percival Whitall III. He was a practicing alcoholic – a severe alcoholic. The only time in my life I have ever witnessed delirium tremens. He was from Massachusetts and had worked as some sort of engineer in the Chesapeake Bay area. When he turned thirty-five he became a trust fund baby, at which point he promptly quit his job and became a drunken bum. I remember taking him somewhere once to pick up a fund distribution. His wife, Dottie, was a pretentious member of a lower socio-economic cohort. I think she had been a waitress or barmaid at some establishment that the good Mr. Whitall had frequented. I believe by the time we arrived at the marina the two had divorced, but they had a complicated and continuing relationship. Yet another sitcom stereotype. I remember thinking that in Michigan you asked what a person did for a living. I found out in the escapist-prone Miami Beach, the appropriate question was not what a person did... it was, did a person do anything?

Matt became the first and only man I have ever slapped. My dad was in the restaurant yacht one afternoon at the bar, and I had to ask him some question. Matt was next to him. Matt, in his ever-drunken, normal state, kept on grinning and grabbing at me. I told him to stop it a couple of times, but he didn't take me seriously. The next time he reached for me, I hauled off and slapped him so hard across the face that bar conversation stopped and my dad gasped. After my newly-found respect, Matt and I became friends, of a sort. When he was not drunk he was a smart guy, and he occasionally gave me good advice. He was the first person that made me feel I was being treated like an adult. He came, he went... the last time I ever saw him he was stumbling across a road. I think he died not long afterward. No physical body can take that kind of abuse for very long.

Besides the colorful marina-mates, life on the freighter became very boring. We were informed that we could not leave territorial waters until after some Admiralty Court reviewed the Detroit River collision, and we had been given no date for that investigation. I could only swim so much, really. I could only cook the fresh fish that Gene would give me so often. So I decided I was going to get a job. There was a restaurant/bar within walking distance. I walked in and was told I had a job, but after I walked out the offer was rescinded. Gene told me afterwards that my limp was the reason, but then he also told me it was a good thing, because the place had a reputation of having waitresses "with benefits." So I got on a bus and headed for the beach, where I got a job as a short order cook at a Royal Castle greasy spoon. I was the night shift girl – there all alone from ten at night to six the next morning. I started on Super Bowl weekend. The place was really jumping – I had not one minute of down time. Not one – not even time to wash a dish. That was my first night. When the manager came in the next morning, he started yelling at me about all the dirty dishes. I told him he should check the cash register. After he counted the money he said nothing more – he simply started washing the dishes.

I came back from work exhausted, but there was so much noise during the day I couldn't get much sleep. My mother didn't seem to comprehend my night schedule, and she was always wanting me to get up in the early afternoon. Anyway, after just a couple of days the manager decided that he needed two on the night shift, so my sister joined me on week two. We came up with a little routine that we performed behind the counter and we got great tips. We had fun working that, but after the second week I was just so tired trying to live on four hours of sleep a day that I called it quits.

Back then there was a very quaint method of finding work... the want ads. Pull out the paper and go to the Classifieds... that's where the job postings were. No internet, no resume-screening software based upon key word search. No... just tiny 5-point font little boxes, full of abbreviations, a telephone number and maybe a company name and address. And that's where I found an ad for a bookkeeper/clerk at a chichi dress store in South Beach, on famed Lincoln Road.

The job was in the corporate headquarters of Lillie Rubin, which were located behind the retail store on Lincoln Road. The South Beach of the early 1970's was nothing like today. Everything in the lower end of South Beach was shabby – even the famed Fontainebleau (where no respectable woman went) had seen better days. There were old hotels running south from Lincoln Avenue on the west side of Collins. Every building was quite run-down, none over three or four stories, all needing coats of paint, all faded pastel with broad porches facing the beach and consistently populated with very old people sitting or rocking the rest of their lives away in the chairs that lined the porches. Small, wizened women in babushkas watching me silently as I walked past them to the bus stop. This was the quiet part of the Beach... down from Lincoln, past 5th Street that led to the southernmost causeway. I was the only person I saw walking on the sidewalk down there. It felt like I was in Krakow or somewhere similar. Lots of old, apparently Eastern European people quietly sitting their remaining lives away, hours on end.

Lillie Rubin was a high-end dress shop – the experience was high-end, not necessarily the clothes. I remember buying a dress with my employee discount – it was polyester. Heavy polyester, but none the less, polyester. The dressing rooms were large – as large as small bedrooms. They had chandeliers in them, and the sales clerks would fetch drinks or coffee for the patrons. The back office consisted of three rooms: the office manager had her own office, the clerks worked in a large bullpen, and the IT guy worked back in the inventory room. I didn't have a desk: I sat at a long table, near one end. I can't remember exactly what I was doing there, except that it entailed using long, narrow boxes full of slips of paper. The office manager's name was Fran: she was a New Yorker, never married, being kept by a married wealthy New Yorker in Miami for his entertainment. She was a stately woman, with always-perfectly-coiffed hair in an elaborate beehive-type hairdo, obviously shellacked to fend off the ever-present heavy humidity. She carried a lot of weight in her face, so that her eyes seemed perpetually squinty. I had a very difficult time finding common ground for conversation with her – our life experiences had been so very different.

Her next-in-command was Millie, a hard-looking peroxide blond whose physique could have belonged to a former boxer. There was another clerk, a kindly older, petite woman that was probably more intelligent than Fran and Millie combined. She kept her mouth shut, her head down, and simply worked. There was little small talk except for Fran's smug tales of her paramour.

As I was wont to do, I applied myself to the tasks at hand. I apparently was doing a very good job at it – enough so that I started to really bother Millie. I was so naïve and dumbfounded that I responded by working harder and faster – which led to being given more work, which led to Millie riding my ass to an ever-increasing degree. The cycle continued: the more work I accomplished, the more irritated Millie got. I never understood what I seemed to be doing wrong, and I did not even consider the possibility that perhaps I should sit down with her and Fran to get to the bottom of it. After a while it didn't matter, though: one day Millie came in waving a gun and was taken away, with the assumption that she had suffered a nervous breakdown.

I never felt that I fit in with any of the other staff, but apparently there were some kindly feelings for me... Fran gave me a surprise 21st birthday party. That was the first birthday party I had had since I was three, and I was so moved by the kindness behind the gesture. I even remember what I was wearing: I had on a pair of grey pinstripe slacks and a sleeveless multi-colored block button-up vest. My very long hair was parted in the middle and held back on either side with clips above my temples. I normally did not wear my hair down, but it was the end of November and a bit coolish. Normally I would simply take my wet hair – wet from swimming – and wrap it in a bun at the nape of my neck for work. It would stay wet until I unwrapped it to go swimming the next evening. Hair blowers had not yet been invented, and my hair, left untended, would fluff out so much in frizz that I could hide the color of my shirt. I know that for a fact because the day I decided to get my hair cut I thought I should let it dry, so I went to work with it down. I was wearing a light blue T-shirt... which was impossible to see if I stood motionless. I looked like Cousin It.

After a few months of working I decided I needed to get my own place. The plastic surgeon across the way owned a small set of apartments. They were at the foot of the 79th Street Causeway on the Beach side, to the north of the Causeway. I was making $80 a week, and the apartment cost $80 a month, furnished. My father was at a bit of a loss at my decision: I saw a side of him I am not sure I had ever seen before. I remember him quietly saying, "I know what I am supposed to do when a daughter gets married. What am I supposed to do if she just leaves?" It never occurred to him that any of us would do anything but live at home until marriage: that's what he did, that's what my mom did, that's what their parents did. That's what most people did, apparently. It wasn't far – only five minutes by car. But still, it was where I would come home to after work.

The apartment was probably built in the 1920's or so. It was a one bedroom – nothing unusual about that – but it had a large kitchen with windows on two walls. The kitchen was the best feature of the place. I decided to decorate it – being on a tight budget, I bought paint: some pretty, dark marine blue that hit somewhere between royal and navy; a bright clear yellow, and some white. I taped off the walls and striped them. I painted the cabinets white and I hung fresh white curtains at the windows. It looked fresh and clean and happy. I had lots of time for projects like that, since I didn't own a television.

My neighbors were Judy and George, a young married couple. They came over to introduce themselves, and after a while I went into the bedroom and opened a drawer, intending to bring something out to show them. I pulled that drawer open and saw the biggest insect I had ever, ever seen – a cockroach. Not a little black, skinny cockroach – no, a big, orange bruiser that Floridians lamely call Palmetto Bugs. Nope – just big, orange cockroaches with wiggling antennae. I will never forget: I was horrified to the point of shaking. I stood in the doorway, pointing my index finger to the dresser drawer, and said as calmly as I could muster (which was not much), "George!! George!! There is a huge bug in my drawer!!" Judy and George got a big laugh out of that one, and reminded me of it frequently after that.

There was a gas station within a block of my apartment owned by a big Irish guy from Boston named Jimmy. He chomped cigars and had a pot belly and was everything you would imagine a big Irish guy from Boston to be. He was looking for someone to keep his books, so I started working nights over there… I really wanted to save up enough money for a car. I got along better with the guys at the gas station than I did with the women at Lillie Rubin's. There was a mechanic named Bobby Stewart – a prematurely grey guy with a good sense of humor. We all kidded and swapped stories, and then one day, Bobby stopped talking to me. I didn't know why, but after a few days of the silent treatment I asked Jimmy what was going on. Jimmy said that Bobby had found out that not only was I Scottish, but that I had a Campbell ancestor. I couldn't believe that was the reason, so armed with that information I went to ask Bobby. Yup… he confirmed that he was angry because I was a Campbell. "Really? Why?" I asked. "Because the Campbell's murdered the Stewart's." "Bobby, that was 400 years ago!" He glared at me and bellowed, "That was yesterday!" Totally couldn't believe it.

I did manage to save up enough money to buy a used car – a 1961 loaded Pontiac Bonneville convertible, white with a red interior. $225 all in, cash on the barrel. Loaded, sure, but most of the load didn't work anymore. The car apparently had a very leaky radiator, and I had to put water in it every morning before I drove it to work. And it was absolutely huge. A friend nicknamed it The Ark.

So I was set and independent: at twenty years old I had my own apartment, my own car, and my own job-and-a-half. It was 1971.

~

In August of 1971 then-President Nixon, on the advice of his advisors, implemented the first and only peacetime wage and price controls in a miserably misguided attempt to stave off inflation, which at 6% was thought to be unsustainable. It was only supposed to last for 90 days, but there were four phases of wage and price controls before it was clear to absolutely everybody that the approach would not work. I had not been at Lillie Rubin a year when the decree went out, so it was of little issue to me personally. However, when my one-year anniversary hit there was no raise to be had. And when my one-year lease was up, the good doctor liked the work I had done so much that he would not renew the lease, intending to rent it at a higher price to someone else, since price controls meant he could not raise the rent on me. I could, of course, move next door and decorate a second apartment if I chose. I was furious. So I was out looking for a new apartment and found one about a block away – a walk-up one bedroom, partially furnished. The woman moving out was elderly and wanted to not have to walk up the stairs. The apartment had a bedroom set but not anything for the living room. I bought the soon-to-be former tenant's white Chippendale sofa, and so had at least something to sit on. She had a brown Colonial-patterned slipcover made for it to keep it clean, and that came with the deal. I had an old steamer trunk that I used for a coffee table, even though the top was slightly crowned. This was another one-bedroom apartment, but it had a narrow galley kitchen along the side of the living room, half open to the living room and with its own louvered-glass door out to the catwalk. There were less than a dozen apartments in the two-story building, and there was only a narrow strip of grass between the back of my building and a similar one in back, wide enough for a clothesline. I remember hanging my clothes one afternoon, singing as I did, and someone popped their head out the window and asked me to continue.

I would go over and visit my parents on the freighter occasionally. One day I went aboard only to find my father entertaining Sloan Wilson: Sloan Wilson of *Man in a Gray Flannel Suit* and *A Summer Place* fame. I am sure they had met in some bar. Sloan was with his wife. I remember Sloan being rather gruff and unpleasant – I remember him saying that horses were not all they were cracked up to be: that they could have bad personalities. I liked his wife: I talked more to her than to him. She had that demeanor common among wives who had quite a bit older, wealthy, but overbearing and maybe inappropriately behaved husbands – that unhappy-but-quiet, sometimes dejected look of sorrowful acceptance of the unpleasant behavior. After a while I bid my farewells and went back home. About a week later I received a call from a literary agent in New York – the firm of Whitehall, Hadlyme and Smith. Apparently, Sloan had called them and told them he thought I could write... how would I like to write a book about the freighter?

I was taken totally by surprise, but being that I am generally up for anything reasonable, I told the agent I would write a chapter or to and send it to him. My mother was jealous: she was a journalism major and thought it should have been her that was asked. Anyway, I did write a couple of chapters and sent them off to New York City. The agent flew down, contract in hand, and I signed it. It was a contract in perpetuity, but that didn't upset me much, since I knew I was not of age to enter into a contract... not yet twenty-one. He left, looking forward to the rest of the book.

I wrote and wrote, but I knew the middle section was terrible. The beginning was good: the end was good, the middle section? Where we were lolly-gagging in the ICW, getting stuck on sandbars on a daily basis? The middle section was like slogging through mud. I knew it, but I sent it to him anyway, since he was bugging me frequently. He came to the same conclusion and scheduled another visit to talk about it. He asked me to meet him after work at an upscale hotel on Key Biscayne. He was in the bar when I got there, and he had very obviously been there a couple of hours too long. He was quite drunk, and he became embarrassingly loquacious. How the lofty firm of Whitehall, Hadlyme and Smith was only him... that Whitehall was a street he used to live on and Hadlyme was some name he made up to sound impressive. How his biggest issue was the affair he was having with his secretary, and whether he should fess up to his wife and drop the secretary or leave his wife for her. Pretty much to hell with the book, ... the discussion was all about his personal situation, of which he had apparently had several hours and way too many ounces of alcohol to ponder. I was totally put off by the debacle, and that was the abrupt end of my first attempt at a literary career.

~

I was still working at Lillie Rubin, but my rent was now higher - $105 a month – and I was locked in at $80 a week because of President Nixon. So I started looking for a better-paying job, and got one at Southeast Bank. When I gave my notice, Fran wanted me to stay and said that she could get me a loan. I couldn't see why I would take a loan over a better paying job ($104 a week), so I left and headed to downtown Miami.

The Southeast Bank was in the heart of the city – so much in the heart that the parking lot was used for the Orange Bowl parade floats. I was working in stock transfer, which at the time was a very manual effort. Stock certificates were sent out as a matter of course back then, even to custodian accounts, issued via type writer. Records were computerized, but only as an after-the-fact system. A major part of our jobs was to review massive green-and-white computer printouts of the transactions we had processed to make sure the data had been entered correctly – we transferred stock certificates by hand, canceling the certificates that were surrendered and issuing new certificates to the new owners. A thin, extremely polite and modest black man named Gilbert Page was a senior clerk, and everything passed through him before it got approved by the supervisor, William Vanderbilt Sherman. There were maybe a dozen young women that were in the bullpen transferring stock certificates all day long: there was Isabel, a beautiful but haughty Cuban woman, and Maria, another Cuban with a kinder and gentler demeanor. There was another young woman from Wisconsin, and the four of us sat in a desk pod, two desks pushed up against two desks. Old grey metal desks with Formica tops, at the back of the bullpen. There were other work pods, but we didn't have much opportunity to speak to anyone other than our pod-mates.

Somewhere within this time frame, life on the freighter totally fell apart. My mother walked in on my sister having sex with the 33-year old house boy from Dr. Sachs' houseboat. Absolutely horrified, my mother [with trademark GREAT DRAMA] flew my sister back to Michigan, threatening to hide her in a nunnery. My father moved the freighter further south, to near Coconut Grove, and he left for Michigan, too. The dream of continuing our world tour was now officially shattered. My father listed the freighter for sale. Every once in a while I slept on it, in a feeble attempt to demonstrate some semblance of life aboard. That stopped rather abruptly for two reasons: the first was seeing a wharf rat. Not a tiny, New York City subway kind of rat. This was a large, humped back, just-like-in-the-fairy-tales, ugly and disgusting rodent. The second was rolling over one morning as I was sleeping on the floor in a sleeping bag and opening my eyes to gaze upon a pair of very large legs right next to me, attached to an equally large man looming over me. I guess it seemed that boarding the ship was fair game. That was the very last time I stayed on the ship.

That didn't mean I wasn't boat sale point person. Anytime anyone wanted to see it, I was on tap to show it. I remember meeting one man at a bar in Coconut Grove. It became readily apparent that he was intent on getting me drunk. I have no idea how my will kicked in, because I have gone by the moniker "One Drink of Wine Wendy" for my entire life, but I was bound and determined not to succumb to his attempts. He did not purchase the boat, but he must have commented on my apparent ability to hold my liquor, because I got a rather concerned call from my mother, wondering if I had developed a drinking problem.

My 1961 Bonneville gave up the ghost shortly after I switched jobs. I was driving home on the expressway one evening after work and the hood, which apparently, I hadn't latched properly after my daily ritual of putting water in the radiator, caught a gust of wind and wrapped itself up over the roof, completely obscuring my view. As the cars behind me were angrily honking their horns, I immediately slowed down, pulled over as far as I could until the next exit, and drove home with my head outside of the window. I called my dad and he started looking for a new car for me - and I was back on the bus. Not very long after, my dad called me up, informing me that I had a new car. A 1971 Mustang Mach I, Windsor 351 engine and all. $2,625. I asked him whether he would come visit me in jail... that much money? No way could I afford that. He drove the car down to Miami and co-signed a loan for me. And he didn't return to Michigan. He bought a couple of 18-wheelers, leased one out, went to commercial driving school and drove the other. And when that happened I was the only one of the family that could be contacted - the only one that could be located. My mother had my sister in hiding - exact whereabouts unknown, and my father was cruising somewhere across the country. I don't think anyone knew where my frequently drugged brother was. Before smart phones and texting, before Facebook check-ins and Instagram, before Twitter, all we had were land lines and snail mail. How positively quaint. So there I was, feeling rather marooned in Miami, fielding potential buyers for the freighter and waiting for other family members to occasionally check in. The phrase "you can never go home again" took on true meaning: I had no home to go back to... whatever home I might have I needed to create for and by myself.

Back at the bank, I managed to meet a man named Tony Canta, and we became very good friends. Tony had been a typist clerk in the army, but the bank was extremely sexist. He put on a suit and got a manly-man job and I, with a couple years of college under my belt and no true clerical skills, became a clerk. Tony and I laughed about it – especially him: he was the one that pointed it out. Tony was gay, so we had a rollicking, fun time together with none of the drama that can come from a "relationship." We went to Disney World right when it opened in 1971 – and we went in my new car. Along the way we hit something in the road, and whatever it was put a hole in something in the undercarriage. Something that made the engine light come on. We limped into a service station off the expressway, and a very kindly man fixed it with a bolt, washer and nut while Tony and I pulled out the picnic lunch we had prepared and ate on the grass next to the station. The service man assumed we were young lovers, and it must have taken him back to a happy time. He commented on how happy the two of us seemed, to which we smiled rather awkwardly, and we were back on our way.

The Vice President over stock transfer was a quiet, melancholy man named Ray Lineberger. He must have been in his forties, I guess, divorced with no children. He liked to sing, and he invited me to join his church choir. I am eternally grateful for that, because I met wonderful friends there. The tiny, perfect-pitch, amazing musician organist/pianist/choir director Betty Rice. Brad and Linda Waller, who were Mr. and Mrs. Gorgeous from Minnesota. He was very blond and was an environmental scientist with the federal government. She, a gorgeous, picture-perfect redhead, also worked for the government. I idolized them – a fairy tale couple. There was Donna and her zany husband Dale. Donna, the first soprano soloist and grounded one, and Dale, off doing his crazy things. There was Gail, the German professor at the University of Miami. And Bill Buckner – William Benson

Buckner – a goofy redhead that was just getting out of high school. There was Karla, raven-haired and pretty, and Bill Trexler, the single associate pastor. The senior pastor's wife, Loretta – a most elegant and pastor's-wifely woman, gracious, lovely… simply lovely. These were good, good people. We had so much fun! I had found an emotional home.

So I settled into my alone-in-Miami life: working at the bank and singing in the choir. I was struck by the overt gender discrimination at the bank: Ray had no problem telling me things like I could go far, but I could never be a bank Vice President: after all, I was a woman. There was a senior guy – I think he was Ray's boss – that fancied himself quite the ladies' man. He would occasionally pop into the bullpen and leer at us with a most disgusting grin. Except for those situations, life at the bank was not unpleasant. Tony worked with a young man that was talking about warrants, and on a whim, I bought maybe $20 worth or so. In 4 months I had more than doubled my money – I became intensely interested in the stock market. I learned that the bank had a tuition reimbursement benefit, so I headed down to the University of Miami and enrolled into the School of Business.

Tuition at the University was steep, so to pay for it, I had gone downstairs at the Bank and had gotten myself a student loan, planning on paying it off via tuition reimbursement right after I passed my two classes – one at lunch and one after work. I learned about the program quite late in the cycle, and the loan officer gave me the forms and told me he would pick them up from me that evening, when I had gotten home and filled everything out. Ms. Totally Naïve here dutifully filled out everything and waited for the loan officer. He arrived at maybe 7 pm or so, and I had the papers on the kitchen counter. There was one place I had forgotten to sign, however, and I went into the bedroom, where my little decoupage desk sat, to fetch a pen. By the time I found one and came back to the living room, that loan officer was wearing nothing but his socks. I didn't try to get past him – I ducked into the kitchen and went out through the louver door, sitting outside waiting for that man to dress himself. He kept calling through the open windows that he would "transport me into the arms of paradise." I just sat outside until he left. The loan came through and I went back to school, taking a class a couple times a week at lunch and then another after work.

My Miami Beach apartment was north of downtown, and the campus was south of the city. After my lease was up I started looking for a place somewhere between school and work, and I found an apartment on 34th Street, east of the airport and fairly mid-center of my two recurring destinations. I had a ground floor "deluxe" apartment in a two-story complex with an unusable swimming pool in the center. It probably was quite a lovely complex once upon a time. My unit was on the end, so I had two walls with windows. That was nice.

That summer the 20-somethings from the choir, Pastor Bill included, came up with a great idea: we would charter a sailboat and take a cruise to the islands. I was up for that! The company from which we chartered had a proprietary ketch design and named their sailboats Shark I, Shark II, etc. We were sailing on Shark 7 and Shark 8, because we had enough people for two boats – 8 per. Each vessel had a licensed captain, but we did everything else. The two crews competed, and I remember passing the Shark 8 while it was mooring for the evening. We decided to pass it, and Marilyn of the perfect boatswain's whistle let loose just as we sailed past, all of us lined up on the gunnel, saluting smartly. We would moor in beautiful bays of uninhabited islands, and sometimes we would berth at marinas in Bahamian Islands. We cracked open coconuts and swam magnificent reefs, the coral so high that we couldn't kick vertically – we needed to skim the water to not get cut. I was over one of the reefs and decided for some reason to go back to the ship. We were never supposed to swim alone, but we were in a protected cove and no one had seen any sharks. The reef must have been a good 30 feet tall, and as I came over the edge, directly underneath me, looking up, was a lone barracuda. He saw me, I saw him. I very calmly kept smoothly swimming – no frantic splashing, no vigorous kicks. Barracudas are mean, and lone barracudas are meaner than most. I got back to the sailboat safely, but I don't think I was ever so happy to board a boat as at that moment.

At the mouth of one of the coves were huge rocks, maybe 20 or 30 feet down. Hard to tell. It was deep enough, though, because I free dove down far enough that the water was getting a bit dark. Down there, behind one of the boulders, was the biggest grouper I had ever seen. That thing was massive! My dad told me later that I could have gotten in trouble down there, but ignorance being bliss, I was fearless. That fish was taller than I was. We ended up chartering again the following year. That second trip was one for the record books: note to self – never leave port soon after a hurricane.

I nearly lost my life on that trip. I had pulled galley duty on our first day out: our departure was delayed because of the hurricane. The seas were very rough, and I was heading up the gangway with two plates of pancakes. I had no sooner handed them both out when the boat rolled deeply. I wasn't hanging on to anything, but as I headed overboard I managed to grab onto a guy wire. Thank God – they would have never been able to see me in those heavy seas.

My little idyllic and peaceful life came to a screeching halt in the fall of 1972. My mother, unable to manage my seventeen-year-old sister, shipped her down to me. Tracy had been kicked out of a couple of high schools, I was told, and my mother was simply fed up. So I took her in. She got a job, since my mother was sending no support, and was taking the bus to and from work. I would drive her to the local high school for GED classes. It took no time at all before she was not coming home after class – she was coming in past one in the morning. I finally told her I was dead-bolting the door at one, which I did. That was no deterrent: she was locked out more than once. She turned 18 on December 28th of that year and left for good. What she had been doing was having Castro, the house boy, pick her up at the high school. She married him as soon as she could. Those were a rough couple of months – me 21, working full time, going to school, and attempting to manage my totally uncontrollable sister. She believes I kicked her out, her with pneumonia. I merely dead-bolted the door when I told her I would. I will never quite understand, even after all of these years, that she thought a 17-year-old should not have a curfew. She never did graduate from high school, but many years later she earned a GED, and then got an Associate degree.

Near the end of the lease on that apartment I met a man, Lynn Forrester, that was selling a condominium down by Dadeland Mall. I started working part-time for him, doing bookkeeping at a car dealership, and he said he would finance the condo sale. With no further ado I bought it, and at 22 was a homeowner. It was quite lovely, and I was thrilled that I could decorate it without someone else's permission. It had cream colored carpeting, so in the bedroom I papered the wall behind the bed in a very subtle beige and cream simple plaid. I had a screened porch overlooking the pool, within which I hung light linen drapes that I had made. The fabric had a white background, printed with a large green fern pattern. Very Florida. I found a chocolate and white cane pattered wallpaper for the kitchen. It looked very clean and crisp. As metallic wallpaper was all the rage, I papered one wall of the dining area in silver – an ersatz mirror to make the room look a bit larger. My mother suggested wallpapering the ceiling of the entrance in a bold black and white stripe, running length-wise, to make the entrance look bigger. It really did. I bought a Plexiglas pedestal lamp, a simple rectangular cube, that was wired for light. I bought a plaster horse head statue, placed it on the pedestal, and that's what greeted guests. I had campaign chests for dressers, room for a table for six in the dining room... it was great. No more worn at the edges, stuccoed Pre-War shabby apartments for me.

I had been attending classes for a year. My dad asked me how much longer it would take me, and I told him nine years. He offered to float me to finish sooner and asked what it would take. I figured I could finish if I took 21 credit hours – 7 classes – each semester for a year. He asked how much I would need to live, and I told him $400. He was surprised and said to make sure to call him if I needed money for a roll of toilet paper. So I went to the school, plan in hand, and was told that I needed Dean's permission to take that many classes. I talked my way into it, and so starting in January 1973, I was a full-time student.

I went to Mr. Sherman, dear Mr. William Vanderbilt Sherman, and told him I was going to quit. He made me the most remarkable offer: don't quit, he said. Come in when you can, he said. I couldn't see how I could turn down that offer, so I stacked my class schedule with classes from eight in the morning until one in the afternoon and then headed down to the bank. I worked there until five. Lynn Forrester at the car dealership didn't want me to quit either, so after the bank I went to the dealership. I got home at about 9:30 at night, slept until 2 in the morning, then got up to study until I needed to leave for school. I became exhausted, enough so I could sleep through the alarm. So I bought a second alarm and put it in the bathroom, set five minutes after alarm #1. I got very good at being able to shut that one off, too, and hop back to bed to fall right back asleep. So I bought a third alarm and put it in the kitchen, right next to the coffee pot. That worked: 3 alarms stacked five minutes apart in three different locations. I remember dozing off at work, but I had my head held up with my right hand while I turned the pages of the big computer printouts slowly with my left... while sleeping. It looked like I was checking records.

As if that wasn't enough, the bank had hired a new clerk: a peppy little firecracker named Nonnie. Nonnie was married and had three kids, but the marriage was terrible. She and her husband had started divorce proceedings, which is why she started working. It was messy, it distracted her, and it cost her that job. Well, one day she asked me if I could babysit the children that night – could they sleep over? I said yes, and that's when I had three kids for a month or so, Caroline, age five, Sean, age three and an eighteen-month curly-haired tot named Elizabeth. They were beautiful children, really. What I didn't know at the time was that Nonnie had gotten wrapped up in a shoplifting ring. She was running wild. Her ex-husband was engaged to a woman, and he was going for full custody. That woman, who said she was all about being a mom, did a 180 right after the wedding and refused to take the kids. The children ended up separated and in foster care. Broke my heart when I found out.

I was now getting up at six in the morning because I needed to take the kids to pre-school before class. One or the other parent, or a grandparent or relation, picked the children up for dinner and brought them back when I got home. I am not sure just how long I would have been able to keep that up. I remember buying them clothes and taking them to church so I could sing. I remember studying by the pool while they played by me... and I remember hearing a splash and looking up to see that little baby girl about a foot under water. I dove right in and plucked her out. She had been in the water such a short time that she wasn't even coughing, but man, it takes no time at all for a baby to be lost. She didn't realize she had been in danger – she didn't cry or cling. I made no big deal of it – she went right back to playing. She had no idea how close she came.

I kept that rather brutal schedule for a full twelve months, and on December 7, 1973, I took my last undergraduate exam. My last semester was quite iffy: my father's last check had bounced, and I wasn't sure I would be able to register with an unpaid bill over my head. I remember going into the Dean's office and telling him I might not be able to finish my last term. He said not to worry – just go register anyway. Back then class registration was in a gym, with long tables set up all the way around. Everything was manual, paper and pencil: you'd walk up to the table that was responsible for the class you wanted to take, and the person at the table would see if there were any slips left. If there were, you were in. I went up to the first table and was told I needed to go over to the scholarship table. What? I didn't apply for any scholarships. I went over and lo and behold, the good Dean had arranged to have $750 waiting for me. He never even said anything to me. Bless that man.

December of 1973 was quite an eventful month. One night, during the week before finals, I answered the door and saw my sister standing there. As I opened the door wider to let her in, Castro came from behind a brick pillar where he had been hiding and burst into my condo. I had been in the bedroom folding clothes, and I went back in. I did not know that Castro had bad intentions. He followed me in and attacked me. I struggled and wiggled, and in the melee furniture was broken and blood was splattered on the wall. I know that from cleaning up afterwards, after the emergency room visit. I don't remember much about the attack, except that I saw my sister cowering in the corner like a beaten dog. I have never seen a human act that way. I also know that he had me over the edge of the bed, and that he was strangling me. I remember thinking I just wanted him to stop, and I remember leaving my pinkie finger nail in his cheek. My leg also came off, because there was a knock on the door, which caused Castro to stop, and I remember hopping to the door and opening it to find two policemen. During the struggle my sister had gone into the kitchen to quietly call the police. Those policemen took one look at me, bleeding and one-legged, and took Castro into custody. My sister told me later that the policemen took a little detour between my condo and the police station and delivered some physical retaliation.

I can't remember having to sign anything or formally press charges. The next thing I knew was that there was an emergency restraining order against Castro, and he could not be within 500 yards of me, and where I wanted to be had priority. The police also advised me to purchase a gun. There was a fellow named Dave that stepped in: he was the one that had taken me to the hospital, he helped me clean up the blood splatter and pick up and discard the broken furniture, and he went with me to buy a blue steel .38 caliber special. He took me to a firing range and taught me how to use it.

I looked a mess. I had deep bruising on my neck that lasted weeks. I remember one of professors seeing the marks – he looked at me with great alarm, but he didn't say anything. The assault trial was well after I had finished class. I don't remember much about it, except that before the trial my sister called me up and tried to get me to get the case dropped. I told her I would not. Besides: it was not Wendy S. Thomson v. Osmar Castro Vega, it was the City of Miami v. Osmar Castro Vega. We went to trial, and I was asked to tell what happened. The judge asked if I had any lasting damage, and I remember stating that my vocal chords were damaged so I was having a hard time singing. My sister testified as a witness – for Castro. I listened in disbelief as she testified that I had attacked him. Of course, nobody in that courtroom believed her. He was found guilty. I felt so very, very betrayed. She told me later it was because she was pregnant. Castro was put on probation, and shortly thereafter my sister had an abortion and divorced him. I think the real reason she lied was because she was terrified of him. He obviously beat her, based upon her level of fear cowering in the corner.

I didn't break down until two months later. I was totally surprised when I walked into the bathroom at work, and as I was passing the mirror I glanced at myself. Suddenly I started sobbing hysterically – I remember gasping, "He tried to kill me!" as I was leaning over, supporting myself on the counter. A woman walked in and looked at me with huge concern – that was enough of a distraction to get me to compose myself. I think I left early that day.

In the midst of all this drama, my mother called me. She was in total shock: my father had gotten up and walked out. He waited until all of us were no longer his responsibility: me out of school, my sister married, my brother off lost in his drug haze somewhere… he waited until all of that was taken care of, and then he left my mother. My mother waited about a week, thinking it wasn't true, but one thing about my father: he was a man of his word, and he didn't buckle. I think he was counting the days. My mother was a total basket case.

~

I was now a freshly-minted college graduate, magna cum laude, with a B.B.A. in Finance. Graduation ceremonies were combined for the year and were held in May, so I simply went back to work as if nothing had happened. I remember my mother wanting to come and visit for graduation, it being December and Miami and everything, but when I told her the ceremony was in

May she was not nearly as eager. My parents' lives were in such disarray that I received no cards or gifts… I had simply completed all the requirements for my degree and no longer needed to go on campus. I remember it feeling so odd to not know there was something I needed to be doing. I had become anemic on top of everything else, so I badly needed a more reasonable life, at least for a while. Come summer, Betty Rice attended that graduation ceremony and told me my name was announced, and where was I? I guess my experiences with ceremony that focused on me had been so negative that I chose no ceremony at all. Of all the opportunities I had, the only time I felt that anyone was proud of what I had accomplished was when my father gave me his National Honor Society pin, and that one instance had been drowned in a sea of not so pleasant memories.

I went back to fulltime work at the bank, in the same job. There was no indication that the bank was going to move or promote me after my academic achievement, so I began looking for a job that would befit my newly acquired education.

I did not have to hunt long: the first job for which I applied was at a real estate investment trust as loan analyst. I got the job, but not before having to spend 8 hours taking all sorts of psychological and knowledge exams. Early in the day there was a sketch of a boy and a man… a pencil sketch, black and white. I was asked to write a story about it, which I dutifully did. There was a vocabulary test buried somewhere in the middle of the day that had words that were progressively more and more obscure: by the last page I was laughing out loud. The very last exercise was that same drawing of the boy and man, with the same request to write a story about it. I remember rather tersely writing something along the lines of, "I already wrote a story about this." I got the job anyway.

I told Mr. Sherman I was leaving. He asked me for a letter of resignation, which I gave him. It was short and sweet: I think I wrote Subject: Resignation. In the body of the letter I wrote "Effective" and then I wrote the date. He looked at it and exclaimed, "You can't do that!" I replied, "I just did." I was not happy that the bank refused to act upon my degree attainment: I was angry that they didn't even discuss a promotional path upwards. I am not sure they even considered that I would want to progress. As I was walking down the hall one day, all smiles because I had just been told I was the successful candidate for my soon-to-be new job, Mr. Leering Sr. VP mentioned that I looked very happy. Never the one for tact or subtlety, I remember grinning as I told him I had finally gotten a decent job. Whoa, was he angry.

In one fell swoop I had gone from $104 a week to $10,000 a year. I felt I was literally rolling in the dough. I bought a 7.5 carat cabochon ruby ring, surrounded by diamonds. I bought new clothes. $10,000 a year was premium pay – jobs for new graduates were normally $7,500 a year. My new job wasn't without its challenges, however. I was the second woman ever hired for that position, the first failing miserably. The office staff – all women – were responsible for making coffee and cleaning up the break room. The men were not so burdened. I learned after a while that the leadership actually had a meeting to decide whether I, as a woman, should be required to take a shift at coffee and clean up, or whether I, as an analyst, should be spared that duty. Thankfully the position held sway.

It's not easy being the first at anything: it's even harder being the second after number one failed. My job was to review commercial building proposals and recommend whether the REIT should invest or not. I knew precious little about building codes or potential topographical problems like culverts. Thankfully I did know something about construction, having lived in it for most of my life. It was baptism by fire: I had to look at plans and market factors like demand, saturation, competition, and financial breakeven occupancy rates. I didn't know it at the time, but these guys were risk-takers extraordinaire. At the end of each quarter they were approving projects they had no business approving in order to show good growth rates. There were shaky developers and razor-thin margin deals. Overbuilding in markets where the required breakeven occupancy fell outside of comfortable achievement probability. I had not developed my voice to challenge any of this: I was new kid on the block, maybe I was wrong and didn't understand the business well enough. I guess I was good enough, though, because I stayed.

There was a VP, John Halvorson, who caused me to change my name. I was baptized Wendy Sue. I hate that name. It never grows up. There I was, trying my very best to be professional in the high-flying world of leveraged financial deals, stuck with "Wendy Sue." Well, John was from the deep South, and he couldn't help but call me "Wendy Sue." Complete with exaggerated drawl. Every time. Why couldn't I have been Patricia or Elizabeth, or even Victoria? Why couldn't I have been given a grown-up, substantial and elegant name? Well, I hadn't been. I was named after Mary Martin in Peter Pan, and that was that. So there was also an attorney at the firm that agreed to draw up a legal name change petition for me... I decided that the "Sue" simply had to go. I adopted my mother's maiden name as my middle name, and Sue became Sura. No more "Wendy Sue."

~

I was alone in Miami, but I had a generally pleasant life. I spent more than one Thanksgiving alone – I would make an entire traditional dinner, but after cooking and smelling it all day long I would wrap it up and stick it all in the refrigerator without as much as a nibble. The next day, I would make up a pie crust or two and put everything except the cranberry sauce in the crusts and make turkey pies. They were delicious! I would put up live Christmas trees, and my sister would come over. I remember she was visiting once and we were looking at a pair of heels I had bought. She tried them on, but her feet are larger than mine. She stumbled and hit the plaster horse head I had sitting on that pedestal in the entrance, and it shattered into pieces. We spent hours gluing it back together.

I started that new job in early 1973. As luck would have it, in 1973 this nation experienced a significant oil shortage. Gas was rationed: sometimes only 10 gallons at a time, sometimes only being able to purchase it on odd or even days, depending on license plate number. There were lines that went around blocks… lines that took hours to get through. Gas stations closed for lack of supply. Of course the economy tumbled – and with it, the REIT for which I worked. Less than six months after I started, many of the need-everything-to-fall-just-right-to-make-it deals had gone south: there was a layoff. I survived. Three months after that, another layoff. I survived that one, too. Then the company declared bankruptcy. I did not survive that: I was jobless.

I had a mortgage, I had a car payment… I needed to change my financial situation in a hurry. I sold the condo in short order. Lynn Forrester offered to rent to me a four-bedroom house in Coral Gables on a canal, close to the University of Miami. It was a wonderful neighborhood once upon a time… a wonderful house, too – once upon a time. The entire area had fallen into genteel shabbiness… the house next door was rented out to three twenty-something guys that made a business of trading in venomous reptiles – that house was full of rattlesnakes and vipers and who knows what else. They had a large green and pink boa named Cathy that ended up in the canal with me once when I was swimming.

I moved into that house, renting out the other three bedrooms: one to Marilyn of the boatswain's whistle fame, one to Suzanne Dow, and one to Bill Buckner while he was home from Florida State. I was pretty much relieved of any housing cost, but I was back in shabby housing. And I took on lots of odd jobs: I sewed boat cushions for zany Dale. I cooked gourmet dinners for the Waller's. Bill Buckner was a great ceramics artist, and he moved his kiln and potter's wheel into the attached garage - I sold some of his pottery. I made a bedspread for some random guy who was a friend of a friend. The economy was terrible, and jobs were very scarce. I did have quite a bit of time to have some fun, though: I threw a Halloween party that year. The guys next door came adorned with Cathy. I made myself into a pirate, complete with glued-on snippets of a wig for a mustache, thick brows and chest hair, a red crushed velvet waistcoat I made from an old Juliet dress, and a peg leg I had fashioned out of an old table leg. I had a friend who had a big green parrot which sat on my shoulder. I had my .38 tucked into the front of my waistband. I made a remarkable Capt. Morgan.

I also had time to fall madly in love with Bill Buckner. We went diving for conch and made conch chowder. We went diving for Florida lobster. We made beautiful pottery ... well, he actually made beautiful pottery. Mine were feeble attempts. Buck – that's what I called him – was the oldest of four boys. His mother, Margaret, was from an old Southern family. She was simply elegant: perfectly coifed, prematurely white, absolutely stunning hair. Perfect complexion. She spoke with such a drawl that the word "yes" came out nearly "yeah, us." The word never came out singly. It was always "yeah us, yeah us." Mrs. Buckner's mother, Jennie Dorsey, also lived locally. She was a wonderful, spry 86-year-old ... another redhead back in the day. She had a remnant of that glorious red hair, right at her crown, which was set off by the white hair that encircled it.

Jenny was born on a plantation in Louisiana in the 1880's. The plantation slaves that were emancipated following the Civil War stayed on, and she remembered them from her childhood. Jenny lived in a very tiny cottage situated in the middle of a good-sized, narrow but deep yard, surrounded on the periphery by a chain link fence with a lockable gate. The cottage front was lined with Jenny's roses. Buck got her a pair of gym shorts for her birthday that year because of a rather amusing incident: she had locked herself out of her gate. Instead of calling for assistance, she drove her car up to the fence, climbed on the hood and got over that fence... at 86. She was that kind of gal. I made her a hooked, monogrammed rug for Christmas – I really liked her.

Buck not only sang, he played several brass instruments. He was a member of the Florida State Marching Band. He was just so very talented – and kind, and funny. It's one of the wonders of the human psyche that people become more attractive the more you like them... the goofy-looking guy I first met started to become a very attractive redhead to me.

~

I sent out many resumes and had several interviews during my stretch of unemployment. I did not apply for – or maybe didn't even qualify for – unemployment, but that somehow didn't bother me at all. I had read that losing a job could take a huge psychological toll, but I came to realize that I apparently didn't define myself by my employment as much as maybe some. I got many interviews, probably in no small part because people felt compelled to meet this woman that had a stint as a navigator. The ship opened many doors. As part of my job search, I took the federal government's PACE test. I laughed very hard about that – I got nothing less than a 97% in all subjects covered – even architecture. That meant that every hiring manager had to interview me for whatever job that was open… all the way from the CIA and FBI to OSHA. There was an opening at OSHA, and per spec I was given the mandatory interview. It was clear from the moment I walked in that I was the last thing this man wanted. He wanted a guy in a hard hat – not me. He tried every trick on the book to try to get me to decline, pointing to the long shelf of regulations that I was supposed to memorize and describing clambering around construction sites. I knew he would find any excuse, and I knew he would not call me back, but I never gave him the satisfaction of crying Uncle.

Being rather bored, I also joined Mensa. I didn't have to take their test, I just sent in my National Merit scores. I went to several meetings, and through that group ended up riding on the back of a Honda 750 up to Fort Lauderdale on I-95. That bike belonged to a fellow Mensa member, and after he learned I had never been on a motorcycle he insisted. I didn't stay active in Mensa, though. It was a very small chapter, and I came to believe that many of the dozen or so members that I had met had not much to hold onto except their IQ, and I started to feel constrained. The organization did put out an interesting publication which had clever jokes at the back. I remember one that really tickled me: it was a parody of singles ads in the paper. This particular "want-ad" had an impossibly hilarious set of qualifications: Ph.D., Nobel Prize winner, movie contract and speaking knowledge of all romance languages. Cracked me up. I remember reading it to my mother during a phone call: she didn't laugh at all. She simply asked me what the five languages were, to which I replied French, Spanish, Portuguese, Italian and Romanian. She sniffed and responded that she thought she was the only one smart enough to know that. Sigh – she obviously was a very insecure woman.

Fall was rolling around, and Buck was going back to finish his senior year. I was sad to see him go. I tried in vain to rent out the room he had, but I got no takers. I relied on rent to make it, and things were not looking good. Suzanne had broken up with her boyfriend and was talking about moving back to Vermont. I visited Buck several times, sitting in the band section at football games. Back then the Seminoles were not the powerhouse they are today… in fact, you could also say that about the Spartans when I was at MSU and the Hurricanes when I was at the University of Miami. Come to think of it, my high school football team wasn't all that great, either. My senior year the only game we won was against our school district rival. I must jinx football teams. Anyway, the games at FSU were so uninspiring that the band members would take people like me and pass us up and down the bleachers over their heads.

With no job prospects in Miami, and with the financials no longer supporting me, I decided to move up to Tallahassee. I might be broke, but at least Buck was there to brighten my day. Buck had gotten me an Irish Setter puppy who I named Shannon. She needed some running space, so I found and rented a very small duplex apartment on a very large lot. I think it was only 336 square feet. It had no air conditioning, and as I sit here I cannot remember a single heat register. However, it was inexpensive. The kitchen had 36 inches of counter space. I had to push the dresser up against the side of the bed, because there wasn't room for it anywhere else if I wanted to get into the bathroom. I hung a thick 6' dowel from the ceiling at the point the dresser touched the bed, climbed up on top of that dresser and macrame'd a room divider. I had to kind of dive into bed. I also got some 2" x 8" boards and a couple of shutters and made a bathroom cabinet, cutting the wood so the shutters just fit as doors. That was one of my better efforts. I moved in late summer, when both the universities and the legislature were gearing up, and I landed a temporary job as a clerk at the local telephone company. At a 75% pay cut.

I was a bit frantic when I first got to Tallahassee. I was flat broke. Broke, like living for two weeks off a 20-lb. bag of potatoes, because that's all I could afford, broke. Broke, like the toes fell off my artificial leg, precluding me from wearing a shoe on that side, broke. People looked at me in horror at the grocery store. And speaking of the grocery store, inflation was still rampant, and prices were going up weekly. I remember standing in the grocery store by the milk and crying because prices had again risen. I couldn't buy a half gallon of milk. I figured that I couldn't work without toes, so I looked and looked and finally found a charity that agreed to pay for a replacement foot. I was able to go to work wearing two shoes.

The job I got was in phone installation. Tallahassee has several very distinct cultures: there are the students that come in for both Florida State and Florida A & M. There are the politicians that come in when the legislature is in session. There are the professors and other highly educated professionals. And then there are the workers – the people that hold it all together. The phone company employees were the workers; all very, very Southern in manner, speech, cuisine and culture. Laura Jessup ran my department. My job was only supposed to last six weeks or so – just until the fall rush was over. Except it didn't: I was offered a permanent job as the clerk in cable and construction. My job was to open and clear work tickets from all the crews working for Jerry, my supervisor. I liked the men. They were strong, kind and rather stoic guys, very gentlemanly... men like those portrayed in old Westerns. There was Riker, who once told me, "Woman, you can get out the entire Declaration of Independence before I can say hello." There was the guy who came out and strung tower cable between my back door and a tree a distance away so I had a dog run. There was Terry, who always had a nice smile for me. And Ben – sweet Ben Tyler.

Buck, his buddies and I had a really great time. We would go to Wakulla Springs and swim in the sinkhole used in the old movie Creature of the Black Lagoon. We took a boat upriver and saw all manner of alligators sunning on the riversides. I had to make sure Shannon didn't bark – the park ranger told me she would be alligator bait. We went diving in remote sinkholes known only to the college kids. We would cook remarkable dinners, going over to Panama City to the shrimp docks to buy fresh shrimp from the returning shrimpers. We picked blueberries from an abandoned orchard we found, and I made fig jam from the fig tree growing in my yard. I was still flat broke: I still have a recipe I called "Poverty is the Mother of Invention Casserole #1," made from whatever I could scrounge up in the kitchen. We even once went out to dinner on a charge card because we didn't have any cash for the grocery store. But Buck used to bring me a white rose when he came to visit, plucked from some garden he knew. That made my day – every day.

By the following fall I had passed my GMATs, had started graduate school, and had gotten engaged to Buck. Since we had both been so involved in the Miami church where we met, Buck wanted to get married there, right in the middle of a service – with hundreds in attendance. Well, okay. We set a date of March 20. I found a dress pattern – very fairy-tale, reminiscent of Princess Diana's wedding dress, and was preparing to get started on it. Buck had decided to attend graduate school at the University of Indiana, so he went north. There was a guy who lived next door that was moving away and who didn't have room for his 10-speed in his van, so he gave it to me. I started night school, riding that bike to and from campus, and took out a student loan to finance it all. Worked during the day, went to school at night, found a choir to join, and started on my way-too-elaborate wedding dress.

I had left the freighter in Coconut Grove, but there was new potential buyer that came up to Tallahassee to discuss it. Some youngish guy. Once again, I had to leave the room for some reason. Once again I returned, only to find this guy standing in only his socks? Again? Geesh. I told him to put on his clothes and walked into the kitchen, asking him if he wanted a sandwich. The boat finally did sell shortly thereafter.

Things were humming along, then along came Thanksgiving. Buck called off the wedding when he returned from Indiana on holiday break, avoiding me but giving no reason. I was devastated. I decided that I would celebrate the coming Christmas the best I could, which wasn't much, with Shannon. The grocery store had fresh dog food wrapped like hamburger. I bought it for her, and after I connected her to her run out back I went into the kitchen to start preparing it for her. Wouldn't she be surprised!! I fried it all up and went to call her in… and she was gone. The cable hadn't snapped, the clip that attached to her collar wasn't broken, and her collar wasn't hanging from the clip. Someone decided they wanted a cute red puppy for Christmas, and they took mine.

I have to undertake a slight segue here and discuss my dog. Shannon Eire O'Callahan, purebred and papered, of both field and show stock. She was amazing. She was my dog, no doubt about it. She listened to no one but me – no one. She tore up my sister's blinds. She stole pizza from the counter with such skill and grace as to be nearly undetectable. She ate half of a New York cheesecake I made and never even got sick from it. She once buried a bone, so frantic she wore off the skin on her snout covering it up, and then paced all night long worried about it. She was the most trusting of dogs – at least to me – letting me cut away the matted hair on an infected forepaw and disinfect it, never pulling away, just occasionally letting out a small whimper. She let a ten-year-old pull her away from her food by her tail, never a snarl. She only once showed any aggression, and that was when I had gotten pulled over by a gumball midway between Miami and Tallahassee in the wee hours of the morning. She was in the back seat, and when I started rolling down my window for the man that approached she was over my shoulder, baring her teeth and growling and barking most menacingly – first and only time, from the day I got her at eight weeks until the day she laid her head down in my lap to die. She moved with me from Miami to Tallahassee, from Tallahassee to Chicago, from Chicago to St. Clair Shores, from St. Clair Shores to Oakland Township. Always my dog, always trusting me totally. Trusting me to guide her down the dirt road after she went blind, happily listening for my footsteps and meandering, righting course when she felt the grass on the side. She wouldn't venture into the road if she couldn't hear my footsteps. Coming up the many steps to the side door for me to draw her blood and administer her insulin injection kindly and patiently, even after the veterinarian said I needed someone to hold her so I wouldn't get bitten. Never happened. I knew it wouldn't happen. She was my dog, and I was her entire world. And finally, laying her head on my lap the very last time, when she couldn't walk up the hill anymore, when she was just tired – laying her head in my lap as I sat on the floor, as she drifted away, me petting her and speaking to her softly as she left me. My entire purpose was to make sure she wasn't afraid. I have had many dogs in my life, but none compares to my Shannon. Best dog in the entire world, bar none.

I had met a very bright, vivacious and motherly woman in the church choir – Rosemary Johnson. Her children were grown and gone, and she rather adopted me. She and her husband Mel came over and we spent the entire day looking for my pup. Never found her. That was the very worst Christmas I have ever spent, bar none. I contacted the three veterinarians in the city and told them to be on the lookout, and also called animal control. And then I simply went back to school and back to work, calling and asking whether any Irish Setters had been picked up every week or so. I was functioning, but what I did not realize is that I wasn't eating. I tried, but every time I tried to eat my stomach would knot up – like having a spasm. I lost twenty pounds in two weeks, and I didn't even notice. And then a miracle happened: an Irish Setter had been found about thirty miles away, very thin, heartworm positive, near an alligator-infested area. I rushed to the pound to find a limp dog who could barely lift her head, filthy and so thin I wasn't sure it was her. They brought her out of the kennel and I looked her over. Still not sure. We walked over to the door, and then she told me she was Shannon. She sat by the door. I had taught her to sit at the door to go out, which for a dog as exuberant as an Irish Setter is nothing to sneeze at. I knew she was my girl.

I took her to the vet, where she was examined and put on medicine. I had to charge the entire bill – I can't even remember how much it cost, but it was enough that I had to pay one credit card one month and a second one the next. Now I was not only significantly broke, I was significantly in debt.

All during this time my twenty-pound weight loss was taking its toll. When you wear a prosthetic it is made to fit a certain weight – like clothing, only way, way more expensive. My leg became too big – so big that once, riding back from school, it fell off right in the middle of the street. I can generally hold it on while walking with my muscles, even if it's too big, but I am unable to properly fire those muscles while peddling a bike. I was putting too much pressure on the bottom of my residual limb, and I rubbed it totally raw. I distinctly remember sitting in my car working up the fortitude to walk into work – it was that painful. Tallahassee's heat and humidity are very friendly to bacteria – my sore didn't heal, so I finally called my dad one night when the pain would not let me sleep. He said I should go to the emergency room the next day to get some antibiotics. Well, I figured if I had to go to the hospital and couldn't sleep anyway, why not go in the dead of night? Fewer people seeking treatment, and then I could just go back to work the next day. So I got into my car at one in the morning and drove through heavy fog to the hospital. The emergency entrance parking lot was blocked off due to construction, but by now it was so hard to walk that I simply could not negotiate parking any distance away at all, so I parked as close as I could, right in front of the construction. I figured I would be gone before the construction crew arrived, anyway.

I left the hospital six days later. I had developed a staph infection which apparently had gotten into my lymph system. I was told the telltale blue line was creeping up my thigh. All I knew is that it hurt like hell. The nurse gave me a shot of Demerol – and I didn't wake up until 26 hours later. Buck had come, and his voice woke me. He needed to move my car. I have no idea how the hospital staff came to call him. When he awakened me, I saw four syringes lined up along the mattress beside me... I was getting sixteen shots a day. My leg was wrapped in gauze – I was told it was weeping. I also was told that I screamed out in pain when they changed the dressing, even though I was knocked out with the Demerol. A doctor told me that I needed to be very careful: I had a "sensitivity to narcotics" – alcohol included. Guess my "One Drink of Wine Wendy" has some medical basis.

On day six I called my father and told him what had happened. He really yelled at me: "What? People DIE from that!!" Anyway, I was discharged, but not after a visit from the billing department. I had no insurance. No car insurance, no health insurance – no insurance. I hadn't had enough time in with the phone company to qualify for their plan, and I was facing hundreds and hundreds of dollars in medical expenses. The woman was very kindly – she asked about my parents, and when I mentioned Dr. Thomson she was all ready to give me professional privilege. I declined because I felt that wasn't ethical – I told her I would pay it off month by month. It took me a long time, but I did it. Sounds rather quaint as I write this – a bill in the hundreds for a six-day stay. Back when insurance was not as widespread, medical costs as a percent of income were much more modest. Just like college tuition.

My next problem was that I was not to wear my leg. For months, and then not the one I had. The only prosthetics maker was in Gainesville, a several hour drive away. So I went to work on crutches. I went to school on crutches. I wore long skirts to conceal my one-leggedness. It was much easier to hop around than it was to use crutches, because having a right arm nine inches shorter, with no thumb, put intense pressure on my armpits. I hopped around the house. I hopped around everywhere I could, to the point that a co-worker reported me as making him uncomfortable. I remember hopping up an entire flight of stairs and not even being winded, which astonished one of the people in the group. And all during this time dear Rosemary came to fetch and wash my clothes and buy groceries for me. She was a true saint.

It was during this hopping interval that my Uncle Gene and Aunt Jean came to visit: they had retired and were making a grand tour of the country in a van outfitted with sleeping quarters. My father also came to visit, describing my apartment later as somewhere where, "You came to the front door, stepped in, and smiled, because there wasn't room to do anything else."

It took four months to get a new leg, but I was back in business. But no sooner than I was once again as whole as I can be, the union workers decided to go on strike. In all the years the phone company had been in business there had never been a strike. There were those in management that didn't believe "their people" would strike, but strike they did. No one was quite sure how all of this was going to work. No one knew if the strikers would get violent with scabs. Terry of the nice smile was a union rep, and I called him aside quietly. Told him I had all of these medical bills and had no insurance – I needed to work, since I had no one to fall back on. He understood and told me he would see I wouldn't be bothered. I did work – I worked 12-hour shifts. I was driven to and from work by a management guy – they wouldn't let me drive myself. I was protected from both sides, but Esther was not. Esther had worked at the phone company for years, was married to an illiterate guy, and had a four-year-old son. Esther supported the family – she was a fundamental Baptist, and if her husband told her to support the family, that was what she was supposed to do. No makeup, modest clothes, "obey your husband" … the whole nine yards. Esther's son had gotten a bad bacon grease burn when he was a toddler, and the union stepped in and helped her out. She wouldn't strike because her husband told her not to, and the union was furious that she would turn her back after all they had done for her. She didn't fare too well after that. The strike lasted maybe three weeks, and then everyone was back to work.

Shortly after all this turmoil my sister called to let me know she was getting married again. It was rather sudden, but I was to be her maid of honor. She was living in Fort Lauderdale at the time, so I took a week of vacation and headed down state. When I got there, a week before the wedding, my sister had arranged very little except an outside venue. She didn't have a dress. A week before the wedding and she had no dress. We spent a day hitting every store we could think of – my sister did not realize that bridal salons didn't carry off-the-rack dresses, only samples. She was in tears. She pulled out a picture of a tailored dress that was only sold in Birmingham Michigan, ironically, and that was the dress she wanted – the only dress she wanted. Without that dress she said she didn't even want to get married, she sobbed. Oh well... off to the fabric store. We bought yards and yards of candlelight peau de soie (my all-time favorite bridal fabric) and yards and yards of matching tulle. I took a couple of sheets from her and made a pattern to match the pictured dress: deep V-neck with a stand-up collar, intricately darted bodice with a flared skirt, no fitted waist, long narrow sleeves with deep cuffs. And I started sewing. I sewed until two in the morning, got up the next morning and started sewing again – repeat until finished. Well, almost finished: at the very end we had to use masking tape on the hem of the petticoat. Ran out of time. Oh: and then she had no veil. Made that. Then she had no cake. Made that, too. I was exhausted. My mother appeared a couple of days before the wedding, but all she could do was worry about what she was going to wear. She was totally useless until about an hour or two before the wedding, when she started helping tape up the petticoat hem... self-absorbed, as usual. All she could seem to think about was whether the magenta gown she had was pretty enough. Did the purse match? Was it appropriate? And I was ass-over-end buried in pulling off the near-impossible.

The wedding turned out to be quite a fiasco: it started to rain hard right before the ceremony, so at the very last minute it was moved. No one had been informed about Plan B, so hardly anyone made the ceremony. There wasn't a reception, really, just a dinner... kind of like a rehearsal dinner, but after the fact. Since I was sadly and forlornly alone, Donna of choir fame "lent" me her husband Dale for my escort. Dale was a hoot – he pretended to tuck a Japanese dinner plate into his tux because it was a very nice piece of ceramic. He spent his evening valiantly keeping me laughing, for which I remain eternally grateful.

That marriage did not last long: while my sister was visiting me in Tallahassee she got a call that her husband, Cesar Augusto Gianella – Colombian by birth - had been jailed on drug charges.

~

Back at the phone company, the manager over the entire area, Jim Hoke, had noticed that not only did I come into work during the strike, I had managed to design a process for myself that got all my work completed by lunchtime so that I could answer phones in the afternoon but study in between. It took the two other women all day. He pulled me off for a little project, wanting me to look for process inefficiencies in another area. I did the work and mapped the process for him. Then he asked me to redesign it – I knew that would mean that some of the union folks that had let me be during the strike would lose their jobs over it, so I respectfully declined. I told Jim that was not something I could do in good conscience, and I told him why. And that told me something about my motivation: I think that since I had no support system, since I had been berated for a significant portion of my life, that I needed to really respect myself. People might not like me – that I didn't think I could control. What I did think was within my power to achieve was garnering respect, and a big part of that was being so very principled that I respected myself.

As luck would have it, my action did not negatively affect me at all. There was a management job opening in Las Vegas for which I was nominated. I was flown up to Chicago, where headquarters were located, for an interview. After I returned, corporate decided that they wanted me in Chicago instead – they wanted me to be their very first Pension Fund Manager. ERISA had recently been passed, over 75% of the pension fund was in company bonds and stock, and law now mandated diversification away from company-related financial instruments.

~

It was winter when I accepted the job in Chicago. The company flew me up for a weekend so I could find a place to live. I found a townhouse in Bensenville with the greatest little address: 10 Meigs Court. I made a reconnaissance survival drive around, locating a gas station, a hospital, a grocery store. So situated, I went back to Tallahassee and prepared my move. There were two men that were surprisingly affected by my announcement: Buck and my dear friend Ben. Ben was a quiet guy, married to a former Army nurse named Barbara. They had two children, a boy and a girl. Ben and I could talk about everything and anything, and we did. We would chat at lunch. We would chat a bit when he called in his completed orders. He had this cute lopsided grin and a great, quiet sense of humor. I gathered that his marriage wasn't the happiest, and we talked about that, too. He knew I was engaged ... he was a good listener. I guess I was, too. Anyway, those two took the news the hardest.

After months of very little communication, and no in-person conversations, Buck asked me out to dinner. I was quite surprised. He took me to a very nice restaurant, and he was all dressed up... he was wearing a three-piece suit - suit and tie. Not sure I had ever seen him in anything but casual wear. He actually looked amazing. He said he needed to explain himself before I left... that he still loved me, but that he loved someone else more, and that person's name was Tom. I was totally dumbstruck. I remember going through the motions of dinner and responding, but it was as if someone else was doing those things - I was in a total blank. Gay? Never in my wildest dreams would I ever have suspected that. I think it's fair to say that I had taken a monstrous body blow. Gay. My fiancé – my former fiancé – was gay. He said he didn't know that until he met Tom. Dinner obviously ended, and I imagine I wandered back to my apartment... I wonder how shocked I appeared.

I remember not being able to sleep. I remember sobbing hysterically, I remember calling a crisis hotline, only to be asked did I have a friend I could call? I guess that, to a crisis hotline person, my situation did not meet their definition of crisis. So I called Ben. At some God-awful hour, sobbing hysterically. I remember him telling me afterwards that his wife asked him if we were having an affair. Silly question, me being engaged and him being married... and me calling because my fiancé had just told me he had chosen a man over me. Lord, I could not WAIT to get out of Tallahassee. I left the last weekend in January, and I heard later that Ben, having missed me that morning, raced after me to try and catch up before I was gone forever.

~

My Mustang was packed with 33 tropical plants and my dog Shannon. I had planned on driving straight through, but as luck would have it I had to get off in Lebanon, Indiana. I had heard there was a blizzard, and I had heard the roads were closed, but that had never stopped me before. Not until the overpass at the Lebanon exit, which was top-to-bottom snow. I had to get off. Lebanon Indiana is a very small town, and the motels were full. The police station was full. The only place for me was at a small church. It was frigid cold, so I left my car running all night long and went in the church, where I ended up sleeping on an uncomfortable wooden pew. Shannon, who had never seen snow or such cold weather before, ended up going to the bathroom in the aisle. How very embarrassing. My tropical plants mostly all froze, even with the car running all night long. The next day the other folks that had been put up in the church left, one by one... going back home. I was awkwardly the only one left. The pastor, kindly but obviously wanting me to leave, too, asked me about going home. I told him I had no home to which I could return. His wife had me over to the parsonage for a spaghetti lunch, and then I said I was going to head out. I was going to travel west until I found an artery open to Chicago. East-west expressways were open – it was just the north-south roads that were blocked. Lebanon is off of I-65 – I headed west on I-74, listening for open roads into Chicago. I had passed I-57 and was heading further west when I heard that I-57 had opened, so I doubled back and headed north.

I got into the Chicago area Sunday at about two in the afternoon. Of course, my furniture was on a moving van, stuck somewhere – who knows where. I had an empty townhouse without even carpeting... my dear new neighbor Mariann came over to introduce herself, and hearing of my plight, lent me a sleeping bag, a towel, some soap, a coffee pot (with coffee) and an alarm clock. I slept on the floor that night. Good thing I had packed a suitcase, because I was due at work the next morning.

HELLO CHICAGO

I learned something very important about myself moving to the Chicago area... I had a miserable time adjusting to living somewhere with no one I knew. Not that I need a throng of friends, but I need someone. Just one. An anchor. I was renting a lovely three-bedroom townhouse, and I spent hours decorating it. I had absolutely nothing else to do. The phone never rang. I paneled one of the bedrooms, hung shelves on two of the walls and made it a library. I reupholstered a club chair in charcoal tweed with beige piping. I painted a large graphic on the living room wall, since I had no artwork to hang. I installed wood shutters in the master bedroom, painted everything taupe, and had a big, Oriental birdcage with finches. I made muslin drapes for the living room, complete with pinch pleats. I made a bedframe from 2" x 10" planks and plywood and upholstered the bed springs to it – a platform bed. It didn't take me very long – it didn't take me long enough. I had nothing else to do: I had never felt so isolated.

The people at work were fine: there was Stephanie, a rather hard-looking woman and single mother. There was Lynn, fresh from New Jersey, who actually believed before making it to Chicago that there were cowboys roaming the streets. The Treasurer, Ken, was a very kindly older gentleman who was rather crestfallen when his best efforts of investing the pension fund over 70% into Corporate bonds was ruled illegal. He really meant well. There was Sandy, a close friend of Stephanie but much younger. Those two had been around for a long time, from a time before the CFO was bringing in people with advanced degrees, like Lynn and like me (albeit not quite.) They were nice, but there were no after work events. Everyone had already established their lives, and I was totally out of my element. It had been very easy to make friends in Tallahassee, but here? At Corporate? It just wasn't happening, for whatever reason. I was engrossed at work, but the minute I left for the evening I was at quite a loss.

There was nothing left to do at my townhouse and I was at loose ends. Someone recommended that I join a singles group at a church downtown, which I did. I bought season tickets for a playhouse in Lake Forest. I started taking private voice lessons from a fabulous baritone, first chair with the Chicago Symphony Chorus. And I became a Big Sister to a cute little ten-year-old - Bekka. I was filling up my time.

My Little Sister Bekka was enrolled by her widowed mother Ceil because Ceil believed her son needed a father figure, and it wasn't fair that the boy got to go do cool things and Bekka didn't. Ceil was another remarkable woman. She was maybe mid-forties, with gorgeous prematurely white hair, worn cropped short like a pixie, and flawless skin. She always looked perfectly put together. She was originally from New York and was a dancer. She had tried out for the Rockettes, but she relayed that her legs weren't long enough. I was only a Big Sister for less than a year, though, because Ceil moved.

I only did a few events with that singles group – I remember going horseback riding. There's a lot of park space by the river, west of town, by the airport. The groom asked if anyone had ever ridden before – well, I had, as a child. Speaking up was quite an error in judgment. He gave me the most spirited horse. Things were going along splendidly, especially since we were riding in woods, so true speed was impossible. We were going up and down the steep banks of the river, and my stirrups were not set properly for me – I need the right stirrup to be long enough that I can lock the knee straight and put weight on that side. The stirrup was set normally, set for a bent knee. The longer we rode, the more the saddle slipped to the left because I would stand to post using only my left leg. Poor horse.

Anyway, there I was, rather lopsided, as we started up a rather steep hill. The horse in front of me stalled, not sure about getting up that steep hill. My horse was not ready for that, and when he saw a tail right in front of him he reared suddenly. Hi, ho, Silver, AWAY!!! I managed to stay on, leaning forward instinctively, and got him under control. I will never forget that. When we finished, the groom looked at that lopsided saddle with a bit of disgust. There wasn't anywhere I could get down and adjust anything on my own, and I wasn't totally sure I would be able to get back on easily. I absolutely know that I would need help getting my right foot back in the stirrup.

Seven years of living in Florida made my first Chicago winter miserable. I was cold – really, really cold. Insanely cold. And I had no winter clothes: no coats, boots, hats or gloves. I bought a coat right away – an opossum-lined, belted trench coat, which in 1977 was all the rage. That coat was so warm that by my second Chicago winter I could only bear to wear it when the temperature was twenty below. The winter wind was so strong that it would rattle the inside shutters in my bedroom. Chicago weather is significantly more extreme than Michigan's, since it doesn't have all the surrounding water to mitigate the heat and cold that blows in from across the Great Plains.

Sometime while I was going through all of this my father sold the semis and had moved back to Michigan. Not having a practice of his own anymore, he associated himself with an office in Pontiac and went back into dentistry and orthodontia. He was having a birthday party on Mother's Day weekend and flew me in for it. I had really lost track of how different his life had become. He had immersed himself with a group of 50-something, single, professional men who had such an active social life that they published a calendar. They decided to do Oktoberfest: they didn't go to Frankenmuth, a couple hours north of Detroit – they went to Munich. Germany. They decided to go skiing: they didn't go up to Boyne Mountain: they went to the Rockies. They did end up buying a house in Charlevoix, which my father put in my name. I didn't ask why. I loved that house. It was right in the city; a couple blocks off the lake. It was an impressive Victorian house, built around the turn of the last century. It had a large, wrap-around porch, complete with a swing. It had gingerbread trim. It had foot-tall, gum baseboards. It was awesome. I was disappointed when he told me that "we" had sold it. This group of high-living men had its cadre of groupie hangers-on, all much younger women whose eyes all glistened green. It was a bit comical actually, even though it was just so sad. These older men, getting their egos fanned by these obvious gold-diggers. Except the men just couldn't see it.

So on this Mother's Day weekend my dad picked me up at the airport and took me to his apartment – it was on Patrick Henry Street. It snowed so much that weekend that the cars were totally covered. I didn't yet have boots, and remember wearing grey suede platform shoes that had the sides cut out. One thing about platform shoes: the thick soles totally insulate the bottom of feet from the cold of the ground.

My dad had bought a cruiser, and it was docked at a marina in St. Clair Shores. We went to the boat on Sunday to open it up – it was a fixer-upper. That Mother's Day was quite cold. The boat in the slip directly to port was in much better shape, and the owner showed up – he was selling it, waiting for potential buyers. He even had flowers in a vase on the galley table. He also had a pot of coffee brewing, and he invited me aboard to warm up and share a cup. His name was Bill, and he took me to a sandwich shop for lunch. He wanted me to try a particular sandwich, which didn't appeal much – I ordered a slice of pizza, I think. He was not happy about my choice, which I thought a bit quirky of him. He asked for my number, I gave it to him, and I left a bit later for the airport. It was eighteen months before I heard from him again.

~

I decided that I would invite my brother, mother and sister for my first Chicago Christmas. It was to be a surprise for my mother, and my brother, sister and I conspired. There was a letter that showed up years later, from me to my brother, filled with excitement and happiness at the prospect. My mother continued to have a horrible time adjusting to the divorce. She actually never did accept it. She had been so miserable that she called the police to arrest my brother when he went to gather some of my father's things. She took my father's tax documentation and burned it. He was getting audited two out of every three years, so he had a devil of a time getting the IRS to believe what happened. The IRS slapped a lien on everything, but after it was convinced that the records had indeed been destroyed, it agreed to take prior and following years and guess at what happened in between. My mother was the epitome of the scorned woman, and she was not elegant or refined or gracious about it at all. That being said, I understand that she was actually completely lost, and was lashing out in fear and hurt. She couldn't decide where to live, so she packed up her worldly belongings and moved them back and forth between Michigan and California – moved them back and forth five times. Her older brother Ted finally told her if she did that once more, he was going to have her committed. She decided California, and that's where she finally landed, some years later.

Anyway, my mother, brother and sister showed up in Chicago for Christmas, but it did not go well. It did not go well at all. Everyone was nervous, I guess, and the three of them smoked. Smoked a considerable amount. There was a visible haze up near the ceiling. I cannot tolerate cigarette smoke, at least not that much of it. They were all terribly affronted when I asked them to dial it down. They took to smoking in the basement, but it merely came right back upstairs. Then they went out back, in the cold. I was the persona non-grata, even though I was hosting the event and doing all of the cooking and clean-up. I got a whole lot of, "How dare you". We all had really grown in different directions: I was a successful business woman with (almost) an advanced degree: my brother was a college drop-out who until the day he died lived off the grid, never holding a tax-paying job and bartering for his meager lifestyle; my sister was a twice-divorced high school drop-out with not even a GED at the time. I am not sure why I turned out so differently.

I did quite well at Central Telephone corporate office. I was running $63 million dollars as Pension Fund Manager. To assist with the asset diversification, the company had hired four investment houses. My job was to oversee them. My immediate supervisor was a great guy named Earl Duke. Earl was from Nebraska or Iowa or somewhere definitely Midwestern. He was a tall, lanky redhead, married with a young family. He was known as the Duke of Earl. He had a very likeable sense of humor – he was just likeable, period. While I was wrapping my arms around the job I prepared an asset value forecast – one year later, when I went in with some results, Earl threw up his arms, started waving them wildly in the air, and reached into his drawer to pull out that forecast I had earlier prepared. "Wait! Wait!" he was saying, as he dramatically shook out that piece of paper. Thankfully I was spot-on. Nobody had thought ahead, and I guess they never did a longer-range forecast. When I first prepared it, I think I took everybody by surprise with the growth curve.

I was making quite a name for myself: one of the very few – maybe the only – women in pension fund management. We were a rare breed: out of a graduating class of several hundred there were only two women that graduated from the University of Miami with degrees in finance, and I was one of them. I published an article in the Pension and Investments periodical and was subsequently interviewed by Institutional Investor magazine. All fancy-like: the interviewer showed up with a professional photographer in tow. I still have a copy of that issue. I was placed in Who's Who in the Midwest. My forecasting was so spot-on that a guy at Harris Trust placed an office bet on my published market predictions and won – I was 5/8 of a point off.

I was tapped to do other things. I wrote testimony for the CFO in a rate case utility hearing and discovered that the opposing counsel's "expert" professor had made a math error in his testimony. That got the CFO's attention, and he became my mentor. He wanted me to finish my graduate degree. I could have chosen Northwestern or University of Chicago: I applied to the University of Chicago and, with the assistance of either a well-placed call or a well-placed letter from the CFO, was accepted. They would not accept any of my existing credits (even though I carried a 3.96 GPA), so I enrolled as a student at large and got Florida State to accept the University of Chicago courses so I could complete my degree. It certainly wasn't a difficult thing to do: the University of Chicago Graduate School of Business vied with Harvard as either #1 or #2 rated in the nation. Harvard was known for its strategy and business cases: University of Chicago was the quintessential quantitative school, home to the likes of legendary Roger Ibbotson.

So I was back to school at night. I only needed six more months of course work. I was in the 190 Program, so named because it was held just north of the Magnificent Mile in a building sporting "190" as part of its address, and not on the main campus. Parking was a nightmare, but I found a couple of young Persian men running a garage (they insisted they Persian, not Iranian) a couple of blocks away. They let me park in the garage, even though they were not supposed to allow non-tenant parking.

There are only a few of things I remember about those classes: I had to read an enormous amount; the only class that was memorable enough that I can remember the work I did was the case study class, taught by Mr. James (everybody there was so snooty that no one called anyone Dr. – they were all "Mr."); and that I got straight A's. I had to read so much that driving home I couldn't stop from seeing double: road signs on top of one another. I simply could not get my eyes to work together. I went to an ophthalmologist and was told that I had eye strain: green eyes are the most light-sensitive, and because I was so sitting-down short the fluorescent light mounted below my cabinet at my desk at work bounced right off the paper into my eyes. I was told to get a little Tensor light and have it shine on my work from left to right and turn off the fluorescent. I did as he suggested, and although I still had eye problems, they were not as severe.

In the midst of all of this my sister called. She wanted to move from Fort Lauderdale to Cincinnati, and could she ship her dog to me while she moved? I said yes, and went to the airport to pick up the poor puppy. That puppy ended up staying with me for four months. No idea why my sister needed that much time.

Also, in the midst of all of this, the summer before I graduated, I got a call. I got a call from Bill of St. Clair Shores marina cup of coffee fame. He was going to be in town for two weeks for a training class, and would I like to go out to dinner? He called me at work, and I remember him prefacing the call with, "You probably don't remember me" – after all, it had been eighteen months. But I did remember him, and we did go out to dinner. And then we went to dinner again. And again. I patched him up after a pick-up game of football. I remember asking him why getting so beat up was fun? We spent quite a bit of time together during those two weeks, and then he went back home to Michigan. Party over.

~

At most B-schools, students are required to take a case study class during their last semester. That was the class that Mr. James taught. We were divided up into teams, and our team was assigned the Vlasic pickle case. I remember coming up with our solution, which entailed the owner transferring equipment ownership which was owned by the family to the company so that the company could use it as collateral to raise money for the expansion it needed. At the end of the class, Mr. James called me aside and stated, "That was your solution, wasn't it?" Well, it was, but I am not sure why he knew it was mine. He continued, saying that in all of the years he had taught the class, he had never seen that solution, and that it would have worked. I was pleased with that. And the very next thing I knew, I was called down to the Administration Building by the Dean. I was offered a four-year fellowship to work on a Ph.D., and since the school knew I was interested in the intersection of psychology and numbers, they suggested I pursue a degree in Behavioral Accounting – it was all the rage at the time; a brand-new field ripe for landmark study. I am positive it was at the recommendation of Mr. James. Well now! I was quite intrigued. What would it entail? Would it take all four years? How much classwork would I need, since I had two Business degrees already? Sniff – "Nobody gets a Ph.D. from the University of Chicago in under five years, unless you happen to be Roger Ibbotson. Nobody."

"So what classes would I need to take?" Sniff sniff… "How much money have you given the University?" I couldn't believe my ears.

"Well, okay. So plan on five years... you are offering me a four-year fellowship. That's fine... I'll just work that last year." Sniff sniff...

"Oh, we don't allow our fellows to have a job." So how in the world was I supposed to live that last year? This was feeling wrong on so many levels... I politely declined right then and there. In retrospect, I am not so sure I was exactly "polite," but I certainly was clear that I didn't think that was for me.

I finished my last exam on December 7th, again – same as undergrad. I remember thinking I should have hired a limousine to pick me up and take me home, but I didn't. I drove myself home and went back to work the following Monday. Graduation would have been back down in Tallahassee, in May, and as usual, I did not attend. I received my Master's Degree in the mail.

Tom Owens, the CFO, had immediate plans to further my career. The problem was, I really liked what I was doing. I wanted to do it longer, but Mr. Owens told me that from a career perspective that was a poor idea. He insisted I become the Chief Economist for the Board of Directors. I took it, under protest, and I hated it. The politics were killing me. I had a cadre of analysts in every area we serviced, and they gathered all sorts of actual data: new housing permits, job growth forecasts – anything that would give us insight into future demand. I took all of that data and, with the help of some staff, rolled it all up into an overall economic forecast for our particular industry in our particular areas of the country. And then the calls would start coming in, from the Vice Presidents of the areas with the lower growth curves. They insisted I revise the numbers to suit their agendas. That's what I hated. I remember thinking that if you already know what you want, why not just fire all of those analysts that were spending untold hours collected real data? The reasons for all of the change requests were never based on different but verifiable data. They were always requested for personal agenda reasons, like, "I need a higher growth forecast." I went from really loving my job to despising it, overnight.

Right about the time I finished my graduate degree I got another call from Bill – would I consider spending Christmas in Florida with his parents? Bowled me over. I never considered that he would be shocked if I said yes, but after the previous Christmas I figured why not? I said I would go… and he was caught totally off guard.

I knew he was divorced, but what I didn't know was that he was living with a woman named Patty. He said he would have to move before he took me down to meet his parents, since I guess they were expecting her instead of someone new. To Bill's credit, he did move – into a house owned by a buddy, Dave. Dave was a Marine, significantly wounded in Vietnam. He had scars all over the place, but he seemed to be a stand-up guy… tough as you expect a Marine to be. Bill prepared his parents for my visit, and he met me at the Palm Beach airport. We were staying at his parent's house.

I was a nervous wreck. When I get really nervous I get a very itchy rash on the palms of my hands – they get very red and then my skin peels off. Odd. Anyway, the palms of my hands were an itchy mess. Bill picked me up in his parents' white Cadillac with a powder blue landau roof, and we headed to Palm Bay, just outside of Melbourne. That's when I met Hutch and Kay.

The dynamics between Hutch and Kay did nothing to calm my itchy palms. The two of them spent their entire lives going at one another. Hutch was a career Army Staff Sergeant who, after retirement, went to work at Harris Corporation. He knew radios inside and out. Hutch was very rough around the edges. He was certified 100% disabled due to severe back issues that made it very difficult for him to walk or stand – and that made him angry and short. Kay was an anorexic, six-foot tall woman taken to wearing blond bouffant wigs. The actress Joan Allen looks very much like her, except that Kay, at six feet tall, weighed only 110 pounds. She was exceptionally sensitive to appearances and her precious possessions... that Cadillac was her prized possession, and it spent most of its life shrouded in a protective cover. Kay had decorated their modest stucco home with more frou-frou than I have ever seen... little china figurines, lace-tiered bedspreads with lace-dressed dolls perched atop, crystal tear-drop lights. The living room was never – NEVER used. It was a veritable museum of frou-frou. The kitchen was wood-paneled and looked out over the enclosed pool. Hutch had converted the carport to a family room of sorts, which is where people congregated. There, or around the kitchen table, or out in the lanai, by the pool. Hutch had a shed out back jammed with all of his amateur radio gear, which is where he spent untold hours. There was precious little grass in the backyard – just a narrow strip that wrapped the pool area – just a couple of feet around the perimeter. The house sat on a corner lot, and the back yard was totally enclosed by a chain link fence.

It became quite clear that Kay wanted Hutch to act in a manner she would consider rich and elegant, and it was equally clear that Hutch took great joy in embarrassing Kay at every turn. Out to dinner at a buffet restaurant? He would refuse to dress up, he would speak too loudly, complain way too much, swear a lot... and Kay would be mortified. They were at each other constantly, picking away. I remember being so shaken by the environment that I went outside and leaned up against the car just to get away from the constant bickering. Bill came out and said that his parents really knew how to mix it up. There was Kay, never without her wig, or her makeup, or her jewelry… and there was Hutch, in an undershirt.

On Christmas day, when we were opening presents, I mistakenly called Bill "Buck" twice. I am not sure anyone noticed, because it was noisy and there was a lot of laughter, but it was as if I could not help myself. I was rather horrified. The reality of this mating dance was sinking in.

I did survive the week, I was glad I met Bill's parents – was more impressed that he actually wanted me to. I liked his young sister Kathy. She was sixteen, still in high school, and a lovely, sunny girl. Not quite as tall as her mother, but possessed of those long, thin and lovely bones commonly seen on models. She was dating a serious young man named John, and they spent their dates competitively dancing. Kay simply adored her daughter – perhaps obsessed would be a better word. There hung a huge, framed picture of her in the living room - it was at least three feet tall. It was the Shrine of the Little Kathy. Bill was sixteen when Kathy was born, and Bill's older brother John was eighteen and heading off to the military. This late-in-life daughter was Kay's wish come true – Hutch was well into his fifties when she was born. Kathy was totally, perfectly, absolutely spoiled. Spoiled, but very sunny. Life had always gone her way.

I went back to Chicago and Bill went back to Detroit. One day, not too long after we parted, he called me with an announcement: "I sent your resume into General Motors." I was a little amused, a little intrigued. A bit later, when I was telling my father about it, he laughed and said, "If you want to get into General Motors, call Pete Elges." Pete Elges, or Mr. Elges to me, was a man that lived down the waterfront from my grandparents. He had built a weed cutter: a square, galvanized metal affair powered by a bicycle that was mounted in the center of the platform. It both moved the craft forward and turned blades that cut the weeds. I remember him puttering over and cutting the weeds between my grandparents' house and Dori's, next door. I had no idea where he worked: I had no idea he was a 14th floor General Motors executive.

It sounded like a good idea, so I called and left a message with his administrative assistant. I didn't realize at the time that the administrative assistants were fierce gatekeepers. After a while, not receiving a call back, I called again. Once again stonewalled. The third time I called I told that woman, "Just tell Mr. Elges this is Capt. Bob's grand-daughter." Mr. Elges was on the phone in no time at all. We chatted a bit, and I told him the purpose of my call. He told me to send him my resume. I thanked him for his time, hung up the phone, and took my resume to the post office the next day.

Not long after I received a call from some man at Fisher Body wanting me to fly in for an interview. I cannot recall his name, but he met me at the airport – a round, roly-poly kind of guy, maybe in his fifties, with a perpetual smile on his face. I interviewed with several people – it was a bit of a whirlwind – and went back to Chicago. A few days later Mr. Roly-Poly called me with a job offer: Auditor with Fisher Body. He mentioned that getting a resume covered by a personal note from Mr. Elges had gotten everybody's attention. Being I was miserable with my impressive-sounding but fairly substance-free position as Chief Economist, I accepted the offer. General Motors arranged to send over a moving company, and I was in Detroit looking for places to live. I stayed with Dave and Bill – Bill wanted me to consider living on the east side.

Bill and Dave came to visit me in January of that year. They picked a horrible weekend: they were caught in a blizzard. The two winters I lived in Chicago were very snowy: 99" the first year and 105" the second. O'Hare borrowed snow moving equipment from Buffalo, New York, and loaded up the snow into trucks, dumping it into Lake Michigan. My townhouse complex brought in a bucket loader, and by the time the season had ended, the parking lot was surrounded by snow piles that reached the second story eaves. It was a snow-bowl. In was in the middle of one of those 24"+ storms that Bill and Dave came. Dave had only brought really nice leather dress shoes, but being the Marine he was, insisted on shoveling the sidewalk. In his beautiful shoes, swearing a blue streak. We seemed to have a major blizzard every other week that started on Friday, continued all through Saturday, and stopped in time for Sunday, whereupon the temperature dropped to minus 20°, with howling winds. Lovely.

My father had, in the meantime, picked up a real estate license. When I flew in to house-hunt he drove me around for an entire day. I remember we were on a narrow road in St. Clair Shores to see a house for sale – didn't like it from the outside, so we didn't even get out. The road was all ice, and my dad put that full-size Lincoln Continental into a perfectly controlled 180° turn, right in the middle of the street. I had never seen anything like that before.

I did find a house: a cute little Cape Cod built in the 1920's, about 800 square feet total, with a small screened porch on the left and a one-car garage with wood carriage doors on the right. It was on a double lot, three or four houses off of Jefferson, very close to all of the marinas. On Downing Street. It was white, with a light blue roof and shutters. The woman who owned it had lived there her entire adult life. She had never married, and now that she was in her 70's she was going to go live with her sister. That house had the original paint, except that it was caked in 50 years or so of heavy cigarette smoke. The fireplace was stuffed with newspapers, then covered with plywood, then hidden behind curtains. It had never been used. The doors all used skeleton key locks. The double sash windows had counter-weights, like my grandmother's house had. My grandmother showed them to me once: she used to hide emergency money on the wire that ran from the window to the weight. The house had original wood floors and the original kitchen. The countertop was made from some linoleum-type material, bright, solid red, that was so degraded that it bloodied anything that touched it.

The first floor had a living room, dining room and kitchen. Upstairs were two bedrooms and a small bath. It had potential… with a $1,500 down payment loan from my mother I bought it, and with my new position I paid my mother back within the year. I moved at the end of February and started with General Motors March 1, 1979.

MY RETURN TO DETROIT

March 1, 1979, fell on a Thursday. I reported to work at the Tech Center in Warren and got processed for employment. I met the people that were in the audit department – at least those that were in the office on Thursday. I was given a key to an office, was informed my formal title was Traveling Auditor, and was told I had a ticket to Rochester, New York, on Monday morning. I did not see the inside of my office for the next fourteen months.

That was never the plan, at least as far as I knew. I had not been made aware I was supposed to travel that much. I had a rather lengthy conversation with my boss, and we came to an agreement of 50% travel. What I did not know at the time was that he meant 50% of the time they would have me in Michigan, some of the time drivable on a daily basis, most of it not. I was in a bit of a panic about Shannon, but Bill agreed he would take care of her. I hadn't taken any time off in between jobs, thinking I could unpack after work. That became unpacking on the weekends. And decorating my cozy little home: under all that grime was a house with much of the original woodwork intact. When we painted the living room ceiling white and painted the walls a cream color, the beautiful wood bannister really stood out. We exposed the pristine fireplace, polished the wood floors and ripped out the old kitchen. We installed Home Depot DIY cherry cabinets and a Formica counter, redesigning the space so we had many more cabinets. I found a really appropriate wallpaper at Sears, and voila, we had a new kitchen!

I say "we," because after a week or two of Bill driving over to tend to the dog, he asked if he could stay there during the week. I was thankful I had someone to look after the place, so I easily agreed. In return, he helped me redo the kitchen. Only on the weekends, though: after six weeks in Rochester, it was six weeks in Pittsburgh, then Marion, Ohio, Lorraine, Ohio... I was gone every week, all week. I came home Friday nights and left again Monday morning. It got to be so constant that a steward on the Pittsburgh flight recognized me.

I was the first and only woman on the traveling audit team. I learned later that management felt the need to get the approval of the male auditors' wives before opening up the role to someone besides a white male. The guys were very, very apprehensive: I think they must have thought I would have loads and loads of luggage, hate trudging around a manufacturing plant... I don't know exactly what they thought, but the trepidation was palpable. I was none of those things they imagined, but even Ms. Socially Inept here realized I needed to take steps to make them feel at ease. That came in the guise of eating three meals a day with them. I am not a three-meal-a-day eater, especially eating out every day, but I was doing what I felt I needed to do. During that first four months I gained 17 pounds – until I felt the guys were comfortable, and I could say enough: breakfast and lunch, but no dinner for me. I spent my evenings in my hotel room, talking to Bill on the phone and knitting. I can't even remember what it was I was making, but I was terribly uncomfortable venturing out on my own – and the venues were not exactly vacation hot spots.

My associates were all men in their 50's: Bill Baker, Mitch Crowl, Jack Patton... nice guys. We ended getting along swimmingly, actually. Jack was the one that took me under his wing the most. He was hysterically funny – a very quick wit. Every morning at breakfast he would start with his jabs, and I finally asked him why. He told me that he figured out that after 9:30 or so he didn't stand a chance, but until then I was fair game. His wife's name was Loretta, and he made great jokes at her expense, calling her "Sir." He told tales of pranks he used to pull: he and a buddy used to pull pranks on each other all the time. At one time they worked in a bullpen, and breaks were very regimented. Jack had come back a bit early from break and noticed a man had crawled under his desk. The man was wearing khakis, and Jack remembered his buddy had khakis on that day. So Jack ran over, jumped on the man's back, and started slapping his butt, rising up and down and yelling, "Hee Haw!!!" – riding a horse. Except that it was the telephone repairman, not Jack's buddy. Not sure Jack ever lived that down.

I dutifully made the rounds: stamping plant, assembly plant, trim plant, forge… loud and huge and gritty. Watching the men take their Friday paychecks, many of whom went right to the bar across the street to spend a goodly portion before they ever got home. Discovering places in plants in obscure corners where the men would fashion places to go sleep, or drink, or both. Empty whiskey bottles tucked into corners. The smell of turkey during the holidays, when some enterprising guys would wrap a turkey in lots of foil and place it on the huge pipes that channeled heat. Once found a little cabin out in the scrap yard, complete with a TV and hot plate. We were always eyed very warily when we walked the plant.

Walking the plant was part of the audit – we also had to walk the perimeter to make sure the property was secure. Plants are massive places, and the property on which they sat was larger still by a large margin. Old machinery was normally just piled up outside somewhere to rust away. They weren't supposed to do that, but getting parts out the door was significantly more important. I remember auditing inventory, and the supervisor in charge was very proud that he could always produce what was needed, right away. Problem was that inventory was bloated because of it. They had things like many large and expensive industrial diamonds that they had been carrying for years and years. I simply could not get him to understand the concept of optimal inventory: how many widgets were needed at any point in time plus lead order time = what you need on hand. Period. Probably only needed one diamond in inventory. Poor guy: he got written up only because his prime directive was to be able to produce whatever immediately.

We were the "bad guys" – everybody loves to hate dentists and auditors. I learned a lot, and in a year, I was promoted to Auditor in Charge.

Back on the home front, Bill proposed. I said yes: I had learned a lot about him, weekends only. That during his divorce his wife got the house, the better car and child support. He had been left with his pension, his boat (which he could not afford) and the Pinto. His wife did not like supporting herself; she stayed at home and lived off AFDC (Aid to Families with Dependent Children) and child support. Bill did not see his children all that often, and he never had them overnight because he had no suitable sleeping quarters for them. He felt the world had really dumped on him. Because money was so tight for him, I gave him the diamonds from my grandmother's engagement ring #2 and he had them reset.

My grandmother had two engagement rings: the first was the "real" one; a very, very modest garnet ring from the Old Country with initials and wedding date engraved in the tiniest font ever on the very narrow band. When my grandfather made it big here in the States he bought her a second wedding set; platinum, with a one carat deep cut center diamond surrounded by several small ones. I kept the "real" engagement ring – Bill used the domestic version.

So I announced my engagement to my parents. We were going to get married in the fall, and we were working on details. Bill's mother was stereotypical Irish Catholic, and because of the divorce he couldn't remarry in the Catholic church without an annulment. It meant a lot to him, so we started proceedings to get his marriage annulled. That was going to take some time, so we were looking at civil alternatives. Marriage in a different faith was entirely out of the question: I think Bill really believed that a lightning bolt would come out of the sky and strike him down if he ever set foot in some other denomination's facility. Anyway, a couple of weeks after my happy announcement I got a call from my father, who flatly stated that if my mother was going to be there, count him out. A couple days later I got the same call from my mother. Bill's parents were in Florida and were not planning on attending, so once again, why bother? The Queen of No Ceremony suggested that the two of us simply elope and escape all of the drama. My godmother Marnie, aghast at my parents' behavior, offered to throw us a reception when we got back. That was the plan, and that's what happened. The very pleasant part was that all of my cousins and aunts and uncles and grandparents came, and Bill's mother came, which forced my parents' hands. They came, and they behaved themselves.

The two of them behaving themselves was exactly the problem. They had gotten into too many ugly, loud fights at parties to which they both had been invited, the worst apparently at my uncle's house. My father could let go, but my mother simply couldn't. She never, never got over it. Not even over thirty years later. My father died in December 2007. They divorced in 1974 or 1975 – I don't know when it was final. I do know he walked out in December 1973. Thirty-four years after he left, weeks after he passed, we were at my uncle's house for Christmas. One of my uncle's neighbors was in attendance – someone we had not previously met. And there was my mother, plying him with sad tales of how her husband had just passed away – the grieving widow. He was appropriately sympathetic until I butted in and told her to stop – that they had divorced more than thirty years prior. He was totally shocked. She looked at me and plaintively cried, "But I loved him!"

That's one of the things that really got my father's goat: my mother kept on calling him her husband, even decades after the divorce. There he would be, at a party, and someone would walk up and start chatting... and would manage to say, "I was talking to your wife just a little while ago..." and then it would start.

We married on a salmon fishing trip to Manistee. On a cliff overlooking Lake Michigan. A storm was rolling in – we could see lightning in the distance. Paul and Mary Parisi, one of Bill's fishing buddies and his wife, were the only people in attendance. I think the storm made Bill more nervous than he would have been – he flubbed the oath. Instead of, "I promise to love and obey", he said, "You promise to love and obey." I giggled, he turned red, backed it up and got it right the second time. And that was it – we went back to the tent. It was late anyway – the sun had been setting, and we were supposed to be on the lake by six the next morning. At one in the morning another fishing buddy, Roy, woke us up by throwing apples at the tent.

I had never been salmon fishing before. Salmon fishing involves downriggers. I was supposed to tell Bill if one sprang. It was really cold and damp that morning, with dense, bone chilling fog. There were fishing boats everywhere, and we were surrounded by foghorns in a choir of different tones, frequencies and timings. I was miserable. Then it looked like we had snagged something on the bottom – the downrigger didn't spring; it was being pulled down. I couldn't even get the words out – I just started saying, "Oh! Oh!" Bill turned around, said we had one, and took the rod and gave it to me. I was sitting in the starboard seat with this big pole in my hands. The salmon decided to get away from us on a 90° angle – and that fish pulled me right across the boat. I ended up in the port seat before I knew it. Didn't even fall into the walking space between the seats. We landed that fish – I think it weighed 23 pounds. That was the only fish I caught.

I do not recommend spending a honeymoon in a tent in the north of Michigan in the fall. Everything gets damp, everything is cold, water must be fetched in a bucket and boiled to do dishes, sand needs to be swept out of the tent, and people have to trudge down to the showers and bathrooms. Coleman stoves just don't do it for me. But Bill's fall fishing trip was sacrosanct to him, so we went fishing. We spent a week camping and then came back – I had only one week of vacation earned and needed to get back to work.

The party Ed and Marnie had for us was beautiful. It was in their spacious home, and everything was so lovely. A lovely cake, a beautiful table with white doves and ribbons... just beautiful. One of the best memories ever.

I was back on a plane the Monday after we returned, just like always. I thought things might settle down, but that wasn't to be. Bill's ex started giving me problems. She would call me at work and threaten to get me fired. She would threaten to throw stones through my windows. She kept on riding past my house. She told me she was going to go after my income for support. What did she even know of my income? How did she know where I worked? I got a restraining order against her and that did seem to stem the tide, but that certainly is not the way to start what should have been a civil, if not friendly, relationship.

I suggested to Bill that he should start seeing his children more regularly. I don't think he ever felt really secure with being a solo parent – he needed to have a partner, I think. I remember first meeting Todd and Amy. Todd was ten, Amy was seven. Amy was thrilled that her daddy had gotten married – she threw her arms around me and asked me if she could call me Mommy. Not a very good idea... not given her mother's behavior. Anyway, visitations became more regular and we started alternating holidays. I was appalled at those little hellions' behavior during our first Christmas together: within seconds every present had been ripped into. I was used to one present at a time, everybody watching and properly appreciating the gift before someone else opened theirs. I learned my lesson, though: Christmas #2 had no labels indicating to whom presents were intended. I had concocted a mental map, certain box sizes in certain paper were for Todd, or Bill, or Amy... only I knew. So whoever picked up a present had to ask me who was to get it. Chaos solved!

Things were progressing fairly well... except that Bill never stepped up and offered to split expenses. I had been footing the entire cost of everything before marrying, which made perfect sense. That just seemed to carry on after he officially moved in. I was aware of it, but I thought that he needed some time to get his feet back on the ground after his divorce. He did ask if I would add him to the house deed, but I saw no reason to do that, since he was living housing-cost free. He came home one night and excitedly told me about a beautiful piece of art he wanted: it was a ship etched in metal within a lovely frame. Sure, I said – we can hang it right here (pointing to a place in the dining room). He asked for half of the cost, which I did not understand – he wanted a picture, fine! Buy it, and we will find it a place of honor. He became quite angry. Should have listened to my gut more closely.

I thought we might avert money issues by having three accounts: a joint account, which would cover household expenses, then his and hers. After funding the joint account each of us could do with our funds what we pleased. Fine, but he was always weird about the shared expenses. It took four years before I could convince him to contribute to the mortgage. Should have listened to my gut more closely....

He was tall and athletic and good-looking. He had very good people skills in social settings. He also knew how to play... and I was very aware that I was deficient in that area. I thought he would be good for me. We had come from very different backgrounds: his populated with salt-of-the-earth types: career military, post office, railroad... no one in his family on either side had attended college. I came from a highly educated background: my grandfather, two uncles and father all had advanced degrees, and my mother had a bachelor's. I didn't want that to be an issue, and it didn't seem like it would be. Except that within six months of getting married we went from having nearly identical salaries, his a little higher, to me getting promotion after promotion and quickly outpacing him. For most of our marriage I ended up bringing home 150% of what he did, and I don't think that sat well at all.

Seven months into the marriage I was offered a position at the Grand Blanc plant as Plant Auditor. We were living in St. Clair Shores; he was working at the Tech Center... and I would have been so far from work. General Motors offered to relocate us, so the house went up for sale and we started looking. Argonaut Realty was a division of GM, buying houses from relocating employees if need be and reselling them. Argonaut owned a small raised ranch on Indian Lake, in Oakland Township, and that's where we settled. It had three bedrooms, so both Todd and Amy had their own rooms when they came to visit. It was tiny, but that didn't bother me. So I would get up very early and head the 38 miles north to be in Grand Blanc in time for the 6AM daily Plant Manager's meeting, and Bill would leave later, heading south to the Tech Center. Our places of employment were over 55 miles apart, and we picked a place as nearly between the two as we could find.

We lived there a couple of years as-is while we were thinking of what we would do. And we decided we were going to breed Shannon. She had a litter of eight adorable puppies. We kept them in the shower off the laundry room – easy to clean up, easy access to outside.

Shannon was a wonderful mother – she was so calm. Todd and Amy were over when the puppies were born, so we had a little ad-hoc biology lesson. Shannon was such a great dog with kids: she didn't even growl when little Amy grabbed her tail and tried to pull her away from her dinner. We sold seven pups and kept a girl – we named her Katy. We now had a pair of setters. Bird dogs. One day we came home to find both of them at the top of the stairs, pointing at the Dutch door that led to the kitchen. While we were at work a pheasant had crashed through the small kitchen window, breaking its neck as it hit the wall across from the window. And there were our bird dogs, bird dogging with all of their might. I decided I would never breed again, though, after I heard through the grapevine that some buyers had given away their pups. That broke my heart.

We had to drive through two miles of state recreation area to get to our house – it was on a little spit of a dirt road totally surrounded by public space. It was very quiet and beautiful back there, high on the ridge overlooking the lake. There was a three-tier set of stairs that led down to the water. We had a little dock and a canoe... no powerboats on the lake. Very serene. The house did have a breathing problem: the builder had made it so airtight that moisture couldn't escape. It had aluminum windows, a moisture barrier all around, and aluminum siding. Floor pillows I had in the back rooms would actually get soggy from the accumulated moisture. We decided if we were going to have to make changes we might as well build our dream home. My dad relished the thought of the project, and he came up with the plans and the engineering. We took away the hill that had made it a raised ranch, so that what was the former basement wall lakeside ended up on grade, and built an addition off the back. It included a living room and master bedroom and bath. In the center of the house, which was a two-story open area, we had a magnificent two-story California drift stone fireplace, a good twelve feet wide, with a walnut travertine hearth on the lower living room fireplace and a smaller fireplace upstairs facing the dining room. We had a slider and transom windows facing the lake and put in a deck that went to the edge of the ravine. The master bedroom and bath were off the living room. The bedroom also had a high, sloped ceiling that matched the living room, but the bath had a regular eight-foot ceiling with a tall sky light. It had a Jacuzzi tub with stairs that fanned out and a separate shower. I tiled the entire bathroom myself, and I was quite pleased the way it turned out. Above it was a storeroom that was secret: accessed via a bookcase in one of the guest bedrooms that opened if you knew how to open it. The carpenters who built it for us joked that they didn't want us to have to kill them. The former basement was transformed into a laundry/tool room and an office. It was logistically perfect: drive in the garage and enter the laundry/tool room, which had a small bath off of it. The next room you hit was the office, where you could put down car keys and the mail and hang up your coat. Everything ended up exactly where it needed to be first time around: no mail dropped on a kitchen counter, no car keys left hither and yon... simply, perfectly designed. I loved it.

We moved the kitchen and made the old area part of a gorgeous dining room off of a large entrance. Since we had a new bedroom, we turned the smallest bedroom upstairs into a den. Those were the plans.

My dad brought a team out and they raised the exterior walls, installed the windows and put on a roof. We were sealed to the weather. And that is how we sat for the next two years.

A couple of things happened: first, interest rates went through the roof. Mortgage rates were over 18%, and other debt was sky-high in tandem. The Federal Reserve was attacking inflation. We had to wait and piecemeal our projects. We did get some phenomenal deals, because home builders and material suppliers were dying on the vine. We bought some gorgeous marble flooring for the dining room and entrance, cash, for some ridiculously low price. It sat in boxes for years.

Our builder was a big, strapping fellow named John VanSteenis. He was the epitome of Mr. Outdoors: spent his summers hunting in Alaska, trophies hung all over his house. He was noticeably taller than Bill, who was a good 6'2" himself. A big, blond, strong, Paul Bunyan-kind-of guy. He was quite a lumberjack: he came over to take out a young tree out back, and as we watched he pointed to exactly where the tree would fall... and there it went. A few weeks after, Bill went out with his chain saw, picked a sapling and pointed to where it would land. He started cutting, and the tree started leaning, and... it did a 180° turn and wiped out the entire middle landing of our three-tier stairs to the lake. So humbled, he requested some assistance with a huge oak tree that needed to come down in front. He decided that he would rope it off to his Buick. He told me to get in the car, with instructions that I was to drive ahead on his say-so. He started cutting, and when he yelled, I drove. To this day I can't decide whether he was trying to kill me or not. That was a massive tree. We had a mill come and take it, getting big, true 2" x 14" boards with enough trim for a new staircase and railing. There was so much wood there that the mill took the tree, milled our wood and returned it, in return for being able to keep the rest.

The wood cured by the side of the house, tarped, for a good two years. Our existing house was opened up to the new addition, but the addition had no heat or insulation. It couldn't get warmer than about 55° in the winter. We would sit huddled under blankets trying to stay warm.

I could understand we had to wait while interest rates were so high. However, in year two the rates came down, and banks started courting loan customers again. It was still impossible to remortgage and get a rate anywhere close to our existing, but we could get unsecured loans. Comerica Bank sent a mass mailing of flyers offering something like 10% or 11%. All the guys at work had gotten them – we talked about it. Pretty much everyone was applying. Well, Bill got a flyer and I got a flyer. I still had bank accounts in my name. Ah, my name…

William Edward Thomas. Wendy Sura Thomson. Our surnames were so, so similar. Our joint account was in the name of William Edward Thomas and Wendy Sura Thomas. However, my personal account was still Wendy Sura Thomson. Back then most official transactions had to be completed in person unless you were comfortable sending original documentation sequentially all over the place, hoping and waiting for it to be returned for its next journey. It was such a hassle being gone Monday through Friday for all of those months that I simply never got around to it.

And then it didn't seem to be very important... I could start signing my last name "Thom" then draw a line and it would suffice for either name. Problem solved.

So back to the bank: I filled out an application for Bill and then I filled one out for me. We both got approved, however he got approved for more than I did. So did the guys at work. Interesting, but I made more than Bill did, so I could not understand the discrepancy. I called the bank and asked why. The very unpleasant man on the other end first said it was because he included my income on Bill's application – not true, I said: I filled them both out. Then he said Bill made more than I did – again, not true: I made 50% more. The guys at work all got the offer Bill did. The guys. I knew the man was lying through his teeth, so I asked him to put the reasons in writing. He flatly refused. So after calming down just enough not to sputter, I filed a discrimination claim with the EEOC. Funny, but not very long after I received a call from a VP at Comerica, explaining that gee, they were going to go the extra mile, do me a favor and give me the same deal they gave the men to whom I had spoken. Do tell. And would I please drop the complaint?

So now we had the money to complete the house. Only Bill had absolutely no motivation to do that. I couldn't get him to budge, so I finally blew and said I was going to get it done. Hire it out. We had quite an argument, and to try and get over it, I suggested we plead our cases before a third-party mediator. One of Bill's closest friends, Bill Trabold, agreed to fill the role of mediator. Certainly couldn't accuse me of stacking the deck. So we went over to the Trabold's house, and I went first. Told Mr. Trabold that the house was stuck in the mud, it was freezing in the winter, and no progress was being made. I remember Bill the mediator stating that these projects can take time, and patience was called for, and how long had it been like that? I replied two years, to which he laughed out loud. I think he was waiting for a month, maybe two... but two years? He said I certainly had a point.

So I contracted out the rest of the work. My fault in all of this was that I simply assumed that Bill would be more like my father, enjoying the building process and being pleased when progress could be seen. I don't know where Bill's head was, but he certainly was not cut from the same cloth. It was starting to dawn on me that Bill strongly preferred playing: fishing and camping, playing softball - he didn't feel the same sense of satisfaction that my dad, or grandfather, or I did creating something. I ended up doing all the work, and he ended up using every minute of our combined "play time." He got very cross that I actually got the job done – I remember him saying that I did everything for him except wipe his butt. Maybe I was making him feel useless, I don't know. He didn't come across that way: he once was saying just how much I would regret not having all of the things he did for me, and I remember looking at him and saying, "Fine. You take care of you and I'll take care of me." So I would cook myself a great dinner while he sat across from me eating a hot dog. And by Sunday my clothes were washed and ironed and my car was washed, ready for Monday. After I washed my car he whined that I didn't wash his. He groused but capitulated - the honeymoon was definitely over.

I was promoted from Plant Auditor to General Supervisor of General Accounting after a year at the plant, which accorded me Executive Dining Room privileges and my own, name-stenciled, premium-located parking space. The first woman in that plant that was ever granted dining room access. That move did not come without issues, though – there was this man – dark hair, big guy – that always had macaroni and cheese with ketchup for lunch. The first day I walked in, he stood up so fast the chair he was sitting on tipped over and clattered to the ground. He swore a blue streak, and within those expletives fell the words, "I guess I will never eat in here again." He was furious that the all-men enclave had been invaded. He stormed out.

There were other issues: there was the very ambitious young cost accountant that wanted the job I got. He would cast barbs such as, "now you'll see how a real plant works," as we went out on the plant floor to check on something, voice dripping with distain. There was the plant doctor that kept on making passes at me. And the team I inherited! I had a couple of supervisors that had maybe half a dozen employees each under them. One supervisor was Dolores, a very high-strung, hard-charging, hard working woman. If I let her come in and vent for a half hour every month or so she would go back out and work her miracles. There was Jim, a very quiet and sweet man who hated confrontation. I had heard through the grapevine that his son had died some time before, and that totally broke the man. His whole personality and demeanor changed. Jim had a woman under him – Shirley – who was a total piece of work. She had seniority, and she thought that gave her carte blanche to do whatever she pleased. Part of her job was to audit invoices to purchase orders before checks were cut. That entailed coordination with Dolores, who headed up that area, except that Shirley decided she wasn't going to speak with Dolores because she didn't like her. Unbelievable. Jim couldn't do anything with her – none of the guys wanted to take her on. So I sat down with her and went over her written job description. Point by point. When her annual review came up I knocked her for not completing that one task of her job that involved coordinating with Dolores. She went ballistic and filed a long and rambling formal complaint. Of course it was baseless: we had her sign the job description that was reviewed earlier. She had no excuse. Actually, the HR manager came in and chuckled, thanking me and adding I was the only one willing to take her on. It didn't change anything material in her pay or position, but she had been put on notice. Helen Keller couldn't run around the dinner table grabbing food off of other people's plates anymore.

Then Christmas came, and a plant layoff came. I had a very hard-working young fellow, Joe, who so appreciated his job. Worked so hard to please. I had come to know that his wife worked at another GM plant, that the two of them had a toddler and a young baby, and that his wife had just gotten laid off. Joe had the least seniority, and I had to lay him off. At Christmas. And there was spoiled brat Shirley, refusing to act in a professional and mature manner, and there was Joe, everything a manager could ask for in an eager and willing employee... and it was Joe I had to call in. I actually was so distressed that I was having a very difficult time, and he interrupted me, gently telling me that he knew what I had to do, and that it was all right, and that he appreciated how deeply it bothered me. That's the downside to seniority-based job security. Damn that Shirley.

The plant's Comptroller was a very earnest fellow named Harold Potter. Harold had worked his way up over many years and was near retirement. He was probably the only person left in senior plant management without a degree, but he had made up for it with an incredible work ethic. He did have his quirks: he was obsessed with having all of the desks in perfect alignment. There had been some sort of morale-related effort at the plant, and as a result people could have their offices painted however they wanted. I chose two-tone grey because it suited the plant. As with many other facilities, this plant had been thrown up for the War effort and was previously a tank plant. There were tales of third shift taking tanks out back to the test track and somehow ending up flipping one over. Anyway, it was bare and utilitarian, especially the offices. Linoleum floors and big paned windows that wouldn't open, half-glass partitions between offices and old grey metal desks. There was no fabric or wood at all in the place, so sound really bounced around. Anyway, Harold hated all of that lack of color uniformity. I think he wanted it to resemble barracks.

Grand Blanc was a stamping plant. It had huge coils of steel that came in through the side bays, right into the blanking machines, and then into the presses. The presses were amazing pieces of machinery: the machines extended through the floor, to the floor of the full-height lower level – they were that massive. Those machines had to have enough pressure to mold steel in seconds, and all of that might made lots of noise. Quality control consisted of measuring the parts for tolerances after they were formed. The quality control guys had jigs into which they would place randomly chosen parts coming off the line to make sure tolerances were being met. If a blanking or stamping machine got off tolerance, the issue frequently wasn't found until after many parts had been stamped. The plant put out thousands of hoods and door panels and fenders a day... with the existing quality control system there was lots and lots of waste, because tolerance slippages weren't found right away. The errant machines would have to be taken offline to be recalibrated. The daily 6 AM plant manager's meeting covered all of the offline machines and scrapped parts – walking out of those meetings, I often marveled that anything went out the door at all.

The machines needed massive quantities of hydraulic fluid and oils to work as fast as they needed to, so the plant was an oily, dirty place. The flooring consisted of 4"x4" hardwood blocks of wood – maple or oak or other hardwood, their individual beauty totally destroyed by the black goop layered over that gorgeous wood. When one cube broke down it was simply lifted out, replaced, and covered in nasty black goop. I often thought that was a terrible use of otherwise perfectly beautiful wood. If a central office executive scheduled a visit, plant management would spend weeks in preparation. They would carefully map out the route and send in cleaners and painters to make sure the chosen route was spruced up. The hapless executive was not allowed to veer off the chosen path, and the schedule was so tight that I remember someone asking about how so-and-so would have time, or the route, to take a bathroom break. Those visits were choreographed to the nth degree.

~

In early 1981, General Motors thought that plant support consolidation made sense, so the accounting departments for the stamping plant, Flint Assembly #1 and Flint Assembly #2 were consolidated in downtown Flint. I became General Supervisor of Accounts Payable for the three plants and had 26 employees. Nobody liked the arrangement: we tried arranging clerks by plant so they could answer any plant question, but the vendors were unhappy about getting bounced around from clerk to clerk. We tried arranging clerks by vendor so they had one-stop shopping, but the plants were unhappy about getting bounced around from clerk to clerk. I was only in that position for a few months, though – I got transferred to Central Office. I became the Practices and Procedures person responsible for writing and maintaining all of the documentation, processes and procedures for Accounts Payable. There were four of us: three mid-fifties white guys and me. No surprise there. It certainly was a much cleaner environment, and Bill and I could drive to and from work together. That was delightful, since we lived so far away. We settled into an easy routine: predictable hours, no more being in a meeting room every day at 6 AM, no overtime, no summer 18-hour inventory marathons during the July shut-down – did I mention plants are not air-conditioned? I was once again actively white-collar.

So things were progressing swimmingly, or sort of. Getting Todd and Amy back and forth from St. Clair Shores for the every-other-weekend schedule was more difficult, and their mother was a combination of sad/jealous that we were doing relatively well.

That was a difficult time for her, since her aspirations were to be a stay-at-home mother, not a working mother. She had no particular skills, so ended up being a waitress. Angry at her situation, she took to playing games, especially around the holidays. One Christmas she hid the children at her sister's. She would deny weekends, saying the children were sick. I remember telling her that we were quite capable of taking care of a sick child, and for that Christmas I called Maryann's older sister and said that unless the children were available at 8 PM there would be a Show Cause filed the very next day. None of this was good for the children, but in these cases, things tend to devolve to the lowest common denominator. The hassle took its toll on Bill, too. Not like you might think: Bill was very conflicted about the children, especially Todd. Bill was not a very mature individual, I was learning, and he couldn't see Todd without feeling that this child had taken all of his mother's attention. Bill actually blamed a baby for taking his wife away. He would be so cross, always yelling, that I remember telling him once that he needed to be a father, but it pained me to see him act in such an angry manner. I said that to preserve my image of him, maybe it would be better for me to go stay in a motel during visitation weekends. Bill then tried to hold it in, but that gave him splitting headaches. He wasn't ready to address the dysfunction in his behavior, so he wasn't ready to go seek help. It was a very painful thing to watch.

Maryann didn't seem to be much more mature: she was very good at guilt trips. The children once said that if they told their mother they had a good time with us, she would start to cry, go lock herself in her bedroom, and the kids would have to fend for themselves for dinner. The entire situation became so uncomfortable that one Friday afternoon, while we were sitting in Maryann's driveway waiting to pick the children up, the police came. The children refused to see their father. We were just sitting there! That spawned a long drawn-out legal battle that ended with visitation and half the child support being halted. We did not see the kids for years after that. Several years. And then I became pregnant.

WORKING MOTHER

I was very surprised and happy. Bill was not, which surprised me. I had raised the issue before we wed, which he dodged a bit, saying it was a bit early to speak of children. It had been over two years without a pregnancy, and I guess because it seemed that it wasn't going to be an issue, the subject was not raised again. I was disappointed in his response, but there certainly wasn't anything I was going to do about it – he knew I wanted to have children.

It was the men at work that were so uneasy – they kept on joking about me going into labor at work. I bought some very business-y fabric and made myself two maternity jumpers that I could wear with my business blouses. Back then the proper business attire for women was a menswear-fabric skirted business suit with a collared blouse and a floppy silk tie: little Ms. Mister. Truth be told, maternity clothes feel like going into work in a nightgown: nothing restrictive about them at all.

I had pretty much given up arguing with Bill about money – we bought some used baby furniture that I paid for, we decorated the nursery and I spent my evenings making an embroidered stuffed accessory to hang across the crib. I was happy, despite Bill grumpiness. He never got over it – he got nastier and nastier. I remember once he was trying to bait me into getting angry. I was ahead of him going up the stairs, with a bunch of papers in my hand, and he was behind me complaining that I never got angry. I turned around and said, "You want me to get angry? There," I said, as I threw the papers at him, scattering all around him. "There. I got angry." I turned around and continued going up the stairs. I asked him shortly after about his seething. I asked him,

189

was he angry? Why? He replied that he was angry every single minute of every single day. Angry that all of his friends were retired, fishing whenever they wanted, and he was not. Of course not: he was in his thirties. Angry that his first wife, in his eyes, deserted him in favor of the red-headed son he so resented. Angry that he got second-hand everything from his older brother. Angry that he was expected to grow up, I guess. Just simply an angry guy, not reconciled to the realities of working adult life.

I was going on maternity leave six weeks before delivery, and that last day, August 26th, the guys at work took me out to lunch. I ordered a taco salad – the one which has the edible taco bowl. I was half way through and mentioned I had never felt so full – I felt like I had eaten a brick. So we stood up to leave and my water broke – right there. In the restaurant. With the fellows that had been joking about me going into labor at work for the last six months. They called an ambulance and took me to the nearest hospital... a small community hospital. My doctor did not have privileges there, so they had to call in someone I had never met. He was old school... said I had to have a C-section, said he only did longitudinal procedures, and that was that. Bill showed up and said the most telling, and some would say, most inappropriate thing: "Don't worry, I'm not mad." He wanted me to know that he wasn't angry that this rather sudden birth would interfere with his sacrosanct salmon fishing trip that was scheduled for the following week. Really? Anyway, I went into surgery and we had a beautiful little girl, six weeks early. Before I was put under so they could suture me up I heard her Apgar scores – a 7 and then an 8 – and I went into my drug-induced twilight smiling.

They brought her to me in recovery. I started speaking to her and she focused right on me, and grabbed my finger. She had curly dark hair... she was gorgeous! We named her Brittany Nicole – we had chosen the first name but hadn't gotten as far as a middle name. My father mentioned he loved the name Nicole, so Nicole it was. Then in a while a neonatal nurse came in and told me they didn't have the proper set-up for a preemie like Brittany, and because her breathing had become somewhat labored they were going to send her over to St. John's in Grosse Pointe, where they had a special neo-natal unit. They told me there was nothing to worry about, she just needed a bit more care, that I would be able to go visit her every day. So I bid my baby girl goodbye, got put in a room, and fell asleep. Bill went over with her and came back later that evening to tell me she was twice as big as any other baby in that unit.

I woke up to Bill's voice in the hall the next morning. I was beaming as he walked around the corner into the room, but then I stopped. He looked awful! His entire face was a strange color, and it was distorted and wrinkled in pain... I had never seen him look like that before. I asked, "Did you go to St. John's? Did you see her again?" He stopped, stood there, and barely managed to croak, "She died."

~

My very first thought was, "Lord, look at that man. I have to be strong because he is not." He said he donated her to medical science... I didn't have a say, and I now had no way to even say goodbye. I was totally devastated. And then I was on auto-pilot. I remember the nurses put me in a private room. I remember having to deal with all of the milk I had that would never be used – that was physically painful. I am pretty sure my father came – I know for a fact my uncle Ted came. And I know for a fact my grandmother came, suggesting that I come stay with her for a while. I remember crying when I told her I wanted to go back home. Mostly people didn't know what to say. I spent the next several weeks getting the information about what happened. The problem with Brittany is that she looked too healthy when she was born, so antibiotics, which apparently are often administered to premature babies, were not given. She had sepsis – a strep infection that got to her heart and stopped it. Her lungs were not fully developed, which was the reason for her labored breathing. The lung issue – previously called Hyaline's Membrane Disease but now called Respiratory Distress Syndrome (RDS). If breathing is supported, RDS will usually resolve itself in four or five days. It was the sepsis – the blood sample they drew didn't happen to have any strep in it, so the hospital merely did the breathing support. By the time they finally figured out she had sepsis, it was too late.

~

For two years after I simply wanted to die. I really did. I was a shadow of a person. I could function when I had something to do – when I was around people. The minute I was alone I would cry. I withdrew from Bill. I acknowledged it to him, in a letter I wrote him, speech being too painful. He was emotionally ill-equipped to support me. I was wooden. I was promoted to the Corporate Treasurer's Staff at the GM Building in Detroit – I was still wooden. And again I lost massive amounts of weight. I remember putting on a camel wool suit when winter came – the waist was four inches too big. And I got another infection, however this time it was internal and it was silent. I ended up with all sorts of scar tissue from it that no one knew was there until a couple of years later.

I was now driving to work by myself, and I would cry from the minute I stepped into the car until I got to work – on the way home I would cry all the way back. I remember really wanting to just die, but what held me back was thinking that my mother – my selfish, totally self-absorbed, unreliable mother – would not be strong enough to handle it. My God Damned mother. The mother that, upon hearing of our tragic loss, did not come. Did not write. Did not even call. She did nothing. She offered no support, no condolence. She did not acknowledge it at all.

I snapped out of it one morning as I was backing out the driveway. Right when I had to leave for work there was a five-minute little motivational segment on the radio that I always turned off because I hated it. However, on this particular morning I had both hands on the wheel, right at the end of the driveway backing into the road, so I was not able to turn it off. And I heard the message, "You can't change what's happened to you... all you can do is choose how to respond to it." I had cried enough. I had turned the corner.

I did have a few relapses. I had started singing in an all-women group led by a bubbly blond named Faith Dippold. There was a lovely, vivacious woman – a pastor's wife – who was speaking one evening about her daughter. She had her baby around the time I had mine. And her baby was premature. And her baby had RDS. And sepsis. However, her baby was born in obvious distress, and the hospital staff acted immediately, administering antibiotics. Same time frame, same issue... but her baby lived and mine did not. That set me back. And if I was caught unaware – if I could not prepare myself for the conversation – I might burst into tears. Brittany was born August 26th. I came to hate August. Everything bad happened in August. I dreaded the advent of the month. Even though Bill's birthday was August 19th. To this day I look upon August with trepidation.

Bill and I did end up going salmon fishing – not to Lake Michigan, and not until October. We went to the Betsy River, meeting up with Paul and Mary Parisi. It was snag fishing on the river bank... I didn't fish. Mary was very kind and gentle – so was Paul. When we got back home, I put all of my baby things away – no Todd, no Amy, no baby. Just my dog Shannon, her baby Katy, a kitten I had spontaneously adopted one cold and rainy October day from a young boy giving away kittens outside the local supermarket, and a nastier and nastier Bill.

~

I was saved by work: I was doing well, even if I couldn't do recommended things like go out for drinks after work with the guys. Bill started yelling at me because dinner was happening later and later. The GM Building was in Midtown Detroit, and it was taking me well over an hour to commute. I remember one night being in a horrible traffic jam because a small plane had made an emergency landing on the expressway... and all I could think about was what to say to not get yelled at. And then there was the overtime... we had to prepare the Red Books for the Board Meetings, coordinating with our New York office. That normally took until one in the morning. One night – or more accurately early morning – the temperature was sitting right at 32°. The paved roads were fine, but once I hit the dirt roads I hit water on ice. My car got stuck on a turn, and after quite some time of unsuccessful rocking I took out the back floor mats, stuck them under the rear tires and managed to get out and go into Lake Orion. It was 2:30AM – and the only pay phone I could find was one outside of a bar that was closing. Not ideal. I called Bill and told him I couldn't make it home, and that I was going to call my dad and ask if I could spend the night. Oh no. Bill said no. He called the police, and Pete the Policeman showed up to take me home in his cruiser. He was properly patronizing, until he got on one of those dirt roads. We started going down a steep hill, and the police cruiser started sliding down sideways. He decided he should turn on his flashers, so there we were, sliding sideways down a water-covered ice hill at three in the morning, flashers lighting up the night. He managed to get back to the police station, frantically telling everyone to call the schools and close them. It was way too late to drive over to Watkins Lake for the night, so I ended up calling the VanSteenises, asking them if I could crash on their sofa. They lived close, but more importantly, they lived on a paved road. I ended up there that night, borrowing an excessively too large, but clean, blouse and some really wrong-color makeup to go into work the next day.

~

The Treasurer's Staff was extremely involved with the shareholder annual meetings, which at the time were held at the Fisher Theater. There was a dais set up in front of the drawn-shut stage curtain. Roger Smith and a handful of senior officers sat at the white-skirted table, and shareholders sat in the theater audience section. What they couldn't see was that the table in front of the senior officers had cutouts in front of each chair, into which were sunk computer screens which were hard-wired to computers in back of the curtain. The computers were loaded with all sorts of facts about the company, and each was manned by one of the many fresh-faced MBA's back stage, whose job it was bring up data so the officers could surreptitiously read off facts and figures from the hidden computer screens. There were runners who went up and down the aisles, picking up questions written on index cards from shareholders. The questions were delivered quietly backstage before they were read aloud by the MC, so the answers were on the officers' screens before the question was read. And there were fresh-faced MBA "plants" who sat strategically close to known trouble-makers, and who would submit cards to the runners not with questions, but with information about the conversations overheard and/or notes written.

The "known trouble-makers" were corporate gadflies that were famous for attending shareholder meetings: there were never many neophyte complainers that made it to the annual meetings. You see, there was this 3" or 4" binder that contained information on shareholders that threatened to come just to complain about their shoddy cars or bad dealership experiences. GM collected dossiers on these shareholders: name, address, picture, occupation, issue – as full a dossier as could be collected. Mostly they were placated, AKA bought off, with a new car or some other remedy, to entice them to not make the trip to Detroit. It was a very effective strategy: my lesson learned was that, played very sparingly, going to the top normally got remarkably good results. I did it once with Comcast: after eighteen months of getting nowhere with the local repairmen, I called Corporate headquarters and asked to speak to the Vice President of Public Relations. Of course my call didn't go through, but a staffer called me back rather promptly. The next thing I knew, I had a two-man crew out for eight hours. They didn't bother to figure out exactly what was wrong – they simply replaced everything – EVERYTHING – from the outside junction multi-home junction box to my junction box and everything inside. And a local supervisor called me and gave me her personal number, in case anything went wrong again. Amazing how that works.

Bill was not supportive of my work life, alternating between saying things like if he had my education he would be making millions of dollars (so why didn't I) and complaining that I wasn't home early enough to fix dinner. I couldn't win for losing.

We spent thirteen years going salmon fishing and going to visit his parents. His mother was a piece of work, I came to learn. I should have known something was up when she was sending him packages of underwear... when he was 32 years old. Not only was she clinically anorexic, she had a real issue with her children. She did not want them married. She picked fights with every single in-law. She picked fights with Jack's wives; Hannie, a very short-lived second marriage, and Carol, wife number three. When there was a divorce, she would ask for the old wedding rings and wear them on a chain around her neck. How macabre is that? Bill's older brother Jack and his wife Hannie had two children; a boy, John Jr., and a girl, Yvonne. Hannie was Dutch, and when the couple divorced, Jack and John-John came to the States and Yvonne stayed with her mother in Holland. Jack was just over his rebound second marriage-turned-divorce and was dating Carol, and had little time for John-John. I remember that we offered to take John-John with us to Disney World, and Kay simply refused to let him go with us. I felt so badly for him. Why ever would she do that?

I was not immune to her barbs: one afternoon she decided to host a tea for the neighbors across the street and next door. As we were sitting there around the table, she smiled at me and said, "Wendy, you should get a nanny for Bill. You are not home to fix him supper, and that's giving him high blood pressure. Since you can't take care of him, maybe you can hire someone who can." Oh my. And I remember Jack getting so angry at his mother for saying something about his wife that he blurted out, "You do not talk to an Officer's wife that way!" Kay got into a physical fight with Kathy's John to the point that he shoved her. She was unbearable.

I should maybe take a minute to clarify names: pretty much everybody is named John. My father. Bill's father. Bill's brother. Bill's nephew. Even my nephew. Bill's brother-in-law. The only outlier was my brother, Jeff. So the nicknames were, in order: Doc, Hutch, Jack, John-John, Jonathan and John.

Visiting Bill's parents was not ever much of a vacation for me, unless we were out and about, like the time we went down to Sebastian Cut close to dusk. We stumbled upon Paul Newman and Joanne Woodward just wrapping up a shoot for "Harry and Son." I wanted to let them pack up and go, figuring they had been working all day and probably wanted to go have some dinner. Not Bill. He went right up and started a conversation with Mr. Newman. I must say that Paul Newman was a very unpretentious person. Bill asked him if the movie was any good, and Mr. Newman replied, "Nah" with a wide grin. What really struck me was his wife. She stood off to the side, positively beaming at her husband. It was so very obvious she was totally in love with the man and was pleased at the attention he was getting. And yes, his eyes were really that blue. And his face was really that chiseled. He was not much taller than me, but perfectly proportioned. The two of them left in separate but matching blue BMW's, apparently for insurance purposes. An extremely gracious couple.

We did take one trip out to California at Christmas. My mother was living with some man – can't even remember him. I do remember the house, though – it was in Westwood, between the expressway and the ocean. It was rather poorly constructed and not in really great shape. All I really remember about that Los Angeles experience was that the traffic was insanely heavy and trying to find a parking spot at the grocery store was a major event. That, and going to visit one of my mom's friends from Michigan that had also relocated to California. His name was Don, and he had a wickedly sharp sense of humor… one that was often at the object's expense, - a Don Rickles kind of guy. I remember him telling me that my mother didn't drive, she aimed. I didn't like the area or the company at all. I remember asking my mother what Don had done for a living, and she really got defensive. She started talking about how well-traveled he was, and what books he read… she was dodging the question big time. I kept asking, and she finally admitted he was a postman. She was embarrassed that she had to admit she was good friends with a man whose station in life was, to her, so lowly. That told me much more about her than him. She had a very hard time looking past exterior markers.

We then visited San Francisco. We ended up there on New Year's Eve and were shocked that we were able to book a room downtown at the Marriott, or Hilton, or some other national chain, with little advance notice. We checked in and walked over to Chinatown for supper. The streets are narrow there, and there were parked cars along the curb. There was a large white limousine right in the middle of the street, stopped and making passing impossible, right in front of the restaurant to which we were headed. As we passed, there was a young man getting out of that limo, a fifth in hand. He seemed drunk. We were seated for only minutes when we heard a loud and rather heavy voice – distinctive enough to be interrupting other conversations. But it was a familiar voice… it was the voice of the drunken man's father several tables over. It was Rodney Dangerfield. Being around him was as distasteful as being around the Newman's was pleasant.

After dinner we went back to our hotel, and at that moment we discovered why it had been so easy to get a room there. It was the closest hotel to the annual Grateful Dead New Year's Eve concert, and the hotel was full of DeadHeads. After the concert they were up all night, roaming the halls and partying in a most joyous but loud – very loud – manner. And then we got a call from Michigan… there had been an ice storm and the power was out. We asked our neighbor to go turn off our water so the pipes wouldn't freeze. That hung over our heads a bit for the rest of the trip, which consisted of a trip to Yosemite, where we thought we could spend a night. That was a huge miscalculation… on New Year's Day there was a traffic backup getting into the park that lasted forever. There was not one room free, anywhere near the park. We went back to San Francisco and flew back from there shortly thereafter… and we were thankful that the pipes were fine.

I did take an independent vacation: my father was engaged to a Bloomfield Hills woman, Mary Lou. She was an excellent cook, very energetic and funny. She loved antiques and would go to London frequently to buy items and have them shipped back. She came from a wealthy family but had a sadistic father – the kind of guy that would put little girls on a boat below deck in stormy weather and laugh when they got seasick. Anyway, Mary Lou was going on one of her London tours and wondered if I would like to go. There would be four of us – a girl's trip. My father thought getting away would be good for me, so he lent me the money. Off we went! We actually had a blast. The dollar was exceptionally strong against the pound, so everything in the UK was relatively cheap. Everything was so crowded that we ended up staying at a hotel near Paddington Station owned by a Greek man who was a friend of Mary Lou's. His clientele was mostly all Middle Eastern. I remember we were looked at a bit askance, but I would go down to the bar in the evenings and get into discussions. I was apparently significantly different than their perception of what an American was, in a good way. Oh, and we went shopping – extensively – and visited the sights. I remember hopping on the subway and going down to Harrod's because my Clinique makeup was cheaper in London than back home. I bought sweaters and silver table pieces and jewelry and a Viyella Blackwatch bathrobe – everything was attractive with such a strong dollar.

The owner of the hotel was having a christening party for his grandson at his home, and we were invited. That was really interesting: I had never been in a private London residence. It was a lovely party, although it was apparent that many of the guests were wary of the unexpected Americans. He was a very welcoming man.

Two weeks in London, with only one sojourn out to Bath to see some semi-circular building Mary Lou loved. On the way back we stopped at a pub not far from Stonehenge. Pubs were supposed to close at eleven or so by law, unless it was a private party. So at eleven o'clock the front doors were locked, and the patrons went from being in a public drinking establishment to being in a private party. It was hilarious how that was simply a matter of course. I ended up speaking at length to some British guy with a Peugeot – when I told him I had never seen Stonehenge, he would not have it. We hopped in his car and drove over, seeing Stonehenge at about midnight. It was perfect – something about the isolation of the spot, the lack of people, the lack of touristy shacks and vendors. At the time there wasn't even a fence, just those stones, standing alone in the glade in the moonlight. Fitting.

Mary Lou had given me a fur coat, being that I was going to be her step daughter. However, my father called off the engagement, and I gave her back her fur. He only said that certain things she had said didn't add up. She may have been a little manic, who knows. His life, his call.

~

On the home front, I was still figuring out what it took to run the household and allocating that amount between us based upon relative earnings. I thought that was eminently fair. He disagreed. It was always a battle. And he groused and groused. He contributed per formula, mind you, but he also became quite passive aggressive. And every year or so, when we needed an adjustment to account for inflation, he would grouse some more, saying things like, "I wouldn't have to contribute more if you hadn't bought that mascara." I would pull out all of the documentation – the electric bill, the tax bill, the phone bill… didn't matter. He was a little boy in many ways. And to this day I do not know what he did with "his" money. I bought the furniture and all of the household stuff. I don't think he drank or gambled his away; he wasn't wearing expensive clothes. He wasn't driving an extravagant car. He had his boat, but it wasn't new. He wasn't squirreling it away. I never did figure that one out.

~

I was on the fast track at work. I was put into a coveted "special" job code and moved from the Treasurer's Staff to the

Comptroller's Staff to start the mandatory job rotation through all of the different departments on the way to Unclassified. I was promoted to the highest Classified category, which gave me a Performance Evaluation Program (PEP) car. That was one sweet deal. It entailed getting a new car every two months, complete with insurance and free gas at the private gas station across from the GM Building. That gas station was discreetly surrounded by opaque fencing. There were no signs, and the pumps were totally unmarked. The only requirement was that at the end of each two-month segment we had to complete a three-page evaluation of the car to which we were assigned. The tags were company tags, so if I had to go into a dealership for warranty or recall work I got the very best treatment: those dealership guys knew my car was a PEP car, and even though they didn't know who I was, they weren't going to take any chances. There was only one drawback to this sweet deal: shopping center parking lots. Not only did I have to remember where I parked, I had to remember what I was driving.

My first stop in the departmental musical chairs game was into Pricing. I was there when the first incentives were dreamt up. Before the mid-eighties, no car company (which covered, almost exclusively, the Big Three) ever dreamed of offering manufacturer's incentives. However, one of our rivals – I can't remember if it was Chrysler or Ford – offered the very first manufacturer incentive. That drove GM wild. We had a flurry of activity trying to not be left behind, and we had pricing proposals up the yang. That doesn't sound like much of a deal, except that we were not very mechanized back then. We had Wang word processors, all independent and single-purpose machines. And we had huge Xerox copiers. So an incentive would come in, and we would prepare a financial analysis. We would write it up with a recommendation, and if it passed department muster it would be distributed to the Executive Committee for approval. That meant about fourteen copies of multiple page documents. When there was an all-hands-on-deck call, each of us would take a page or two of each incentive request, run adequate copies, and actually walk around fourteen "stations" which were lined up on file cabinets around the room, walking in circles, depositing our pages on each pile until every package was done. And since we had five car lines, and since Pontiac ended up competing with Chevrolet and Buick, and since they were all run independent of each other, we would have multiple redundant incentive packages. And then we would make the Fourteenth Floor run, taking the packages to each Executive's office. I did an awful lot of walking back then.

GM was in a financial mess, but it was hidden from view for a long time. The Treasurer's Office in New York would prepare the financials and the forecasts for the Board, but the process used was developed during "what's good for GM is good for the country" days. GM Corporate only hired newly minted MBAs for their financial and market forecasting staffs, preferring to not have anyone tainted by anyone else's business practices. And in New York, many decades earlier, some arrogant Harvard fellow recognized that GM's earnings per share were so consistent and predictable that he could forecast earnings per share and work up the income statement to income and expenses. It worked for years and years, but because GM had become so insular and arrogant, because they did not want to introduce anyone that would look at that peculiar process and say, "What???," the office did not recognize when it stopped working. The CFO would get the bottoms-up analysis and have the staff add a fudge factor to get the EPS where he wanted it to be. By the time I was in Pricing, that CFO was fudging over a dollar per share, going from negative to positive, in the erroneous belief that any particular quarter – or year - was an anomaly and that the ship would right itself within the next three months. When the truth came out – when the Board finally asked some hard questions, that CFO was fired. I ran into

Bob Hendry at the North American Auto Show Charity Preview, who was named the succeeding CFO. He told me that he was given the former CFO's work and asked to come back with an analysis. Bob did, and he nailed the problem. He told me that he was told point blank, "If you do anything like that, you are fired."

While I was in Pricing I became pregnant again. I was thrilled! This pregnancy was different: I had no morning sickness: I had whenever-I-got-hungry-sickness, to the point that going home one day from the grocery store with Bill, which was maybe a ten-minute drive, I told him to pull over. Right now. I couldn't even make it home. It was also an interesting pregnancy, in that I came home at three months with a prescription from my doctor which said, "R/O twins." When I got that I simply left it on the kitchen counter where I knew Bill would see it. The look on his face was priceless. That being said, an ultrasound did rule out twins – my dear son was not curled up nice and tight in a fetal position. Oh no... he was stretched out on his back, head against my spine, legs horizontal to the floor. No wonder I looked seven months pregnant! I wonder if he had his hands behind his head.

My grandmother was excited, but she was failing. My father had bought her a condominium but had subsequently moved her into his house because she needed more tending. She developed bladder cancer and ended up in the hospital. She was definitely old country, and she was totally unfamiliar with modern medicine. I remember going to visit her when she was first admitted for surgery prep. A nurse came in to ask her questions and asked her who her doctor was. My grandmother said she didn't have one. The nurse, believing my grandmother was a bit senile, thought that if she went at it a little differently she might extract an answer... she asked when my grandmother last saw a doctor for a routine physical. My dear Maggie, in her wonderful Scottish brogue, said, "Thairty years ago." The nurse started to say, "Now,

Mrs. Thomson..." and then looked at me. I grinned and said, "Thairty years ago." It was true. We are not doctor-going folk. Then the surgeon came in, and he was a handsome one. I watched in fascination as my grandmother skillfully engaged in the gentle art of flirtation. She was an expert! I was a little bit shocked, quite amused, and quite impressed at how accomplished she was.

I will never forget waiting with my father for the results. My dad was saying that at my grandmother's age, she probably needed very little anesthesia... and shortly thereafter the doctor came in mentioning what a tough old bird Maggie was, and that they needed extra to put her under. And then, going to her room after she left recovery, my father was walking me down the hall telling me how, with that extra anesthesia, Gram would probably be really groggy... when we heard her clearly, and loudly, telling the nurse what she would and would not accept. It was hilarious, really. Gram, who was such a proud woman, who had never seen modern medicine, did not understand how catheters worked. She was mortified that she might pee all over the bed. She was mortified that she was bed-ridden. She was mortified that strangers were looking "down there." She wanted nothing of it at all.

After her operation Gram went into a rehab/nursing home... the one that my mother's parents had been in years before. She met a gentleman in there, and they got along very well. They would sit holding hands in the living room. My grandmother was a beautiful woman, and I was thrilled that she seemed happy with him. That being said, she was tired of living. She would tell me that she had had a good, long life, and she was ready to leave. I kept telling her to hold on – my son was due May 5th, and her birthday was April 28th... I kept telling her to hold on, I was going to give her a wonderful birthday present! But then winter came, and I was seven months pregnant. The doctor told me I couldn't walk on ice – and there was ice on her nursing home sidewalk. I could only call her.

It was the dead of night on February 12th when I got the call. They put a feeding tube in Maggie, against my father's wishes. And then I got a second call in the wee hours of February 13th - Maggie had passed. I swear to this day she willed herself to death. She did not like being physically dependent, and she did not like the indignity of requiring nursing staff. She did not like that her normally impeccably clean nails (she used to dip them in bleach) were not cleaned well enough by the nursing staff. She just did not like life anymore, so she decided to leave.

Our son Chris was born on what would have been her 87th birthday. I would indeed have given her a wonderful birthday gift – a healthy wee bairn.

~

Christopher and I came home from the hospital on day three – he was borderline jaundiced, but all I needed to do was to sit him in sunshine for a day for everything to clear up. Katy took him in stride, but the K-Mart cat, Spook, did not like the intrusion in the least. I could see down the stairs from the den where I would breast feed my newborn... that cat would look up the stairs and wait until we were settled. Then she would take one clawed paw and, making sure I could see her, very deliberately grab one of my favorite white occasional chairs and rip away. That demon knew there was nothing I would do at that moment. By the time Chris was six months old, those two occasional chairs were totally ruined.

I have heard about parents being exhausted with newborns... I relished every minute. Because I was breast-feeding, I had 100% of the child care duties. Chris was not a difficult baby – by six weeks he was sleeping a good six hours through the night. It was very peaceful, sitting in his darkened room feeding him in the middle of the night. I loved it, actually. The only thing a bit disconcerting is that he was not a cuddle-bug: he was a very matter-of-fact "feed me, put me down and let me sleep: I have a lot of growing to do" kind of baby. I also got the distinct impression that he came into this world with a "you and I are equals: let's negotiate" attitude.

A few days after I got home, my mother and sister surprised us by arriving to "help." I was quite shocked, since neither of them were there when Brittany died. It was pretty uncomfortable, because I needed no help – I had everything totally under control. I not only had everything under control, I was relishing the role. There was nothing that I could suggest for them to do, and I think they both felt awkward. While they were visiting, my mother picked up her mother and brought her over to see the baby. From that visit I have a four-generation picture. Beyond that, I can't remember much of that visit. It was a nice thought, though…

I went back to work after two months, taking Chris to a daycare center. That became a logistical nightmare: I had to get up at 4-something in the morning to get everything together and get to the GM Building in time. It went from difficult to impossible when the three major – and only – arteries were closed or significantly constricted, two because of construction and one because of the need for emergency bridge repair. My commute was taking two hours each way, and I told Bill it was killing me. We needed to move closer in. At first he was not keen on the idea, because he loved where we lived. However, we started looking at houses, and when he indicated he was interested in a house across the street from the Oakland Hills Country Club, we jumped. Our house sold in a very short time, and all of a sudden we were in a roomy, four-bedroom split level colonial. Per usual, we ripped out the existing kitchen and put in a new one. Other than some paint and new carpeting, the house didn't need much else. We both cut our commutes in half.

I just could not understand Bill... I had been very careful to let him choose the house, since I was the one asking to move – he went from choosing the house to complaining he hated it. I didn't know where that came from, really... I guess I came to the conclusion that it was an indication not of the house per se, but of his overall unhappiness. I started making excuses to be in different rooms than him, doing different things: oh, I have to do the laundry. Oh, I need to read Chris a bedtime story. Oh, I need to wash the windows. I certainly could not spend weekends with him on the boat. He had gone and joined the Coast Guard Reserves, which he enjoyed. I think he enjoyed the uniforms the most. Anyway, we started going our different ways, except for vacations.

Bill's brother Jack had left the military and gotten a job in national security in Washington DC. We decided to rent an RV and take an East Coast tour. Bill had been born in Holyoke, Massachusetts, and he wanted to show me where he had grown up. His dad was also career military, so Bill lived in a couple of different states, all on the East Coast. We made the grand tour – Billerica, MA, through Boston, over to Rhode Island, down the coast to Maryland, and then into Virginia, baby son and Irish Setter in tow. Bill was very excited to show me where he grew up, marveling at how much larger the places seemed when he was a child: "That's where I saw the biggest spider EVER! That's where I road my bike to school. That's where we played baseball." Quite the trip down memory lane.

We ended up in Virginia to visit Jack and Carol, his third wife. Jack adopted her then-teenage daughter, and the three of them were making a lovely life for themselves in Chantilly. Bill always resented his older brother for getting things new, while Bill got the hand-me-down's. There was quite a bit of tension between them – one-sided - and Jack unsuccessfully tried to get Bill to let go. That was something Bill was unable to do. I have never met anyone so adept at holding on to a perceived past slight. I think I actually liked Jack's personality better than Bill's – Jack seemed so much more at peace with life. Carol was much more reserved, and it took me longer to get a feel for her. She was totally devoted to her daughter, her husband and her home, in that order. She was working full time but put a lot of time into her home life. Everything was immaculate and just-so. I ended up with a lot of respect for her – she is a very lovely, refined and loving woman. Jack did well: third time's the charm.

Back to every-day, I was very content being the 100% parent. I ferried Christopher back and forth to daycare. I did the doctor appointments. It was all on me, and I didn't mind in the least. He was a physically precocious child: at exactly seven and a half months old, he cut his first tooth, took his first step, and started to crawl – in that order. He was walking at 9 months and was off the growth charts, high end. And he loved his fire trucks. Or, should I say, "Fie Tucks." "Fie tucks, Mommy!!! Fie tucks!!!" We couldn't pass a fire station without him going totally bonkers. It was so cute. And he called himself FooFoo. I would try to get him to say his entire first name, syllable by syllable. "Chris." "Tis." "Toe." "Toe." "Pher." "Feh." "Christopher." "Tis-te-foo-foo." Hilarious. I was so enjoying my little boy.

When Chris was nearly two, my grandfather came up from the Keys to visit. He had long since retired and had moved into a beautiful home on Duck Key, living with his former secretary Dorothy, her also-a-spinster sister Esther, and their father Archie. My grandfather, Dorothy and Esther in tow, met us at an Italian restaurant that had a glass case full of toys near the hostess station, and I was so worried that my grandfather would go away with a bad impression of this toddler. When we piled out of the car, Chris' shirt had come out of his shorts. He hated tucking in his shirt. I looked at him and asked him to tuck his shirt in. He asked why... I said that when he walked in with his shirt tucked in so nicely that everyone would look at him and think, "Now there's a little boy whose Mommy loves him very, very much." He didn't say another word – he simply started tucking in his shirt.

I actually bribed my son that night, telling him that if he was a very good boy during dinner, I would buy him a Batman toy that he had spied in that glass case. I never did anything like that, and Chris was so surprised that he took me up on my offer – and right before dessert he leaned over and asked about that toy. I got right up and went to buy it for him. Evening – and reputations – saved. Never know how a couple of spinsters are going to react to a rambunctious little boy.

My grandfather told me a lot about himself while watching Chris. How I had my hands full, and how it was genetic. Four generations – that's what he said to me. How when my grandfather was a little boy, he was also a handful. How he couldn't keep his mouth shut when he enlisted, and how many times he had to march all night long in full dress parade – Blackwatch kilted - because of it. How it took him so long to learn how to keep his mouth shut. It is genetic, for sure.... Same thing got my father in Dutch during WWII. Same thing has gotten me in Dutch more times that I would like to admit. Same thing has gotten my son in Dutch. Apples do not fall far from the tree, that's for certain.

And it was that trait that derailed my meteoric Financial Staff rise at GM. All due to a Director that eventually got himself fired for graft and corruption... he was a bad apple. Trouble was, I figured that out before the Corporation did. I had the gall to challenge him, and before he got caught he saw to it that I was derailed. There was nothing secret about his intentions, he actually told me that if I pursued the issue he would ruin my career. He was furious. But that was a bit later... I hung around the Financial Staff long enough to have a second son – my blondie - Golden Boy, Kevin.

~

Kevin was actually an ounce heavier than Chris when he was born but was more than two inches shorter. Chris seemed to have gotten every single available drop of melanin from Bill and me: he was darker than either of us. Kevin was an indication there was no melanin left to give: he was so fair his chest veins were very visible against his marble-white skin. He was born with some water in his lungs, so he was put on a feeding tube since he couldn't hold his breath long enough to suck. I was a nervous wreck – I got myself down to his neo-natal special care unit on day two to hold him, me with IV tubes and him with his arm in paddles with tubes. I was petrified I would lose him. The nurses couldn't understand my concern, but Bill told them to let me go – that I had to go. The issue passed within 48 hours, and we got him home. He was a bit fussier, but still, at six weeks, was sleeping six hours a night. Chris was about two and a half, and he was such a good big brother! I remember having Kevin in the bassinet in the family room, with Chris playing with his toys. Chris wanted to go outside, but I told him we couldn't until Kevin fell asleep. Chris played very quietly for about ten minutes, tiptoed over to the bassinet and peeked in, and whispered to me, "Baby is asleep, Mommy. We can go now." He called his brother Baby for a good five years.

One thing about Chris - when he made up his mind, that was it. For good or bad. He potty-trained himself at exactly 10:25 AM one morning when Kevin was about a month old. We had been practicing, but Kevin started to fuss in his crib while Chris was in the bathroom. I told him to stay there while I went to tend to the baby. Chris followed me into the nursery, butt naked, and started talking to me. But then his eyes got big and round, he started saying, "Oh! Oh!" he went back into the bathroom, and that was that. Period. No training pants, no protection at night, no accidents – nothing. That was that.

I went back to work after maternity leave, but an infant care center had opened close to work, so I would take Kevin with me downtown so I could go over and see him at lunch. He came with me for a full year. I remember one night coming home from work - I got a flat tire on the Lodge Expressway near the Seven Mile exit. It was summer, and it was a hot day. I pulled off, grabbed Kevin, and walked until I got to the exit ramp, walked up it, and went to a Kentucky Fried Chicken restaurant and asked if I could use their phone. That's not the best part of town, and I got some very strange looks, me in heels and business suit, nine-month-old in arms, perspiring in the heat. Bill came and changed the tire so I could get home. Very thankful we didn't still live so far out when that happened.

As much as Chris was off the charts big, Kevin was small. He hated formula, and so at six months I was giving him ice cream and yogurt to supplement his breast milk instead of formula. My two sons, rather ying and yang: Chris of the much darker complexion and reddish hair, Kevin of the porcelain skin and towhead blond. One near the 99th percentile in size, one near the 10th. But if you looked at their features, they looked like the same boy in different colors. No mistaking them – they were definitely brothers.

When Kevin was not yet five months old, Bill's mother died. She had congestive heart failure, a result of her anorexia. We got the call that she was critically ill, so Bill booked a flight and headed down to Florida. He was in a layover when the second call came in: she had passed. I gathered up the boys and all of the baby gear and headed to the airport. We were quite the scene… I told the woman at the ticket counter that I needed to get on the next available flight due to a death in the family. The boys and I got there not too long after Bill. Kay had lost another couple of pounds, and by the time she died she weighted 104… six feet tall and 104 pounds. She was nothing but a skeleton. To me, it seemed the only one that appeared heartbroken was Kathy.

While Bill and I were busy with our lives, Bill's ex had remarried. She was a scion of an old, original Detroit family… one of the first French farmers on the east side. In fact, there's even a road carrying the family name: Allard. Her second husband was also a scion of a grand old family – a Glancy. This Glancy, however, was quite the black sheep, not attending Princeton, not becoming a CEO, not becoming a financier like his grandfather, father and brother… this Glancy drove a car hauler. Todd hated his stepfather, and pretty much out of the blue he asked if he could come live with us – and it became my three sons. Todd was twenty-one, taking some classes at Oakland University, caddying for Bill Laimbeer and loving basketball.

Todd had grown to be taller than his father – a big, broad-shouldered redhead. He and I have always gotten along but moving in with us was a disaster for him – Bill just couldn't lay off. If Todd ate dinner with us, he ate too much food and drank too much milk: if he missed dinner he was chided because of "all the effort that was devoted" to its preparation. Todd simply couldn't win for losing – Bill just could not let go of that initial misplaced resentment. Todd was not with us for even a year: it was just too much for him to bear. I felt sorry for him… he was a bit lost, admittedly, but he didn't deserve the constant verbal abuse. The unfortunate thing about the entire situation is that Todd never fully recovered from it... he was always driven to do better than his father, to prove himself a worthy person. It did not serve him well in many areas of his life. Although he made himself a financial success story – a millionaire entrepreneur - he fought the shadow of his verbally abusive father until the day he died: at 47, in his sleep, from a heart attack.

~

After Todd left, my father came to visit... he had retired and moved to Florida. The previous March, coming back from vacation to Detroit, he went to get his car at airport parking, stepped in a big pile of slush, and decided that was it. He was like that. I bought a condominium for him in Stuart and rented it to him. He had developed an atypical melanoma on his back, however – it was not brown or black, so by the time it was biopsied it was large. He had a foot-long section of his back skin removed – ¾" of an inch, in an arrow-shaped form. It was so large that he had grafts taken from his thighs to fill it in. After he recovered from that ordeal, one that required some full-time nursing care, he went for an experimental immunology treatment at Duke University. This was in the late 1980's – it was *really* experimental. However, there was a 60% chance that the melanoma had metastasized, so my dad figured he had little to lose. He came to visit because he wasn't sure he would see us again. He had to have injections while he was staying with us, and they were brutal. He needed a double-barreled syringe, administered in his upper arm. He would develop a big, oozing sore at the site of the injection, which was extremely painful for him. The sheets would become a mess from the oozing sore, and I had to strip the bed pretty much every night. If I touched his arm by mistake he would recoil and wince... it was that bad. One benefit, however, was that Bill didn't dare carry on while my father was with us. That experimental treatment was a success story, my father went back to Florida, and we were back to a four-person family.

I had pretty much reduced contact with the rest of my natal family – I would invite my brother to Thanksgiving dinner every year and buy him a shirt for Christmas – 15-1/2 32: I will never forget that size. He would come about six hours late, so it actually got to the point that I would tell him we were eating at one in the afternoon so he might make it for six. He had become a rather lost soul: he never held a job. He bartered and mooched, but never held a job. Never married. He had an on-again, off-again relationship with a woman named Debbie, but I only met her once. He was in his own little world. My mother was busy repeatedly moving coast to coast trying to find happiness, never realizing that it comes from within. When she was in town I saw her occasionally, but not often. Too dangerous for my well-being: I also don't swim with great whites or keep a pet cobra – there are things one needs to do to stay safe. My sister was in California – she had married a third time, to a man named Dwight Jackson. She had called me just about the time I became pregnant with Kevin to announce that she also was pregnant, and that it was my fault since I had cute little Chris. Her son was born about three months earlier than Kevin. I might have this story wrong, but I believe I was told at the time that she had divorced Dwight, then got pregnant by him, and then remarried. It's a bit difficult to keep her husbands straight. Anyway, Dwight, Tracy and baby Jonathan came to visit for a few days when Jonathan was several months old. They seemed pretty happy at the time. They were still together when I had to fly out to Los Angeles for work – I had been running the dealer discount program, and a Los Angeles dealer had entered into arbitration because he thought GM was shorting him. I was an expert witness – I flew out with a staff attorney named Judy, Kevin in tow. GM prevailed, but that's not the most significant thing about that business trip. My mother was in California at the time, working as a sales person at the Design Center. She had some pretty famous clients, like Kenny Rogers, Placido Domingo and John DeLorean. She had undergone a knee replacement on the knee she had damaged when I was a teenager. She did not take well to therapy, refusing to do the exercises prescribed, and was using a cane. Without the movement required to regain flexibility, her knee had gotten stiff and did not bend enough to allow her to walk up a flight of stairs. We were at Tracy and Dwight's, and my mother had her leg propped on a barstool. I mentioned that since she was having a difficult time with flexion maybe she should simply take advantage of gravity and get her knee to bend while sitting. She said it hurt. She then played ultimate victim, stating that she was a cripple, and that no one wanted to buy furniture from a cripple. Dwight took one look at her, looked at me, muttered that he didn't believe that she had said that to me, and left the room. I looked at her in what was probably a mixture of indignation and disgust, telling her I was the last person in the world to whom she should say that.

Tracy and Dwight did not stay together very long – I got a call when Jonathan was just ten months old. My sister was divorcing Dwight and wanted sole custody. California does not easily entertain sole custody, requiring proof that withstands the scrutiny of the system to deny any parent joint custody. That infuriated my sister: she claimed Dwight was using drugs, to which the court responded, "Prove it." My sister instead left the state with Jonathan, which resulted in a felony parental kidnapping charge being filed against her. She showed up at our doorstep on a Saturday, baby in tow. She wanted me to keep Jonathan while she tried to get out of the mess she was in… she wanted to file for divorce in Michigan. She giggled and mentioned, "like you kept my dog!" To this day I don't know why she ever got the idea she could file in Michigan, since she had not been a resident since she had been seventeen. Anyway, babies develop separation anxiety at that age. I looked at her and said that she and Jonathan could stay, but that she was the only thing familiar to that little boy. I would have to see if I could get him into daycare – unlikely since infant spots needed to be reserved months in advance. That, and I had not asked for time off from work. I told her that Jonathan would be in great distress – she was his only link in this entirely new world. He didn't know me, he didn't know Bill, and he certainly wouldn't know any daycare provider I might be able to arrange. I also told her that if what she said about Dwight was true, all she had to do was go back and prove it. She was a fugitive, for heaven's sake! It wasn't going to get any better with time.

On Sunday Tracy took Jonathan, saying she was going up to Lansing and would be back. Bill and I left the light on for her, but she never returned. This being somewhat of a family crisis, I had spoken to both my mother and father the evening after Tracy had gone. They said she wasn't intending on returning, but that's not what she told us. Little naïve me, contradicting both of them – "No, she said she'd be back."

I have come to believe my sister sees the world through distorted lenses – she interprets things differently than most. I remember when we were little girls, I "saw" a Mt. Vesuvius deep in the pit of her stomach… she had a volcano ready to erupt inside her. Maybe I "saw" that as a way to explain the temper tantrums she threw. Maybe because it was the way she learned to happily lie in order to not cause a scene and then do whatever she wanted to do in the first place, even though time and time again the world proved her judgment poor. Maybe it's the string of decisions she has made that made her life difficult, and her rationalizations. She was too smart for high school. She was too smart for college. She had the ability to convince herself of rather outlandish things, like the time she swore that the owner of the restaurant for which she had recently become a hostess was going to give her an ownership position. Give her, as opposed to allowing her to buy in. Now, what entrepreneur (happily married entrepreneur) would simply give away something like that: give away something like that to a hostess he had fairly recently hired? Of course he wouldn't - of course he didn't.

There were other broad hints along the way, but I never wanted to "go there." I guess I was in denial, or simply so blind – like the time she called me at work, hysterical, screaming over the phone, "How come you survived our horrible childhood?" How she and Jeff would commiserate about how their childhoods were the cause of their separate but equally difficult adult lives. I remember telling her that those years were long gone, and it wasn't the experience haunting them – it was them allowing those memories to continue to inflict damage - that was the problem. She didn't like that. I guess Jeff and Tracy had confronted Mom about that at some point, because I remember my mother commenting that Jeff and Tracy told her they had terrible childhoods. Her comment to me was, "How could they say that? They grew up on a lake!"

My mother was having her own significant issues. The three of us were serially disowned at any perceived slight. It was pretty much, "who's turn is it in the barrel?" It became a farce. One of her friends told me that she threatened to hang herself, and some people with whom she worked told me she was neurotic. She was so very lost, but she was so terrified of confronting the fact that she had some pretty significant emotional issues. She refused to acknowledge the possibility and seek professional help. She was very much a wounded and frightened wild animal, lashing about and charging at everybody and everything in her path.

And speaking of people that needed some professional help, Bill was still so desperately unhappy. He said he hated the house, so I went looking. I didn't even take him with me as I did the ground work. I asked him what he wanted: he wanted a big basement and a big garage. Fine. I went looking for a house with a big basement and a big garage. I found one – a house with a four-and-a-half car, extra deep garage with hot and cold running water, with an outlet for the whole-house vacuum and a furnace. A house with a 3,000 SF basement. Big enough? It was huge: five bedrooms, dual central furnaces, dual central air conditioners, dual water heaters. It was a definite twofer house – lots of two of everything. It had been on the market for over a year because it has some really strange features: for a house that big, two people couldn't be in the kitchen at the same time. The house had started out as this guy's dream home, but he ran out of money. So it had amazing bones, but cheap lauan doors, cheap trim, cheap linoleum flooring in the kitchen abutting amazing ¾" beveled hardwood floors. It also had other design issues: couldn't get to the basement without either going out into the garage or going down rickety, narrow circular stairs that you practically fell into coming in the front door. But it had the basement, it had the garage, and it had over an acre of land. We made a ridiculously low offer – and it was accepted. We were moving to Wabeek.

The odd thing about moving to Wabeek is that we were only about a mile from where I grew up. We were a mile north of the house on Walnut Lake I loved so much. I passed my old bus stops all the time. I never wanted to click my heels three times and go home, but there I was: after the freighter and Florida and Chicago and St. Clair Shores and Oakland Township and the Oakland Hills Country Club; I was back to my old stomping grounds. So maybe now Bill would be happier... it's not like I didn't try. I really did try – I really did try to make it so he would be happy. I responded to his complaints, checking off the requirements he gave me. The problem was I don't think he actually knew why he was so unhappy, so everything I did was for naught. I was asking him one night why he wasn't happy with this huge house. He said it didn't have a gate. A gate? Really? So I started going over all the things he said were wrong with the last house, and everything he said he wanted, and he got very short with me and snapped that he could live in a shack. I looked at him and said, "Well, what is it? Do you want a gated estate or a shack?" He blustered, but it was then I determined with absolute certainty that there was nothing I could do to make him happy. I had done the best I could; it was not the house, it was not me... it was him. I gave up at that moment and decided that I would just carry on being my old cheerful self, happy with my kids... doing my thing, working, mothering - he could join along or go sulk. Whatever. Not my issue any more.

~

He knew. He knew I had given up on him. We just didn't talk about it. I had told myself I would *not* be a divorce statistic... how could I pull this off? Well, I went back to being somewhere else. Gee, I need to go put up wallpaper in the kids' rooms. I need to do the laundry. I stayed so clear of him. I thought I was doing a good job: the children wouldn't hear any arguments because I was somewhere else all of the time. I thought I could pull it off – so that was my home life. And I took days off work to go teach French to the three-year-olds at the daycare center. And I would bring home evaluation vehicles and take Chris on Mommy-Son "dates." One of the cars was a right-hand-drive, lime green gull wing Japanese sports car: when I drove up to daycare the teachers couldn't keep the children inside – they all came streaming out. One day I took a Porsche for the evening, took half a day vacation and took Christopher to see Peter Pan at the Fisher Theater. Another time I took him to see South Pacific: I thought he would like the soldiers. I took him to an upscale restaurant that had a several hundred-gallon fish tank. Todd took him to the zoo... I took the both kids to the zoo. I took Chris to soccer, where, at the tender age of three, he didn't do too very well. He got bored and would watch the butterflies and look for four-leaf clovers. He was defense, and he just couldn't bear waiting for the ball to come down field. And all the while Bill was home sulking. Oh well... this bus keeps a schedule: either get on or get out of the way. After ten years, we had only a shell of a marriage.

~

Bill's older brother Jack died unexpectedly in 1991. His schedule was to get up before Carol, go make a pot of coffee, leave a couple of coffee cups out on the counter, and spend some time on the treadmill before work. He was following that routine on September 9 – when Carol came downstairs she saw the coffee cups, but no Jack. She found him slumped over the treadmill – he had had a massive heart attack. We were all shocked: he was only 48. We enlisted the help of Virginia Trabold to babysit, and Bill and I went to Virginia.

The first man to show up at the wake was the head of the NSA. I have never felt a power aura around anyone like I did that man. I remember him saying that he would make sure his "people" showed their proper respects. The service was held in a chapel right outside Arlington, where Jack is laid to rest. I was hastily recruited as a soloist – I sang the Malotte "Our Father" – a very dramatic piece. It rises at the end to a very strong finish, and at the very, very end, just a few notes from the finish, I started to cry. Bill rushed up the aisle, and afterwards people said they didn't know I was the sister-in-law. I was very startled at Bill's actions – it really felt that he was trying to protect me. Maybe I never gave him enough opportunity to do that.

Jack had a full military honors funeral… Carol was grief-stricken, but always the perfectly poised and collected lady around others. Laura was young still – a teenager. She adored Jack. His death hit her hard.

I was not happy doing the typical Financial Staff rotation: I actually hate the idea that once you accept a position, agreeing to the specific position and requirements, all of a sudden you became owned property, shuttled around at the whim of a faceless Corporation. And that's how it felt. So one afternoon, unusually, I had brought lunch from home because I had some errand to run at lunchtime. That hardly ever happened. And as luck would have it, there across from the refrigerator was a job posting for the Strategy Department. GM had entered into a consent agreement with the government to end a discrimination probe, and as a part of that all jobs above a certain level needed to be posted. I knew a guy in Strategy – worked with him on some previous analysis. Bob Clark. I called him when I got back from my errand, and he said fill out the paperwork, but the job is yours. I crossed the T's and dotted the I's and filled out all of the paperwork... and felt really bad for an earnest man named Tony that was putting in so much effort with his paperwork. He very animatedly told me how he was going to do his very best to land that job. I couldn't tell him that it was for naught; that I was a shoe-in.

I can do numbers, but I absolutely adore strategy. I like big, complex, intricate puzzles... I like finding answers that fit a myriad of constraints. That department was a bit of an anomaly: there were two sections, the analysts that were responsible for the various divisions' business plans, and then the rest of us – the ones that did the free-form thinking. GM did not understand the true purpose of business plans. General Electric did: Jack Welch did. Jack's view was that a strategy set a strong direction, but not the path that would get you there. He understood that there were inevitable unknowns along the way that may help or hinder progress. To him, as long as everyone had a clear understanding of the direction, they could assess opportunities against that and decide whether to accept or reject. It's rather like telling a bunch of people that we are heading North West. As long as you know you need to head North West, you can walk along the river if you need the water or head through the forest if you need wood – as long as you head North West. GM's idea of a business plan was a very thick tome for each division, each filled with detailed forecasts and projections and other minutia. Hundreds of pages each. These plans were never integrated into one overall strategy, and they were never referenced as time went by to see how well they were working. No – they were locked up in a room within an area that itself was locked, within an area itself again locked…. I needed to go through five locked doors to get to my desk. And the business plans were behind locked door #6. The analysts responsible for reviewing these plans became more schoolmarms that anything else, critiquing the plans for all the wrong markers.

Then there were the rest of us. There was Jim Powers - James Powers, Ph.D., the one that had worked on the Manhattan Project. When he got bored, he got a degree in Theology. Then he learned Chinese. Then Japanese. That man had grey matter oozing from behind his ears. Man, was he brilliant. Then there was Tom Crumm – a brilliant, if eccentric, engineer. He kept on coming up with ways to improve production via innovative plant layouts, using individual robot carriers for a chassis instead of one car/one plant assembly lines and plug-and-play dies that would slip into frames, so a plant needn't be shut down for weeks to retool for a different car – in fact, any plant could simultaneously build pretty much any car using some of Tom's ideas, since there were no longer assembly lines and dedicated stamping dies, but various assembly stations that allowed for great flexibility. Plant shutdowns for retooling could have become a thing of the past. There was Doug Marshall, who also held a Ph.D…. really have no idea how his background of being a University of Michigan History professor and a nominee for a Pulitzer Prize was cogent to our merry little band. It was a very stimulating group of people.

I made a significant personal discovery one day in the coffee room – one that became a hallmark to me. We were simply chatting, and Jim finished my sentence for me. And then he did it again. I kind of launched on him, and afterwards wondered why I had over-reacted. I came to the conclusion that I was reacting as if my thoughts and feelings were unimportant: like when I was a child. My startling ah-ha moment was that it wasn't Jim Powers' job to understand my history: it is my job to try and make sure whatever I have been through doesn't get in my way. To this day I strive to follow that principle.

It was in that stimulating environment that I made what I consider to be one of my most significant contributions. It was Bob's idea: why don't I look at GM's financial position six years out? The New York Treasurer's Staff never forecast past five years, but in year six two significant things were going to happen: The Financial Accounting Standards Board (FASB) had mandated that starting in year six, corporate balance sheets would have to book unfunded health care liabilities. That was going to send GM into an overall deficit position. The second important item was that GMAC had a huge amount of debt coming due. At this point in time, GMAC was barred from the commercial paper market over financial concerns. Refinancing that coming-due debt was going to be very difficult to manage.

So I took it on. However, I took a little different tack: what would EPS need to be, right now, to be able to manage those two events? To not head into negative equity territory, and to be able to retire the debt coming due? I used very, very favorable assumptions: that GM could forecast the same sales volume from a $43 billion capital plan using only $34 billion. That productivity would improve at a 0.5% rate each year. Even at that, GM would have needed $11 EPS in 1992 to hit the mark. I can't remember what EPS was at the time, precisely, but it was a small fraction of that. I remember giving the analysis to Ron Pirtle, the then-Director. He said it couldn't be – I answered that it was only math:

change any of the assumptions and I will re-run the numbers. He took it without changing any assumptions. Not too long after the Vice President of Finance, Leon Crain, came down to the department to announce we were being dissolved. Rumor had it the New York office was furious with what I had done – they were caught with their pants down. So much for all of those Harvard MBA's. The solution wasn't to face the issue together: the solution was to shoot the messenger.

That was not the first time our little merry band had developed logically rock-solid analyses for the betterment of the corporation. But that was exactly the problem: we were rock-solid logical folk… we were Spock's in the face of a whole shipload of emotional beings. I remember once, when Hughes, a wholly-owned division, sold a satellite communications system to Chrysler and its entire dealer network. The CEO was furious that we would be selling to our competitors first. So I was the analyst on that team… the problem was EDS, another wholly-owned subsidiary. EDS was telling us that we couldn't buy that from Hughes. What? Is this a child telling a parent what to fix for supper? It was a perfect marriage: Hughes wanted to sell and install a turn-key system: EDS wanted maintenance contracts. So what was the problem? I ended up in the Vice Chair's office one afternoon, trying to persuade him ever-so-nicely to get his unruly children in line. Really: both firms were 100% owned by GM. If GM wanted to buy a system from Hughes and give the maintenance contract to EDS, it should jolly well be able to do that. Say the word! The Vice Chair's response was that he couldn't do that because "he had to eat lunch with these guys every day."

I remember another time, when we had worked feverishly to analyze the relative positions of all of the various GM divisions and subsidiaries on the famed four-square quadrant so beloved by consultants. We charted the growth and revenue potential of each entity, using circle size to denote the amount of capital we were intending to invest in each. The chart conclusively – extraordinarily, exaggeratedly – revealed that we were intending on pouring the vast majority of available capital into the poorest performing, most slowly growing and most highly competitive sector. We had presented it to the Executive Committee just days before Robert Stempel was in New York trying to get the analysts to not trash the stock too badly. He called us up from the analyst's meeting – he was using the chart to describe how we were looking at future strategy. It was for naught – the executives never intended to use that analysis as a roadmap. I remember asking why – nobody could quarrel with the facts underlying the graphic. I was told it was because the executives could not imagine anything else – that they had oil in their veins. They could not imagine being a General Electric… a company that pursued its strategy of diversification using a simple benchmark: if GE could not be #1 or #2 in an industry, it would not be in that industry. GE had no problem envisioning a GE that was no longer light bulbs and small appliances. GE became a financial powerhouse, a builder of turbine engines…. It became so much more; so different than its beginnings. GM just did not have that level of brazen and bold imagination.

When Leon Krain told us the department was being dissolved he singled me out, saying that the Treasurer, Heidi Kunz, wanted to speak to me. Leon is South African by birth, and it must have been his delivery; everyone thought I was the only one that needed to look for another job. I was a bit panic-stricken. It wasn't until two years later, when I was teaching a class attended by the GM HR person with Leon, that I learned that, of the entire crew, I was the only one they *knew* they had a place for. I just didn't stick around long enough to take them up on it.

Oh: and about that analysis that ended up dissolving the department? It did go into the famous "Black Hole of Calcutta"... that place where all things uncomfortable go when no one can dispute the math but no one wants to face the ugly truth. I know it was read and taken to heart by at least one person, however: years later, when I was reading an article in the Wall Street Journal, Rick Waggoner was quoted saying something that told me he either thought just I like do, or spoke just like I do, or had read my analysis and remembered it. My kind of thinking was novel in the hide-bound culture of GM, and what he said focused exactly on the analytic basis of the spreadsheet I had prepared. I read that sentence over and over again, feeling remarkably amazed that my work had perhaps stuck in the mind of the man who was to be GM President. And then I watched as GM proceeded to sell every valuable asset it had to try and float that heavy, impossible anchor... as if it was a desperate gambler that kept on doubling down after a string of losses dug too deep. It came as no surprise to me that GM eventually declared bankruptcy. I wish I had been wrong.

~

1992 was a year of turmoil at GM: it also was a year of turmoil on the home front. I learned that my strategy of always being in a different room was not working on Mother's Day. As we were driving to dinner that night, Chris piped up from the back seat, "Mommy, Daddy doesn't like you very much, does he?" Surprised, I asked him why he said that. Chris replied, "Because he is always yelling at you." I told Chris he should ask his father, which he did. Bill replied, "She's not bad for a girl." Chris smiled and said, "I told you so." So much for my strategy.

Shortly thereafter something happened: I cannot remember what it was, except that Bill was not participating in something festive – maybe decorating for some holiday? Anyway, I became so totally frustrated with his pouty, passive-aggressive behavior

227

that I took his clothes and threw them into the basement, angrily telling him I had had enough, and that we needed to go to marriage counseling. Chris was crying, telling me that it would be alright. I felt terrible – a five-year-old should not be trying to protect an adult.

So off we went to marriage counseling. To Dr. Campbell. He was a calm man. He spoke to us separately and spoke to us together. I remember him telling me that he couldn't decide whether my strongest trait was intelligence or determination. He thought that we should reconnect: he gave us homework. We were to do little thoughtful things for one another. Little things, like maybe leaving the garage door open for the second one to get home. Just little, thoughtful things. I did my best. Bill's version was to say things like, "Gee boys, Mommy smells good tonight!" in a way that intimated that the opposite was the norm. He was snide and nasty and so very passive-aggressive. When we returned to counseling, Bill admitted that I was good at the assignment, and that he wasn't. I remember the therapist asking Bill to take notice of how I smiled and was happy while describing the little things I had done for Bill – how it pleased me. The doctor asked me what it would take to get Bill back upstairs. Can't remember what I told him, exactly, but I know that all I wanted was to be treated like a valued and loved wife. There were measurable criteria set, can't remember what, but Bill did meet them. So we were back at the therapist's, and I said the criteria had been met, to which Bill replied that he wasn't sure he wanted to come back upstairs. I think it must have been the way he said it: I clearly remember the therapist telling Bill he felt like knocking his block off. That was his exact phrase. Anyway, on to other things… was there anything else we could talk about? Was there anything else I might like? I mentioned that after thirteen years I would like a vacation where I didn't have to boil water or clean his father's house. One where I could actually relax. Thirteen years of Florida and fishing, with one trip out to California and one RV trip out east. I didn't think I was asking for much. Guess I was wrong.

On the way home Bill was screaming at me – screaming so long and so loudly that by the time we pulled into the driveway, he had actually lost his voice. "What do you mean, you don't want to go to my dad's? He won't be around forever." I replied that he should go then – take the boys too, if he liked. He then screamed, "And I bet you think I should pay for it, too?" Twenty-five minutes of shrieking rage. We got into the house and I said I was done. We were over. That was it.

~

We went back for one last session with Dr. Campbell to inform him of my decision to call the whole thing off, and then we had to start planning for separate lives. Bill threatened this and threatened that: he would sue for custody. I told him he had every right to do that, but he should know that I was prepared to spend tens of thousands of dollars to fight for the boys. I knew I would win: I think he knew I would win, too. All I had to do was get him on the stand and try to answer questions like, "Who is the children's pediatrician?" "Who are their teachers?" "What size shoes do they wear?" He would have fallen flat on his face, and I think he knew it. He did not ask for custody. I actually sat down and drew up a strawman settlement: he would get everything he had purchased (his account), his retirement, his savings account and his pro rata percentage of every joint asset – house included. I think he knew that he would never be able to do better than that, and throwing money at lawyers would simply make the pie that much smaller. He would move out after the house was sold and closed, so I could pay him his portion of the house equity. He accepted, and we got an offer on the house quickly: a doctor that lived in the subdivision that liked our house better. Bill found a house in West Bloomfield, and I found a condo on the north side of Gilbert Lake. Things were humming, and then the house sale fell through – the doctor could not get approved for a mortgage. I spoke to our mortgage broker, and because interest rates had fallen, I was able to refinance the house with little increase in monthly payment, pay Bill off and keep the house. All of that happened approximately one month before Leon Krain paid our department that fateful visit. No wonder I didn't stick around to wait for Heidi Kunz' call.

SINGLE PARENT

It wasn't just me that took Leon's words to mean I needed to go look for a job – it was everyone. One of the guys, Jim McBride, set me up for an interview with a friend of his – Chris Bridgeman – who ran a consulting arm under the aegis of EDS: Manufacturing Consulting Services. I went for an interview and got the job. It happened so quickly that I didn't have a car to get there, since I was losing my PEP car privileges. GM allowed me to tag a PEP car in service: a Bonneville that was being driven by a friend of mine, Tom Drumgoole. I called him up and asked him to pile on the miles, but in the meantime GM lent me a Cadillac. Just like that, fourteen years to the day I started at GM, I left to become a consultant.

Consulting was perfect. I loved the work – loved figuring out answers to problems. I did so many different things: I helped develop coursework for Benchmarking and taught the class – that's the class that GM HR person took. She was very surprised to see me there. I designed an engagement that was focused on change management, getting the client group to understand their differences and their strengths, and how those personalities merged to create a working environment specific to the particular group participants... I probably could have done more with that work. I based it upon the observation that people reveal certain parts of their personalities based upon the company they are in: with some people I am funny, with others I am quiet – what I become is in part a function of how I perceive I am being received. In a work group, then, there is a distinct group personality that is tailored by everyone's similar perceptions. Understand that and the work group has tools to work more effectively together. There was a great guy, John Meier, who had a strong Columbia

University math background. He really was impressed with the results.

It was an eclectic group: Charnell Havens, strong insights; David Townsend, deep process thinker; Maria DeKeyser, the hardest worker I think I have ever met; Marianne Sekora, the uber-efficient admin that kept everything together. All led by Chris Bridgeman, who is one of the most decent and honorable human beings I have ever met. Great, great guy. Wonderful manager. The kind of leader you would fall on a sword for. The offices were not downtown – they were in Southfield. So not only was the job great, the commute was much shorter.

My life was work and kids: Bill would not take our sons for any weekends or vacations – not for the first two years. Wednesday night dinners only. I believe he did that to spite me – to make it so I had no weekends free for my personal social life. Besides thinking what a silly, petty thing to do, I didn't mind. However, it became apparent that the schedule was disruptive to the boys: I was told that they misbehaved terribly on Thursdays. I finally told Bill that he could either see the boys more often, so he was not a once-a-week dinner novelty, or he could see them not at all. Take your pick. He said he would do every-other weekend, but then he added, "but no Wednesdays!" Sigh. Whatever.

I had become very dissatisfied with the kitchen, so I contracted with a friend's husband and his father to remodel it. The original layout had a wall between the kitchen and the informal eating area, but was half open to the formal dining room. From the formal dining room what was visible was the kitchen sink. Nothing like having a sink full of dinner preparation pots and pans visible from the formal dining room. That, and the cabinets were cheap laminate – with a chocolate brown laminate countertop. And vinyl flooring. Very dark, very dated, and very unappealing. So it all got ripped out: ivory pantries were installed between the kitchen and formal dining room, and the wall between the kitchen and the breakfast nook was removed. I put in an island with the sink facing the slider so I could look out to the backyard while working at the sink. I lightened up everything: ivory cabinets with rounded doors on the corners, ceramic tile for the floor and Corian counters. It was a long process, and I had to wash the dishes in the powder room sink. It was difficult to deal with that and the dust and the youngsters, but I was determined. In late August the floor was in, the cabinets were installed and the island was half done... the plumbing was not in. And right at that point, on August 23rd, I saw Mike Glynn, a VP, and Chris Bridgeman heading to my office. They had very worried looks on their faces: my hysterical mother had ended up on the phone with them, she not having my work number. My brother had been killed in a car accident, and I was the only one within thousands of miles.

I remember sobbing as I started to leave. Mike and Chris would not let me be alone: they assigned Marianne Sekora to be by my side until family arrived. Marianne went with me to the funeral parlor to make arrangements. She was a God-send: I had no experience in such matters. Work gave me a car for the family that was arriving – even picked them up at the airport, if I remember correctly. Work paid for the food for the wake; work had the food brought to my house and set out on a piece of plywood that the contractors brought over. Those contractors hastily connected the kitchen sink water – and then the drain pipe, forgetting it was also disconnected, after I had filled one of their tool boxes with water as it sat under the sink. My employer was amazing – and it didn't stop there.

My mom, dad and sister arrived. After twenty years of feuding and silliness, my parents were so shocked that they actually stopped their feuding, right then and there. At the time of his death, my brother had been in the "disowned" penalty box... no matter. My mother had lost her one and only son. I remember thinking that she never showed any internal consistency: I had a copy of the hand-written latest-edition will in my office – when you love someone, you don't go off disowning them on a whim. Not if you are a reasoned, mature adult. I had learned that he was disowned this time because my mother had visited him and had berated him mightily for the way he was living, saying she would scrub toilets before she lived like that. They got into a fight: she fell and broke her arm. She said he pushed her: he had said she fell. Either scenario was plausible.

So everyone showed up. I found places for everyone to sleep. I was so wound up I couldn't sleep: I got up at 2 AM and cleaned while everyone else slept and went back to bed for a while several hours later. When I got up, my sister was on the phone in the office. I walked into the family room to find my mother on the sofa, gray-faced and clutching her chest – she was having a hard time breathing and said her chest hurt. OMG, I thought – she's having a heart attack. I went into the office and asked my sister to get off the phone so I could call 911. The ambulance and fire truck roared up not long after. By then my sister had disappeared with the car: I called work and two people came out: Marianne, to take me to the hospital, and Norm, who took the boys to daycare. I didn't know where my sister had gone, but she was gone the entire day. Turns out my mother did not have a heart attack – she had extreme angina. She was discharged from the hospital on the 25th, in time to be in attendance for the viewing. We had a half-open casket... the undertaker had pieced my brother together remarkably well, being that (as I found out later) he had been decapitated and was missing a couple of limbs. He had been motoring along on a little Vespa scooter on a country road in mid-Michigan one evening, going over to a friend's house to mooch some dinner. A teenager, two months into his license, had decided to open up his full-sized

Oldsmobile on that country road that evening. By the time he hit my brother he was going well over 100 MPH. My brother went through the front windshield and out the back window – he never knew what hit him. I remember that evening of the 22nd: I remember the weather was perfectly glorious. I remember standing on the back deck and thinking what a lovely, peaceful night it was.

After the service we had brunch at my house. I saw people from MSU: Ted Strunk was there. He asked if I was "going tomorrow." I had no idea what he meant by that. None at all. I had been very busy – pretty much everyone from my work showed up to show their respects and to support me. I remember Chris Bridgeman remarking about how electric my family was… he couldn't believe I grew up around that all of that energy. I heard that my sister was rude to people who were there for me. I was just so eternally grateful for the support work was showing me… much more support than I was getting from my family.

After it was all finished, my brother cremated and laid to rest with my maternal grandparents at White Chapel, it was only my parents, my sister and me… the boys were asleep. I was cleaning up while the three of them were sitting at the kitchen table. I was exhausted, but there I was, doing my usual Cinderella role, while they were conversing; totally oblivious to the work I was doing and to the work that remained to be done, never offering to help. And then I heard my sister start talking about a little roadside remembrance she had arranged for the next day – where Jeff had been killed. That's where she had been that day when she took off before my mother was even taken to the hospital. And then I lost it. I don't lose it often: I lost it when my brother would not stop picking on me once when we were children; he couldn't hold onto me, even though he was a boy and was nearly two years older. I was a veritable tornado. There was the time when my boss at

Centel called in to the office to ask me to cover for him to his wife: he had been on a bender and hadn't made it home. There was the time that I found out John Vacketta had lied to me about a raise the Treasurer's Staff had proposed for me that he talked down to less, all the while preening himself to me about how he stood up for me. That episode - right out of a movie. When I found out, I stormed right past his admin as she was telling me I couldn't go into his office. Flew right by her and marched right up one side of John Vacketta and down the other. How dare he so bald-faced lie. The level of energy I can exude literally blows people away, and I can become such a force that I almost intimidate myself.

So there I was, washing dishes as the King, Queen and Princess took no note, discussing an event of which I was not as much as informed. So I threw down the dish cloth – threw it right down on the counter. "Is that what Ted Strunk was asking me about?" "Yes." "And you didn't think to even mention it to me?" Oh, I was becoming more and more furious. My sister turned to me and snarled, "You aren't invited." An incredulous me replied, "What??" She then let loose. "You aren't invited. I hate you!! I will never see you again. I wouldn't even visit your grave except to spit on it." Oh man. I lost it. I was yelling. They had never heard me yell – I realized that afterwards. Never. I had always kept everything in, never taking the bait. Not now. Not tonight. My father was dumbstruck. Can't remember him uttering a single word. My mother got up and came over to whisper, "I'll call you tomorrow." I yelled at her, too: "What, you have to whisper? I'm not good enough?" My sister was yelling that they were leaving, and I was yelling that, "You are the one choosing to leave. I am not kicking you out – which is probably the story you would tell if mom and dad weren't here to see it." What a row. Oh man. All I could think of is Cinderella no more. For all I have done, this is not how I deserve to be treated. No more. Never again.

Sometime after that, my mother found a letter from me in Jeff's belongings – it was a letter concerning getting together in Chicago for that one Christmas. It was all happy and bubbly – she handed it to me, saying in a surprised tone, "It wasn't you, was it?" I answered, "It never was"… who knows what tales were told that lead my mother to believe that I was the one deserving the hate of my sister. I thought deeply about what had transpired: I came to the conclusion that I did not know my sister; and furthermore, it was clear she had no idea who I was. Her operating assumptions were far from reality. I decided that with the emotional and physical distance between us, it would take a Herculean effort to mend the situation. So I decided to let it be: she would never know me as I am, and I would never know the woman she had become. The one difference between us is that I realized we were veritable strangers: she thought she knew me. And as I thought about the events surrounding my brother's death, I kept going back to Chris Bridgeman's comment about the energy he sensed in my family – and then something I had done years before made some sense. I had been given a challenge at work: by just listening to a person's recorded statements, I was asked to identify the emotion they were feeling. Interesting – no reliance on body language. I got everything right except anger. I have a hard time recognizing anger. With Chris' insight it all made sense: my definition of anger was based on my family. Anger was defined as hammers flying across the room. Anger was shelves of stuff smashed to the floor. Anger was sinking a belt hook into an arm. What other people recognized as anger was, in my book, merely slight irritation. I still have problems recognizing anger, but at least I now know it's a weakness of mine.

And all of this happened in August. We buried my brother on my late daughter's birthday. The fight happened on my late daughter's birthday. Even Todd died in August – and we buried him on the day my brother died. I told you I hate the month of August.

~

How much can a person withstand in one day? I imagined myself standing on a beach, alone, in a typhoon. The sea salt mixed with the salt and sand-blasted my skin as I stood facing the ocean. Palm trees were collapsing on both sides of me, but there I stood, facing the storm, my dress being close to blown off in the maelstrom. Standing. I kept standing – I never turned away, and I never fell down.

My family left to go back out West, and then the calls from my mother started coming. Frequently. She was obsessed with the thought that the young driver needed to be punished. She insisted I go to every court hearing of his. She wanted me to get that driver's parents to write her a letter of apology. I told her I wouldn't take that on – I did attend every hearing, however, and dutifully reported back the happenings. I went more because I thought my brother should have someone there on his behalf – he shouldn't be alone.

My mother was very unhappy with the outcome: the young man was sentenced to several weekends in jail, a ton of community service, and a requirement that he had to go to the local high schools and get up on stage to tell everyone what he had done, and how it had affected him. He was only seventeen – he was a high school jock with no history of problems. He would have to live with what he did for the rest of his life – getting up and recounting his tale in front of his peers must have been so very painful for him. I felt sorry for the lad, but it was not enough punishment for my mother.

My time in Manufacturing Consulting Services was fairly short-lived: EDS, the parent company, had purchased the A. T. Kearney Management Consulting firm, and we were transferred to it. That was quite a culture shock. ATK had been a private firm, led and owned by the partners – organized like a law firm. Different practices, different policies, different benefit plans... and once-a-month pay. That first month going from bi-monthly to monthly was painful.

ATK had a policy that they only hired MBA's, and they only hired from four B-schools: Harvard, Michigan, Chicago and (I think) Stanford. MCS had manufacturing experts and engineers besides those of us on the more strategic side. It was a bad fit. The partners got together and went through everyone's credentials, accepting only those that met their prior criteria... all except for one Jeff Tucek, who had a lock on a manufacturing dies specialty and was extremely sought after. They kept him because of the money he could bring in. Most of the existing MCS personnel didn't make the cut: not Maria, not Charnell, not Marianne. John Meier did, as did David Townsend and Chris Bridgeman. And me. David left shortly to head out on his own.

We were moved to lofty offices on the 22nd floor of one of the Southfield office towers, joining the existing ATK Automotive Practice.

The raft of young MBA's regarded us with some suspicion and melding the two groups together took some time. My first Kearney engagement was led by a woman who lived in New York. She patiently explained the Kearney Way of developing, and then, testing hypotheses. The thinking was second-nature logical, but there were forms and ways of presenting the data that I needed to learn. I remember that I wrapped up draft #1 on New Year's Eve and sent it, late at night. The boys were asleep and I had nothing better to do. She was concerned about how I spent my NYE. I did well enough, though, and was 100% billable for the entire time I was there. That was key: billable hours were almost the entire end-all and be-all. My second engagement was at GM Research: GM had pulled together a global team to develop four likely scenarios of global trends: my job was to take each of those scenarios and take them out thirty years. This one I did from home... this one was solid research and internally consistent thinking. I loved that engagement – right up my alley. Very complex, many constraints... perfect. It took me four months – my bibliography was hundreds of entries long. I researched economic conditions in all of the major countries. I researched industry trends. I simply dove into it. Something happens to me when I get involved in such endeavors: I think I cross the synapses between my right and left hemispheres and go into that co-processor I have. When I put work down and try to come back to it, at first it seems very foreign: it takes me a while to get back in the zone. And so it was for this engagement. It was almost as if I was walking the streets of these forward scenarios and observing what was around me. A couple of things happened as a result of this engagement: first of all, I got the attention of all of the GM experts that had worked on the project by pointing out an inconsistency within one of their scenarios, and correcting it with an internally consistent alternative assumption. That got their attention. Then I took out each of the scenarios thirty years, backed up by the research I had conducted. The head of the Automotive Practice, Bram Bluestein, called the consulting "brilliant." A cadre of GM Ph.D.'s asked Kearney if I could be made available so they could study the way I think, because they had never seen anyone think like I do and they were fascinated by it. Kearney answered "No," but that piece of work made the partners at ATK stand up and take notice.

I was assigned a mentor – a senior partner named Al Morrison. He was a very nice man. He lived in Ohio – Bram lived in Chicago – it doesn't matter where consultants live. They fly to work every week. Al's favorite view of consultants was that they come in two flavors: those who work to live and those who live to work. ATK favored those who live to work. We went out to dinner one night, to the now-closed Fox and Hounds restaurant, where Al told me he had always been a live to work kind of guy. His wife raised their family, a single parent all week long, every week. He told me with some significant remorse that he had a son that was having some issues at home – Al told me he kicked his son out of the house over the phone. Al knew I was a parent of youngsters, and he also knew that I was not interested in jetting all over the world for work. There were consultants that would go to great lengths to earn bragging rights for the most miles flown in a year. I think the minimum was 250,000 miles. I was on one engagement with a team that included a man who lived in Paris: it was Christmastime, and the engagement had taken part of the team - his part of the team - to Mexico City. He booked a round-the-world trip to get back home for the holidays. Why not? All of these engagements were hourly plus expenses. I was getting billed at $300 an hour plus expenses. ATK was making a bundle off of me. I didn't mind much – I totally, totally loved the job.

I had some wonderful engagements, mostly around process design. One was to help GM Customs and Tax: the government was auditing GM. There is an arcane rule about shipping used manufacturing equipment to an overseas plant for use in production, some of which would end up back stateside. GM would ship totally depreciated manufacturing equipment – large stamping presses, for instance – to China for GM China's use. Customs says that if you move a piece of equipment overseas at no charge, you have to estimate how many pieces that piece of equipment will make over its remaining life, estimate how much of that production will be coming back to the States, and pay a tariff on the proportionate value-add from that free piece of equipment. It's an accounting nightmare. However, GM had not kept track of what got no-charge-shipped, and as a result they had an entire team trying to figure out how much GM owed in tariffs. Our job was to understand how that happened and design something so it wouldn't happen again. We had a twelve-foot whiteboard in an office, and we mapped out the process GM had for getting a piece of equipment to China, step by step. It was fairly long and arduous, but when it was documented, I stood back and told the lead consultant, "I know what the problem is, and I know how to fix it." She looked at me a bit surprised as I continued, "The problem is they are trying to fix it after the fact." Way at the beginning of the process, right when the plant engineer was marking a piece of equipment for export, he filled out a pink "No Charge Shipper." There was a little box on that small pink slip that, when checked, indicated that the equipment was leaving the United States. I knew all about No Charge Shippers from my GM plant days. That little box was being totally ignored, since it did not help the guy in the plant with his job. Mark that box and the problem is solved... an easy and accurate paper trail is established. The person that owned the required information could enter it once, and presto-chango, problem solved. More than half of the subsequent existing steps could have been eliminated with that one, simple step. When the lead consultant was explaining that to the tax attorney liaison, she actually used the phrase, "fix it after the fact." It was the perfect, logical solution... however, the GM attorney was very reluctant to inform the guy over the plant engineers that his assistance was requested. Have to eat lunch with these guys, you know. That attorney wanted some answer that he could totally control, and he didn't trust the plant engineers. But for twenty-two million dollars I think I would have made the effort to explain just how much money the corporation could save with one little nano-second of a check mark. I have come to the conclusion that most of the world's process messes could be fixed by following two basic precepts: data has a natural owner, and data should only be entered once. Use those two precepts when designing a process, and it is very likely the resulting process will be the most efficient and error-proof process available.

~

When the dust settled at ATK and the team that would be staying on was firmed up and integrated, ATK addressed salary structure. And those of us that made the jump were given massive raises – compared to the top-notch MBA-schooled individuals Kearney had hired, we had been significantly underpaid. I was now flying high.

~

That was all well and good, but Chris was starting to cause his teachers fits. Absolute fits. I guess I had better luck with him, so while I believed the teachers, I couldn't imagine it - didn't see as much of that at home. One day, when he was in first grade, I got to school about 20 minutes before class was supposed to end and stood at the door silently, watching the class. There was one little girl assiduously cleaning off the desktops, the rest of the children were sitting on the floor cross-legged as the student teacher was reading a story... and there was my son, doing handstands off the desks over by the window. Ms. Gallup – that was her name, the red-headed Ms. Gallup – politely asked Chris whether he was going to come over and listen to the story or continue what he was doing. Silly teacher. You never give my son an option unless you mean it to be a real option. Of course, given the choice, he chirped, "Keep on!" I stepped into the doorway and said four words, "Chris, go sit down." He stopped, frozen, turned and looked at me, and silently went over and sat down. And there he stayed, legs crossed, for the rest of the story. Ms. Gallup came up to me later and said, "That was amazing." It was then I could say, and she would understand, that I simply did not see the same behaviors the teachers did.

Chris' behavior did not get any better. He hated behavior modification techniques, because he knew what they were and he was not interested in playing the teachers' game. The school said he was ADD. I took him for my own diagnosis, which came back borderline. However, I had been influenced greatly by my uncle Gene, his son Tom and daughter-in-law Jannie. Educators – incredible, inspired, electric educators. I believed educators were rock-solid, like the three in my family. So Chris was started on Adderall. He hated it. He told me it didn't do anything, and he proved it to me one day. He would get green stickers or red stickers, depending on his behavior – one in the morning and one in the afternoon. He faked his morning medicine and got a green, took his afternoon medicine and got a red. "See? I told you." There was only one teacher that inspired him to achieve – one that he went back to visit even after he left elementary school. Both my sons had Mrs. Semanas and loved her.

Chris got more and more difficult. He got kicked out of every summer program I had him in: KinderCare. Beverly Hills Racquet Club. Pontiac Yacht Club. By the time he was ten, he was taller than I was – and he didn't want to go to school one day. He pinned me to the ground. I called the school and told them what happened, and they sent two people to fetch him. That little event got him put into a two-week day-program stint at a mental health facility. They said Chris had Oppositional Defiant Disorder. Then the school changed his diagnosis to Emotional Disorder. His medication dosage kept getting higher and higher until it was giving him Tourette's tics. I found out that he was taking his lunch money to buy candy and give it to other kids in order to make friends. That totally broke my heart.

The school called me in one day to tell me that I should stay out of my son's education, because I would call his teachers every

Thursday and ask if Chris' assignments were done. If not, he was grounded until the following Thursday. I kept that up for months. The principal, Ed Bretzlaff, told me that come Thursday, Chris would start getting upset, knowing he was going to be grounded again. I retorted, "Well, that's great! I would be really worried if he was happy about that." The principal's response was that they would keep him after school for 45 minutes every day. I asked whether he would be required to complete his work. I got no response, and when I pressed the issue, I still got no response. That principal was not interested in my son learning what was required: the 45-minute drill would only be window dressing. Oh man – I learned that they would pass him if he answered just every other question or math problem. That they would not make him write essay answers, turning everything into multiple choice for him. I was livid. How was he ever going to make it in the world with that kind of education? I said that was not going to happen anymore – if he needed to take his tests in a quiet room alone, fine. If it took him extra time, fine. The school would NOT hold him to lesser standards. That's like allowing a man to drive without glasses just because he was myopic. No, the requirement is glasses, because you have to see to drive well. You need something to help, fine – but that does not relieve you of basic responsibility. I told the school social worker that she was banned from talking to my son, since she was making him feel that he was permanently disabled. The very nerve!!! And I took him off the meds. I had mistakenly thought that these people were better equipped to creatively meet students where they could best learn, but obviously they were only trying to make their jobs easier. The school district responded by moving Chris to the Max Program for Emotionally Disabled (ED) students in Hazel Park. I didn't know any better at the time, so I didn't fight it. He was there for eighteen months.

I remember the moment it all changed. It was Christmas break, and Chris was standing at the kitchen counter while I was at the sink. He looked at me and said, "I am not learning anything at the Max Program – I want to go back to normal school." I said I would make that happen, but I told him that he was behind in his studies. Did he want to move laterally, into the proper grade but need extra assistance, or did he want to fall back a year and be "normal?" He wanted to fall back a year. "Fine." So come the 2nd of January I called Hills Middle School and asked to enroll Chris. He needed to switch schools to pull this off – no more West Hills. I was refused. I called somebody at the Max Program and told them Chris would not be coming back. I then went to the middle school and asked the principal for a set of books that Chris could start using until I got everything settled. He refused, but he did sign a piece of paper I had brought with me indicating that I requested the books and was refused. Now we were officially civilly disobedient, and I was probably officially a negligent parent.

There's a county-wide school administration organization that is involved in all of the individual school districts in the County, and I called there to get my son back in school. I was flatly turned down – flatly turned down until I said, "I want an administrative hearing." Those are magical words. The haughty intermediate school district person went from a haughty, "No way!" to a frantic, "Oh no!" I had her. I knew I had her when she next said, "Do you know how much work that is for us?" They went from a "No way" to a FedEx, Saturday-delivered plea for me to withdraw my demand. I would not cave, and the next thing I knew, we were in a meeting room with fifteen against three: Bill, Chris and me. I pulled out all of my consulting stops and passed out a PowerPoint presentation to all of those clowns – all of those clowns who are so eager to put people into neat little boxes. My argument started with a definition of disability… I got them to agree that Emotional Disorder was pervasive and permanent… as was ADD. And then I asked them which was it? Was he ED? Was he ADD? How did the diagnosis change, who was the expert that gave the diagnosis, and which was it? They were dumfounded. Then they started with how bad it was to hold a child back, to which Chris answered it was his desire. I rolled over those "educators" in a verbal Sherman tank, and I did it purposefully and shamelessly. And guess who won. Chris started at Hills Middle School shortly thereafter. The rest of his life was at stake, and I would just not have it any other way. Period. He says now that I probably saved his life that day. He had such presence about him, and such self-control: a kid was goading him one day, and Chris just smiled and told him he wasn't worth it. Chris was six feet tall already and weighed 200 pounds – he wasn't anyone you'd want to mess with. Big enough to simply walk away.

Chris has always had remarkable self-control. Remarkable. Like the time he toilet-trained himself. And the time he decided he wasn't going to suck his thumb anymore – at five years old, after every sock-over-the-arm, funny-tasting-stuff-on-thumb trick known to man. He just decided one night he wouldn't anymore, and that was that. Trouble with that level of resolve is that it goes both ways, which is why all of that behavior modification stuff was useless in the face of such inner strength.

Bill showed up at that hearing because I asked him to, and because he had been given a terminal diagnosis a couple of years after we divorced. He was given ten years... he had cancer that couldn't be entirely removed. We didn't tell the boys. I read and read about the possible effects of a boy losing a father in high school, and I decided I needed to build my boys so strong they would be able to manage it. I was so involved with them – so involved in their interests, as much as I could be. Every game they played. Every school production they were in. I was building them strong. I had their backs, and I think they knew it. They have both told me, unsolicited, that I have the strongest values and principles of anyone they have ever met, and when asked for one word that describes me, it is "caring." Lead by example... make them strong. If ever there was a reason and purpose to life, I had it – in spades. And I put all of my determination and intelligence behind that. My personal Jack Welch-type strategic plan? Simple. (1) Get my boys successfully to adulthood. (2) Be able to retire someday. Short and sweet.

My father, meanwhile, had been moving around: he tried Florida, Mexico, California, and then back to Florida. He did come visit, and he kept in contact. He had such a way about him: when he heard that Chris had pinned me down, he sat Chris down and very, very calmly explained that he was retired, didn't have to work – he really wouldn't mind going to jail. Which would happen, because if he heard that Chris had hurt me that would be it – I was his daughter, and he would go to jail protecting me. My dad always had a way about him that made you believe Every. Single. Word. he said. No questions. And Chris believed him.

My dad got his pilot's license and started building airplanes: experimental airplanes from kits. He was back and forth with his band of buddies, and he became enthralled with one of the groupies that hung around those guys – Donna. He proposed to her and bought her a beautiful engagement ring with a wraparound wedding band – which she wore before the wedding. She was bad news: I knew it, but never said a word. I went down to Florida for the wedding. That marriage lasted maybe two months – he was going to move back to Michigan for her and her teenage son. I invited all of them over for my dad's birthday, and only he showed up. I had to quietly put away the extra table settings. He didn't know where she was... she had stolen from my dad for her cocaine habit, and once my dad found out, it was over. He felt like a fool and then pretty much swore off women for good.

He didn't stay in Michigan for long: he moved to a small town in California – Chula Vista - very close to the Mexican border. That's where he was living when I sent Kevin to spend a week or two with him. Kevin needed his guidance: he didn't have the same issues that Chris did, but he had more anxiety that showed up sporadically but briefly: as a youngster there was a time he washed his hands raw because of germs. That lasted less than a week. He was very afraid of bridges and mountain driving. When the boys were maybe ten and eight, respectively, I drove them to Virginia so they could be in their cousin Laura's wedding. Carol had asked Bill to walk Laura down the aisle, the boys were ushers, and I sang. Kevin was so afraid that I would fall asleep driving, he stayed awake to keep me awake. At eight years old! And after he called me one day when he was in middle school with a story of a man in a red car trying to abduct him – and me taking him to the police station to file a report, only to discover it was a false report – I not only got him professional help, I sent him to my father for a time. Kevin loved it dearly. He loved going to Carl's Jr., he loved kicking around the airfield, he told me he killed black widow spiders that were in traffic cones using a magnifying glass (ewwww) – it was a Huckleberry Finn type of adventure, only California style. One of the best things I ever did.

And that condo I had bought for my dad in Stuart? I ended up with it, and I rented out to a working man until the complex went 55+. I then rented it out December – March, usually, and the boys and I would spend Thanksgiving and Easter there. The other condo residents went through something that very much resembled mitosis: those that liked children and those that did not. They split and pulled away from each other. We did not get along well with the haters. I remember once a trio of elderly gentlemen came to my door to inform me that skateboarding in the driveway cum parking lot was not allowed. I asked them to bring me the association rules. They left and returned a bit later, nothing in hand. Not a rule. They said, though, that they had seen it on the condo television station. No proof. I told them that until and unless they could produce that document, my boys would skate in the lot. They were not too happy with me, and I was not too happy with them. These Condo Cops with nothing else better to do but complain.

We had a tradition when we were at the condo: we would make a Wendy's Frosty run every night, and we would go over to the driving range/putt putt/go-cart/batting cage center at least once. We went to the beach, we went to Disney World, we visited their grandfather Hutch, and their aunt Kathy – we kept summer clothes there so we didn't have to pack. Just get on a plane and go. We totally redecorated the place: all new carpet and all new furniture. St. Vincent de Paul came and got the old appliances and furniture, but we had other remodeling detritus that needed to be thrown out. Problem was, there were only small, in-ground trash receptacles in the complex, jealously surveilled by the Condo Cops, peering out windows. So we would load up the rental car at night and head out to find available dumpsters. The boys thought that was hilarious.

We visited Florida for several years, until I got a cold call one early December day – an unsolicited offer to buy the unit. The offer was over twice what I had paid for it, so I agreed. We closed on December 31st. The following spring two hurricanes hit Stuart straight on. My unit was in a marina – sold in the nick of time.

~

Summers were the difficult time. I had the boys in the KinderCare summer program – until Chris got kicked out. I had hired a woman that worked at the Max Program as a housekeeper. I hired her as a nanny to take the kids over to the country club for a couple of summers, which I had joined specifically for the boys – it had a great pool and tennis courts.

The kids got a kick out of ordering lunch and putting it on the member tab. That was for the time the boys were not at Howe Military Summer Camp, which lasted six weeks. I tried the kid program at the Beverly Hills Racquet Club... that lasted maybe three days for Chris. Ditto the sailing class, in which Kevin positively excelled. He was a faster sailor than the University of Michigan Sailing Club instructors that taught the class. I bought him a little one-design Optimist, which he christened the "Fly By You 2." We became a sailing family, joining the Pontiac Yacht Club. We had a little Escape, which was an easy-to-rig single-sail craft, and I had half interest in a Lightning, a three-man fully rigged racing craft – vangs and cunninghams and all – with a mainsail, jib and spinnaker. The boys crewed a lot, mainly for a master sailor named Mark Whatley, and my boat partner Gary and I normally puttered in the back forty. The best we ever did was sixth place. In our defense, that particular club is home to the largest Lightning fleet in the world, and it claimed amidst its members nationally ranked competitors. It was those guys in the lead all of the time, and then the rest of us bringing up the back. It was against those sailors that Kevin, at the age of 12, won the Commander's Challenge, in which crew and helmsman switch roles. Kevin, with Mark Whatley as his crew, beat everyone – and they were all adults. He's in the national Lightning yearbook for that victory. He was one hell of a sailor. I was asked to join the Board, which I did, but passed when asked to start the steps to becoming Commodore.

~

I kept a well-organized and tidy home life: always cloth napkins and a tablecloth; home-cooked meals, rarely restaurants. I would cook on the weekends, making enough for three meals at a time. I would freeze the extras, and after a while we had a freezer stocked with home-cooked meals. Szechuan shrimp tonight? Beef stew? Lasagna? We would get home and we were only fifteen minutes away from a homemade dinner. I would sometimes get up early in the morning to do laundry and to make pancakes or muffins for breakfast. My boys noticed how hard I worked: one morning I woke up to a note from a first-grader Kevin, written in phonetic English: "Dear Momma, I oup uo didite gite up so eule. Uo r a hode wekor. Her is some many for you. Love Kevin." He left a couple of quarters on the paper, laid at the foot of my bed. And when Chris was older, and I was saying that old Momma standard, "What are you going to do when you are grown up?", he retorted, "I don't want to grow up and have to work as hard as you do." Worth it – very worth it. My boys had a high-quality childhood.

Bill and I stayed in contact and had a workable relationship: I did his taxes until he remarried in 2002, and he came over whenever there was some sort of equipment emergency. He had become engaged to a woman named Caroline, and they purchased a home together. I thought he crossed the line when I came home after singing the Christmas Eve midnight service to find the both of them in my kitchen, but I didn't say anything.

One Saturday morning there was a knock at the door: it was Bill and Caroline with two birds. Apparently Caroline loved her birds, and had several birds too many. So, unannounced, they decided to give two of the birds to us. Grrrr. One of the birds escaped while they were bringing them into the house, but Nibbles got in, and Nibbles stayed. Nibbles the Cockatiel, unable to fly due to an unfortunate run-in with Bill's dog. It wasn't two weeks before I got a call before work: it was Bill. He and Caroline were not getting along at all. They were splitting up. I heard his side of the story. And then at work later that morning, I got a call from Caroline. Bill is a mental case. They were splitting up. After that second call I bemusedly wondered why I ended up their respective sounding boards.

I had joined the professional choir at Kirk in the Hills and had been singing there for some time. A soprano and alto, Jeannie and Marguerite, had solo gigs over in Grosse Pointe one Good Friday, and I went to hear them. Afterwards, Marguerite invited me over to the director's home for an afterglow. I went and decided that I needed to introduce myself to Fred, being that I had crashed his party. I went up to him and started my introduction: that I sang with Jeanne and Marguerite over at Kirk in the Hills. He offered me a position in his Chorale, which was soon to embark on a concert tour of Italy. He followed it up with, "you'll have to audition, of course," whereupon Marguerite leaned over and told Fred, "She doesn't need to audition." That was that: I was going on tour in Italy the following summer.

Todd had recently come to live with us: not his father, not his mother – me and the boys. Maryann came over to plead his case. She said something that disturbed me: it felt as if she was giving me her son. She even said we looked alike (so not true). I knew she had been involuntarily admitted for psychiatric care twice, so I found out the name of her psychiatrist and told him my concerns. That was the best I could do: I didn't want a possible suicide marker to go ignored. I asked Todd to be in charge of the house while I was gone, and the boys would go with Bill. Todd was not very domestic, though. I can't remember the cause, but one day I was driven home by the man that was President of the Kirk's Men's Club. He had two children, a boy and a girl, the same ages as my two. He was very engaging, so I asked him if he might perhaps check on the house every once in a while, to make sure nothing was amiss. Thinking I had everything covered, I prepared for my Italian adventure.

~

I adore Italy. The Tuscan hills and walled cities, the marvel that is Florence, the Amalfi coast, the enchanting Venice. Our first stop was Siena. There was a Countess living in Grosse Pointe, a friend Fred's, who allowed us to stay in her 700-year-old enclave, high on a steep hill outside of Siena. There were wild boars in the heavy woods heading up to the villa. Simply glorious! I was at a bit of a disadvantage, as my luggage had been lost: I ended up buying a sweater for the chilly evenings until my suitcase arrived on the second day. We were in Siena when they were setting up the enclosures for the annual Paleo di Siena – the famous horse race. We performed in the Siena Cathedral, a magnificent medieval church. I love singing in those old churches: the reverberation lasts many seconds past the last note. It's absolutely awe-inspiring. We were performing Haydn's *Lord Nelson Mass*, and we brought our own chamber orchestra as well. Lots of time for sight-seeing, lots of great food: what a delight! After Siena we headed to Florence. Our four-star hotel had double shutters on the windows: a set inside and a set outside. I was rooming with Marguerite: the first morning we were awakened by absolutely glorious singing. We were across the street from the Opera House – not the new one, the old one: the Teatro Comunale. What an amazing way to awake! We got tickets for that night: for Verdi's *Aida*. Now I know why opera is so popular in Italy: it is Opera meets Las Vegas. The Triumphal March had topless women and all manner of animals that paraded around twice! Most of the characters were in gauzy Egyptian-styled garments, but the two leads were a bit too portly to pull that off. They were therefore artfully, but totally, covered up in heavy Elizabethan-looking costumes. At the end, when the tomb stone was slowly being pushed into place, the only thing I could think of was that those two would last a long, long time before they starved to death.

We had an afternoon to see the sights: walked across the Ponte Vecchio with all of its gold vendors; we went through the Uffizi. As we were standing in line at the Uffizi, an Italian man was walking excitedly up and down the line warning us of gypsies. And there they were: the gypsies. Dressed as one might expect. They looked to be three generations: a haggard, bent-over older woman who was begging (she reminded me so of the evil witch in Snow White, disguised to sell apples), a woman who I assume was her daughter, and a bare-chested toddler of about ten months in her arms. The babe had a half-eaten apple but dropped it. It rolled in the dirt, the mother picked it up and gave it back to the babe. Yuck. Apparently, they had a scam: while the old lady was begging, hand extended, the younger woman would attempt to pick-pocket. There was a baritone from our group who had taken out his passport and wallet and moved them to his front pocket, keeping his hand in his pocket over them. He said he felt the woman's hand in his back pocket, where he normally kept his wallet. I'm not sure those women were very successful: we had been warned and were on guard.

One afternoon, four of us - Jeanne, Marguerite, Martha and me - were sitting in an open café. We were approached by a couple of good-looking young men. They had a leather factory; would we like to see? We went and ended up buying a bunch of stuff: I got a gorgeous red leather swing coat and a beautiful black and red leather bag. We walked out of there many shekels lighter – but the merchandise was simply stunning.

I was humbled by our entourage that evening. We were at a restaurant for dinner, and I got up to use the facilities. When I returned, the entire group started singing "Windy" by the Association – in four-part harmony! I'm sure I turned beet-red. "And Windy has stormy eyes, that flash at the sound of lies"… very à propos.

We sang at the Florence Cathedral and then headed to Assisi. We were there before that devastating earthquake that significantly damaged the Basilica. I love Assisi. Walking around, it was easy to see why St. Francis loved nature – so very peaceful there, gazing down to the green fields far below. We sang in the Basilica. It was the 4th of July, and after the concert there was a small group of people standing outside. They wanted more – especially this little black-kerchiefed, smiling woman. We sang a short reprise. More! We sang Windy. We even sang the Star-Spangled Banner for her. I wanted to hug that little black-kerchiefed woman.

We had two other scheduled engagements: at St. Mark's in Venice (which has an amazingly long reverberation), and at the Vatican. We were scheduled to sing in the Sistine Chapel, but that got canceled at the very last moment because of a change in the Pope's schedule. I am frankly not exceptionally fond of Rome, but Venice? Venice is simply magical. Rome is crowded and touristy – unless you take a walk. One Sunday morning I took myself out for a stroll. The streets were totally empty - I ended up at this old abandoned villa: I don't know how old it was. It was a two-story edifice shaped like a "U", the second story had an arched catwalk with a stone railing overlooking the courtyard. It was in shambles, in a glorious, ancient sort of way, and had marble statuary and broken columns pushed over and scattered around: all I could think of was that this gorgeous place; these gorgeous pieces of ancient Rome, tossed around like old wine bottles in some New York alley. That's how rich the history of Rome is. That was my favorite part of Rome.

That trip – that entire trip – was wonderful. No, wonderful does not come close to how I feel about it. Astoundingly fantastic. That might come a little closer. I loved every minute.

~

I came home to a problem. My problem was that man I asked to look after the house. Todd told me he was always there! I never meant him to watch so closely. He picked me up from the airport –

256

it was late, and he asked if he could sleep on the floor in the family room. It was truly late, so I agreed. I went to work the next day, picked up the kids, made dinner… same routine. Jack showed up. Wanted to watch some sports event on TV with the household of men with whom I was living. The boys and I needed to go to bed and the game was not over. Jack asked if he could stay to watch the end – I found him on the floor the next day. Something was terribly amiss here. I should have been less naïve – I should have been more suspicious.

Jack was going through a divorce. Everyone at church knew it – he not only was the President of the Men's Club, he was an usher. Slowly the truth came out: Jack had lost his job and was pretty much homeless. What to do? There was another usher at the church – David Lau – who owned an insurance agency. He said that if Jack got his credentials he would hire him. Jack had a degree in finance, so the deal was I would pay for him to get his certification and David would give him a job. And that's what we did: Jack was a smart guy and got his credentials. David gave him a job. And I agreed to him stay in the basement until he could save enough money to get his own place. However, it didn't work out that way.

I found out way, way too late that Jack was a narcissistic, bi-polar sociopath. Charming – really, really charming. Really good-looking, too. That certainly did not hurt. He said he needed a car to get to work – and his car really was on its last legs, anyone could tell. So I bought a used Mercedes station wagon and let him use it. And then one day, while I was at work, I got a call from the police. Jack was hiding in the basement (was not at work), and the police wanted my permission to enter the house to arrest him. What??? I called Jack and convinced him to give himself up. He subsequently called me from jail and proposed to me. That was definitely from so far out in left field – what was this man thinking?

But he sure had a golden tongue, he certainly was smart, and he was damn good-looking. The answer was definitely no, but there was something about the man that kept me hooked.

Jack was arrested for back child support. His explanation of not being able to pay it because he wasn't working was very plausible – all he didn't do was tell the Court he was unemployed, right? He could make this right with his new job. David, the church and I could help this guy get it together. That's what we are here for, right?

The short answer was no, but I didn't truly understand that for many months. He always had a great excuse, a great plan. He lost his job with David by Christmas, because he did not close one single sale. I had his children John and Betsy over for Christmas, buying them presents. I knit them Christmas stockings to hang so they would feel at home. I thought that trying to normalize Jack's interactions with them would help. I tried everything I knew how to try. By Easter, when Gaye, his ex-wife, asked if I would have the children over for dinner, I agreed immediately. Jack never showed – it was the four children and me. I had no idea where he was. Come to find out he knew his con was wearing thin, and he was out finding another mark to sucker – and her name was Marty.

I knew he was breaking into my house when I was at work – things were moved, things started going missing. Like the silver tableware my grandmother gave me, and a laptop computer. I had never given him a key, but I figured he had copied one. So I called up a locksmith and was home one afternoon, folding laundry in the bedroom while the locks were being re-keyed in the front. I heard a noise from the bedroom deck – there was an enclosed deck off the master bedroom, totally encircled by six-foot bushes. I heard a noise, and right then I just knew it was him – and this was how he was breaking in. But I didn't know exactly how he was doing it, so

I quietly waited – the blinds were drawn, so he had no idea I was home. He had figured out there was enough clearance between the top channel and the door that he could lift up the door – and that door weighed a ton – lift up the door high enough that the latch would clear the locking mechanism. He simply lifted up the door. Once I saw how he was getting in, I went over and yanked open the blinds. That man cleared the railing and the bushes and tore off. I put paint sticks on the tops of the sliders until I could arrange for all five window walls to be replaced with sliders that had metal rods that went up and down into the frame when the handle locked.

I called the police more than once on that man. I called them when he took the Mercedes without permission. I called them when he stole the silverware and laptop. The police showed me a rap sheet that was six feet long. No kidding: I was at the police station when the officer came around the corner with this long, long piece of paper. Jack was bad news.

He didn't like being shut out – I had the life and the reputation he wanted for himself. I was in the basement one day cleaning the kids' playroom when Jack came through the garage and down the stairs. The boys were unaware - even though they were upstairs, the stupid house design, with access off the garage without ever entering the house, hid the intruder's presence. Jack grabbed me, threw me down on the sofa, and covered my mouth with his hand. I wiggled free and screamed as loudly as I could. Chris and Kevin came flying down the stairs – absolutely flying. Kevin, my ten-year-old little Kevin, went right over to the phone, ready to pick it up his eyes fixed on Jack. Chris – my big, strong, protective Chris –went right up to the man, who by now had stood up. Chris walked up to Jack – 6'2" Jack - walked right up to his face. He had a remarkably confident little sneer, one side of his mouth upturned. Chris, my thirteen-year-old Chris, self-assuredly looked

Jack in the eyes and quietly said, "Get out." Just those two words. Jack ran out, and I got a Personal Protection Order. And I sued him for stealing the silver and the computer. Very interestingly, sometime between his being served and our first court date, he returned my belongings to my attorney's office, after he was sure she had left for lunch.

But Jack would not let go. He would call constantly, so I got caller ID and screened my calls. He showed up at the yacht club one night when I was sailing and tried to let the air out of my tires. A woman working on the refreshments saw him and called the police. He would look into my windows at night and then leave threatening letters in my mail box to let me know he was watching. I was actually escorted to and from my car by an armed guard for two weeks at work. Jack stole my mail, getting credit card information and ordering himself suits. He adopted my education on his resume. He was a total nightmare.

And then one day, shortly after Thanksgiving, I got a call from a stranger named Marty. Could we meet for dinner? At the Hideaway? Sure, I said.

Marty was on to Jack. She was emotionally a little fragile, I could tell. She wanted to kick Jack out but was terrified of him. Would I help? Gee – all 118 pounds of me, not too good at that. Didn't she have any guy friends that could help her? She said she was from up north, all her family and friends were up there. Oh well… here we go. I said I would. So the next weekend I showed up at her apartment to give her moral support. One thing I knew about Jack, though – after the PPO he was afraid of me. He couldn't believe I was standing there in the drive, but he did leave. I have no idea where he went, but I think he knew that I would not hesitate to call for reinforcements if need be. After all, Jack was nothing but a coward.

Two summers later I took the boys down to St. Petersburg, where the three of us became certified skippers at the Annapolis Sailing School. Three or four days into it, as we were sitting at a pizza parlor waiting for dinner, I decided to check my home voicemail. There was a call from the Troy Police Department looking for some Volkswagen Jack had. I was pretty powerless to do anything from Florida, but the minute I got home I contacted them. The story was far from pretty: apparently, Jack had gone to the Secretary of State and changed his address to mine somewhere along the line. The mail lady told me a couple of months later that Jack would walk up to the mailbox every day while I was at work – she was curious, because he always walked up to it from down the street. She snooped around and found out he was parking across the parkway and walking the couple of short blocks to my mail box, taking mail before I got home. He had taken his driver's license to a Volkswagen dealership and left his license while he took the car for a test drive – to Colorado. The police came over to the house thinking I might be covering for him, but no – I let them look all over, showed them my now-expired PPO and told them the story. That's the last I heard of that until over a year later, when he had been arrested and charged with a felony – larceny by conversion over $20,000. The prosecutor asked if I would testify. The answer was a resounding yes.

I refer to the prosecutor as Amazon Woman. She was tall – very tall, maybe 6'0" – blond, and fierce. Quite intimidating. She came over to prep me and was asking some really unusual questions, until it became clear that Jack had said we had been married. Nope. Anyway, I did testify against him... and within a week I had received a letter from the prison – Jack, trying to sweet-talk me. I gave it to the prosecutor, who was gob-smacked that he would have the gall.

Jack was convicted of the felony. I don't know how much time he spent in jail. He contacted me a couple of years later using a false email name, asking about a racing series the boys and I had started at the yacht club using the Portsmouth Ranking System. That got me written up in *Sailing Magazine*, which was the premise of the initial email. He pretended to be a well-known sailmaker and made up a Yahoo email address using the sailmaker's name. It only took me two emails to realize it was Jack. I got the real email of the sailmaker and forwarded the imposter's email to him. For many years I would Google Jack's name annually to try and figure out if he was anywhere in the area. What I found was that he moved around a lot, being arrested (at a minimum) in Kentucky, South Dakota, Montana and Colorado for things like fleeing and eluding, disarming a police officer and impersonation. I think he must have finally been sentenced to a long stint, though – his online presence and trail had gone cold. His son seems to have some of Jack's characteristics – he was arrested in Colorado. His daughter became so embarrassed that she legally assumed her mother's maiden name as her own.

The entire "Jack" affair shattered my feeling of safety at home for quite some time. I always considered home to be my fortress, where I was safe. It took me years to feel that way again.

~

During these years I would fly my mother in for Christmas, or at other times just because. She never took the initiative to visit herself. It was during one of these fly-ins that we had occasion to drive by Bedford Villa, a nursing home in Southfield – the nursing home where my grandmother passed away. My two uncles had been taking turns taking care of her, but they were both in their seventies and wanted to move to Arizona permanently. My mother declined taking her mother to California so she could have her turn with the elder care, so my uncles were preparing to move

Grandma to Arizona. Within a week of the scheduled move, Grandma passed away. My mother had a broken something-or-other... an arm, a leg: I can't remember. Anyway, she missed the funeral. So there we were, driving by Bedford Villa, when I casually remarked, "There's where Grandma was when she died." My mother angrily said no, but I knew I was right. "No, that's where she was. Ted and Gene moved her from Lake Orion over six months ago," I said. My mother became furious – she carried the argument on for a good two weeks, well after she returned to California. I knew why she was so angry – it was because she felt so guilty. She did not know where her mother had been living for a good six months – that means she never called, she never wrote... she had no idea. You know, she often would say to me when I was young, "Wait until you have children. You'll see." Well, I did have children, and then I had concrete proof... I never reacted like she did. And when it became clear just how much she had ignored her own mother, I felt a big sense of release.

For years and years, I had tried to be a "good daughter," but somehow now I felt I had permission to stop – I mean, if my mother didn't even know where her own mother was, what was my obligation? At the end of the two-week verbal-turned-email argument, she still trying to justify her egregious self-absorption, I simply gave up on her. Silly of me to get angry anymore for what she wasn't and could never be. From that moment on I rarely initiated a phone call - only in emergencies – and I mostly did not pick up the phone when I knew it was her. Oh, I sent gifts for Christmas, Mother's Day and her birthday, but that was the extent of our relationship. She had laid a path of expected behavior which I followed in a fashion, but for entirely different reasons. And she never thought to come for either of the lads' high school or college graduations – never even crossed her mind.

My absence was noticed, however, and she hated it. She would call friends to cry and complain, and they on occasion would call me. They could not fathom the extent of her emotional black hole and would try to get me to call the mother that told them she loved me. But then, it is really difficult for normal people to get their arms around someone so emotionally deviant. She would tell people it was because she was an alcoholic – she consumed all of her calories in cheap boxed wine. It never occurred to her that it was her behavior that drove me away. Not just her behavior – it was who she was that drove me away.

~

Kearney did everything in Technicolor. Big everything: big salaries, big offices, big expense accounts. Big staff meetings – a multiple-days-long staff meeting, held in the State Theater. Formal dinner dances at country clubs. Larger than life. The staff meeting I referenced had a legendary Motown quartet as entertainment. There were awards given: the show theme was Goldfinger. I was nominated to be a presenter – I was given a gold lame evening gown (with silicone breast enhancers) and shoulder-grazing chandelier earrings to wear. I was escorted by two of the better-looking consultants, they in tuxedoes. (Better-looking is a gross understatement.) One thing about Kearney: for all of the years I was there, its staff consisted of 75% white males: less than a dozen women consultants, with the remainder non-Caucasian males. I would sit in gatherings and count. So you can imagine the reaction we got as we entered from stage left, me with a studly gentleman on each arm, in front of an audience that had consumed liberal amounts of wine and cocktails.

On day two, after dinner, there was a karaoke contest. We had a woman in the administrative staff who was known to be a singer – and then there was me. I heard that people were placing bets, so I went to her and suggested we do a duet – I did not want to compete with her. I knew I would win, and I knew she had little else to boost her self-esteem. A duet it was. We held out until five minutes before the contest was to end, then we got up. We sang "When I Fall in Love," by Nat King Cole and his daughter Natalie. My sweet singing partner was having a difficult time, so I gently guided her – and we won. Hands down. We won a bottle of champagne, several hours of a limousine and dinner for six at Fishbone's Restaurant. I rounded up "the girls" from work and we celebrated. That was quite fun.

I had some other very interesting experiences at Kearney. I was once asked to judge a competition at the University of Michigan B-School. Those kids were so respectful and eager. I was flown to Chicago for a whirlwind round of new candidate interviews. We got together after hours and voted the candidates in or out. There is something not quite right about judging someone up or down based on how they conduct themselves in a fifteen-minute interview… good for out-of-the-box impressions, but not good for assessing longer term performance potential.

And then there was the day-to-day, highly logical but almost borderline sociopathic approach to business. I really had a basic dislike of that part. Consultants would get together and plot how to get an idea implemented: Split client employees up by identifying who could be convinced, who that would be fine with a polite "agree to disagree," and who that just needed to be neutralized. We would actually plot it out on a white board: categories of recommendations across the top and client individuals down the side. Step One: remove from the list those whose opinions just didn't matter. It was Machiavellian – effective, but just so Machiavellian.

And then there were those two young men who had a competition between them. They had Xeroxed a picture of a slice of burnt toast – the consultant that got the most people laid off in their respective engagements would win the Burnt Toast Award. And they laughed about it. I really had a hard time with that – how very cold.

Kearney has an "up or out" culture: they did not want anyone that was content to stay at a Managing Consultant level. Al Morrison counseled me that I needed to aspire to Principal, and that the sixty hours I was working a week was not enough. Kearney is amazing in regard to personnel: no hard feelings at all. They actually love placing former consultants into client companies. They continue to have a very strong Kearney Alumni community. I was not interested in living to work, so by mutual agreement we decided we would plan my exit. I had conducted several engagements at the GM account of EDS, and after the third one I was challenged to put my money where my mouth was. I left Kearney and joined EDS proper, ending up in Troy. That was the first time in decades I could keep off the freeway to get to work. The timing was wonderful.

That's where I was working when Chris decided, after many unsolicited comments from even complete strangers, to go out for football. And when I say unsolicited, I recall one incident when we were approached while eating dinner at the country club by a man who asked Chris if he played football: that he should; moreover, this guy's cousin was the coach at Seaholm and would love to talk to Chris. Chris said at the time that he was going to get a sign and pin it on his back: "No, I don't play football." But after all of those comments he decided to try. On the third day of August three-a-days the coach came over to me, leaned over into the car window, and asked if Chris was my son. "Here we go," I said to myself, "Chris is going to get kicked out of this, too. What did he do?" I merely answered yes, waiting for the shoe to drop, when the coach said, "Do you have any more boys at home?" I replied to the affirmative, to which the coach said, "Promise me you'll let me talk to him. I saw Chris and I said, "Hallelujah!! Thank you God!!" Football it was.

Chris had Coach Loria for one of his classes. Loria was the Varsity coach: freshman football had a different coach. Chris was pulling his usual "I won't do it – can't make me" with his schoolwork, so after a few weeks I told Coach I would have to pull him out. Coach said, "If I come in every morning at 6:45 and tutor him, will you let him play?" I thought about it – here's the Varsity Coach committing to tutor my son every day for the entire football season? I agreed. And that is exactly how it came to be that Coach Loria pretty much saved my son.

Chris was a natural. He quickly became a star, making Varsity his sophomore year. He made the papers. All of the other MHSAA division coaches knew his name. He was a defensive end, and he was lethal on the field. He had found an identity and something he was really, really good at doing. And I was so grateful that I joined the Football Boosters Board as Treasurer. Together with a few other amazing mothers/professional women, Julie Gust, Pam Johnson and Cathy Sparling, we managed to raise over $150,000 for the football team. The football program was so grateful that they bent the rules a bit so I could stay on for Treasurer an extra year.

The team was named the Lahser Knights, and I got the idea that these knights needed their own standards, and the press box needed large forked flags on all four corners. So I made them. I ordered yards and yards of yellow rip-stop nylon and made standards for each player. They were shaped like shields, 36" tall, with dowels at the top with plastic cord from corner to corner so they could be suspended from the tops of the chain link fence. The boys were allowed to choose from about three or four different designs I had developed, with their names at the top and their uniform numbers dead center. It took me forever to do those: I used magic marker to color in the designs, names and numbers – two coats. Then I sprayed each with polyurethane. I would have four or five strung around the breakfast nook in varying stages of completion. When those banners were hung for home games it was a very impressive sight. The Knights made the playoffs every year my son played, making it to the semi-finals once. That is an amazing accomplishment for a team that had historically been at the bottom of the pile. Those were the Lahser Knights glory days. Five of those lads ended up being recruited for NCAA football – and my son was one of them.

> DC Adamic – Ashland
> Chris Faison – Toledo
> Montez Perkins – Northwood
> Greg Raspberry – Northern Michigan
> Chris Thomas – Northern Michigan

The recruitment process is dizzying. Long weekends and great sales pitches. Chris was recruited by five schools that I can remember he visited: I don't know if there were other offers that he declined out of hand. The Northern weekend was the last, and Coach called me up and said I needed to go this time. Chris and I piled in the car and off we went – 422 miles north, across the Mackinac Bridge, and then WNW to the shores of Lake Superior. The recruiting weekend was quite the show. There were fairly elaborate dinners and parties for the prospects. The coach teamed each recruit with a player who was responsible for their entertainment. The coach also made sure there were several comely young women at the dinners. There was a bus tour for the parents, paid accommodations at the downtown hotel, and lunch where every table had a dean in attendance, expounding on the great programs to be had. Sunday was offer day. We sat around waiting for names to be called, and one by one the lads would go into an office with one of the coaches. They walked out with offers in hand – or not. The offers were not formal until Signing Day, but Chris had been successfully recruited, and we had said yes.

~

Chris and Kevin had been two years apart in school, and after I held Chris back that margin shrank to just a year. As big as Chris was in ninth grade, Kevin was small. He really was that 99-lb, 5'1" kid that was a late bloomer – and it didn't help that he started school at the age of four, so he was one of the younger lads. He didn't want to go out for football, but Chris said he would have to do all sorts of down-ups if Kevin didn't sign on. So Kevin did – and his first year at Lahser was inauspicious. He was living in the shadow of his big older brother; so much so that he was always called "Little T" instead of his name. Chris said the other guys often asked him what happened to the younger brother. It wasn't an environment within which Kevin could be his own man, that's for sure. His grades were also suffering, so one spring day I sent him over to Orchard Lake St. Mary's for their annual spend-a-day program. My thought was that it would "scare him straight," but at the end of the day, as we were sitting in some administrator's office, Kevin said he really liked it because the classes were small and the teachers didn't spend all of their time simply writing on the blackboard. I was shocked, but St. Mary's it was. We discussed Kevin's relatively poor performance at Lahser, and taking that with his young age, we started him in the ninth grade. The name is officially St. Mary's Preparatory, complete with a huge 125-acre campus with dormitories for the live-in students, all-male, official school ties and navy blazers with St. Mary's crests on the pockets, and even a nationally ranked rowing team. Rowing. White dress shirts only, unless you were a senior - then you could wear light blue dress shirts. Dress shoes, dress slacks, ties, belts, short hair – the whole nine yards. My Sunday nights were occupied with ironing five dress shirts and five pair of khakis. A fair replica of the lads in *Dead Poet's Society*.

St. Mary's had a classic educational structure: seven periods, five days a week. No "blocks" or other newer educational design. Math, English, some foreign language, History, Science – very traditional. And mandatory sports. Also very strict: during that first fall, my son lost his temper and stormed out of class one day. He spent six hours the next Saturday – starting early – raking leaves on campus. He never did that again. He got a quality education: nothing like driving ninth grade boys home, listening as they discussed ancient Greek history in the back seat.

My sons both responded emotionally to their high school years: if they liked a teacher they would get A's: if they didn't like a teacher, they would flunk. Truly. I remember one of Kevin's report cards – either A's or E's: nothing in between. I was flummoxed at that, but it was what it was. Both of my sons are much more natively intelligent than their high school records would indicate.

Being that Kevin needed a sport, he picked up lacrosse. He excelled at the game and made varsity as a sophomore. However, the varsity coach, John Alexander, simply did not like him. I didn't know that for sure until later. So when the coach moved Kevin back to JV, I told him it was so he could get more playing time. But more playing time didn't happen. I drove Kevin over to 6 AM practice every morning, and sadly watched at afternoon games as he would scrounge around the sidelines to pick up any available jersey, wearing a different number every game. It was heartbreaking. I wrote John, asking him why. I hated to see my son so rejected. I got a ridiculously untrue response: that he didn't show up for practice (totally not true: I drove him), that he was suffering from not having a father in the house, and a few other totally invalid points. I responded to every allegation with facts – and when I got to the "fatherless home" part, I remember saying that's why I sent my son to school in an environment awash in testosterone. I was absolutely furious. The lacrosse team was short on staff, however, so I managed to get Chris in as a coach assistant. Chris validated my concerns. It came to a head when, at the lacrosse banquet, my son was listed with no first name and no jersey number in the program. I sent that program to the Headmaster and announced that from that point forward I was a parent assistant: I would take care of communications and make sure other administrivia was managed properly. I was positively livid. And the following year John Alexander got fired.

Kevin was named to All-Region as a junior and was also MVP – offense. That's my son! He was not allowed to play his senior year because he re-did ninth grade, but lacrosse is a spring sport, so the scouts show up for players' junior season. And that's how Kevin came to be recruited.

So I had Chris in football, lacrosse and wrestling; I had Kevin at a different school in lacrosse, and I had Lena in softball. Lena – the young woman that wrote me during the summer between Chris' sophomore and junior years. She had been a casual friend of Chris' from middle school, being one of the movies-bowling "pack" of friends that hung out together. She and her younger brother had been removed from their home by the State and placed in separate juvenile homes to get them away from their alcoholic and abusive father. The mother was told she couldn't have her children back unless the father was no longer in the home – and she chose the husband over her children. Lena wrote and asked if she could live with us and finish high school. I asked the boys about that, and they thought it wouldn't be such a bad idea. It took me until shortly before Christmas to get everything finalized – the parents were against the idea, but the grandparents were all set to testify against their daughter and in favor of me. I did get guardianship, and Lena moved into the apartment downstairs.

I had finished off the lower level a few years earlier to accommodate all of the football/wrestling/lacrosse players that were very often around. It was a full, 2,000 SF apartment: it had slate flooring, its own large kitchen, media room (65" TV with Bose surround sound), sauna, family room, fireplace, weight room, bedroom and bath. I also had the spiral staircase removed and opened up the wall that was blocking the garage staircase to the house. Now access was "normal" – there was a landing with a door to the outside and a door to the garage, open to the upstairs family room next to the fireplace. No more having to go out into the garage to get to that set of stairs.

So Lena moved in downstairs, and a week before Christmas she had a planned visit with her mother – they were going to go together to see her brother, who was still in a juvenile home. She returned with a kitten – she had seen it at a vegetable stand and simply took it. Oh my… we don't simply take things that are not ours. I made Lena contact the owners, who said they wanted the kitten back. Trouble was, the kitten became ill with a respiratory problem and ended up at the vet for a while. The original owners thought twice, and that's how I came to have a second cat. I named him Shady because that's how he was obtained.

I told Lena that she needed to keep her grades up, because her parents were simply dying to be able to say, "I told you so." The parents wanted Lena to stay in that group home, saying that everything was her fault… it was her fault that her father threw her down and gave her a concussion. Lena got a 3.716 GPA every semester. Every one. That being said, she really needed help. She was scratching "I hate me" in her abdomen with a safety pin. She was one lost little girl. I sent her to counseling twice a week, but she still had significant issues that ended up hurting her to the point that she now has no desire to go back to any high school reunions.

Lena was a challenge for me. She was struggling to survive the best way she knew how, but I don't think she trusted most adults, me included. Her values were so different: I understand where they came from, but I was not used to a child who believed they needed to manipulate and use people to survive the way Lena did at the time. She has grown so much since then, and I am very proud of her, but those years were very difficult for us all. We all needed Lena to go to college – for her, for me... for us all. Besides being in the Color Guard, Lena played varsity softball, and her coach wanted her to go out for a college team. Lena chose not to, which I think was probably a wise decision, if only because Lena is under 5' tall. It took us forever to find a prom dress in a size petite zero for her.

Lena lacked the confidence to apply to various schools, so one day when she came home from school I announced, "Guess what you did today?" She replied, "What?" I said, "You applied to Grand Valley, Oakland, Central, Eastern and Western." I had applied on her behalf. She was accepted at nearly all of them, and the best school was Grand Valley. We were a little behind the eight-ball and missed the dorm signup deadline by one week, so I took her up one icy day shortly thereafter to get her signed up for a dorm room. Lena was going to college. I believe she is the first woman in her family to have a college education.

That last year – Chris and Lena's senior year – was a logistical nightmare for me. Fall was okay: just football. Chris fractured two vertebrae but played through playoffs because he didn't want to let down the team. He didn't tell anyone. After football season, though, after the doctor visit, wrestling was definitely out. When spring hit, it was Chris in lacrosse – Lahser,

Lena in softball – Lahser, and Kevin in lacrosse – St. Mary's. Each sport plays two or three games a week. I was spending half-games with one and tearing over to spend half-games with another. I had to take vacation days to buy groceries. And then Lahser played St. Mary's. Chris, long-stick defense; Kevin, attack-offense. I told Chris that if he went after his brother hard I would march right down on the field.

I was not a soccer mom: I was a football/lacrosse/wrestling/softball mom. Building them strong the best way I knew how.

THE DAY EVERYTHING CHANGED

I was at GM's headquarters in the RenCen, on the Detroit River, when those planes hit the Towers on September 11. I was there for a meeting with my difficult GMAC client when the news hit. I remember asking whether the meeting would be canceled – the client laughed and mentioned my work ethic. I remember leaving Detroit: the tunnel to Canada is right next door, and I was stuck in a traffic jam on Jefferson watching all of the Customs security vehicles roar past, lights flashing and sirens blaring, as they hurried to close the border. I wasn't afraid at all: I was a bit wooden in my response to the events of the day. Like I was watching from a different place. That day didn't make a significant difference in my life, really, until three years later. Didn't make a huge difference even though I was called to sing at the funeral of one that had died. I was saddened, but not shaken.

Sometime between 2001 and 2004 I had been asked to assist in developing an IT governance approach, which ended up getting patented. I loved that development process: I was in a room with Kathryn Dodson, and all of a sudden I lit up. She could barely keep up documenting the process I designed in about two of three hours. I loved it, she loved it: and then I became quite interested in process design. I was christened Demand Creation Executive, and my job was to come up with things we could deliver. Health care was a hot topic, so I developed a streamlined process that (after some significant research) could have taken $300 billion in non-value-added administrative healthcare costs nationwide. I wrote it up, and at the suggestion of somebody at work, submitted it for presentation at the Health Information Management Systems Symposium in Dallas. I made some very uncomfortable waves with the existing Health Practice at EDS – stepping on many toes.

They poo-pooed my approach – until it got accepted for presentation at the HIMSS conference. Then all sorts of people took note. I was called down to GM, walking into a room that had every GM stakeholder there: even Blue Cross and the Purchasing Department. They were ready to sign on the dotted line – give them a proposal. I was also asked to fly to Washington DC to meet with the staff that supported some large government platform. And I even got a call from the White House. The White House! So there I was, sitting at my desk on day, when I picked up my phone to hear a polite operator ask if I would could receive a call from the White House. Gee, no – can I get a cup of coffee instead? OMG!! The White House staff assistant said if I could get GM, Ford and Chrysler together, the White House was willing to publicly announce the effort there – at the White House. I was hot.

There was a Vice President that had deep ties to several healthcare CEOs – his name was Ken, but I can't remember his last name. He asked me to hold off on the GM proposal until he could talk to Wellpoint. The EDS PR department sat me down and was preparing a big media splash. I dutifully held off on GM, taking the heat for dragging my feet while waiting for Ken to do whatever he thought he wanted to do. I got two calls from GM, wondering what the hell was going on. I wrote Ken twice asking for direction, and finally I told him that I was so disappointed that we had made EDS look bad. And the big PR push? A sales guy named Nevin Mitchell told them to drop it. Anne Marie Bondarelli, the PR person, was furious. No one ever told me why EDS decided to not pursue this opportunity, but I have my suspicions. The approach was very disruptive to the status quo; current insurers were trying to protect their turf and their own, proprietary systems, which were coincidentally supported by EDS.

This whirlwind of activity happened in November – December 2004. I was making day trips to DC and Dallas – and that required flying – 8 flights in a two-month timeframe. And flying required the TSA. The TSA does not take kindly to amputees. Janet Napolitano used to sniff that only 3% of passengers are fully searched. I would like to clarify that statement: it is 3% of the flying population, 100% of the time. Please understand that amputees like me cannot board an aircraft without egregiously intrusive, full-body assault. Every. Single. Time.

Amputees cannot escape full body checks. My first flight out of Detroit was a nightmare. McNamara Terminal was relatively new, and the security area was also new. No matter that I told the clerks I was going to set off the metal detectors... I was told to follow a couple of middle-aged women into Concourse A, where I stood and watched while they took three rickety office cubicle dividers and leaned them up against one another and a wall – right in the Concourse, travelers walking past. I was then told to take off my trousers. Now, at the risk of too much information, it's better for me to wear pantyhose under suit trousers so the fabric doesn't get stuck between my body and the top of my artificial leg. So there I was, stripped down to my pantyhose in the middle of Concourse A. The women obviously struggled with asking me to take off my pantyhose - since I had nothing under them, they decided against it. I was absolutely livid. Livid! That day trip was to DC, and coming back I had my breasts felt up by this rather large, rude woman. Fit to be tied. I cannot begin to tell you how humiliating that was. I would not let it rest; I contacted the *Detroit News* and told them my story. When I walked into the 2005 Lahser Football Banquet, I was told I was on the front page of the *Detroit News*. A Marine Lance Corporal from Texas ended up reading about it and took the time to search me out – he called me, furious at what was happening to me and to his mother. He alleged that the TSA was itself violating the Patriot Act by terrorizing the citizenry. There is a huge undercurrent of hatred in this nation –

hatred that the government has turned on its people, especially the disabled.

It never got better. The HIMSS Conference was the last in that string of flights, and by that time I had the telephone number of one Sandra Cammaroto, Director of Disability Screening at the TSA. Our first phone call was cordial – she said I could ask for assistance with screening. So the next time I flew out of Detroit, I dutifully asked for assistance. I was met by a kindly black man who was going to escort me through screening. What I thought was going to be a check-only-what-alarms screening was nothing but – that was the Full Monty. The screener told me she wanted to impress the Boss… he was so embarrassed he had to look away. Nothing like having a stranger's hands publicly down your pants.

My second call to Sandra was not so cordial. She started on her same schtick, and I quickly came to the realization that she did not remember me at all. I was so in her face that she became quite unnerved. She was screaming, vacillating between telling me she had all sorts of staples on her torso somewhere and that she was going to hang up on me. But she never did – I am certain she had no idea of the vitriol that exists in "the real world." I asked her about the discrepancies between what she had told me and what happened to me – she admitted that her department and the screening department were not coordinated. That certainly did not calm me down. So I wrote an email from my Dallas hotel room, at two in the morning, declaring that I was going to fly home the following day, and that I would not allow any more sexual assault upon my person. It is sexual assault, by the way – in any other setting short of prison that's what it is called.

When I got to the airport I was locked out of the check-in kiosk. I presented myself at the counter, got my boarding pass, and headed to security. I put my belongings on the conveyor, declared I was going to set off the alarm, and went through the metal detector. Of course, beep beep beep. The clerk came over with a hand-held and determined that my right leg from knee to ankle was the only area that alarmed. So far, so good. However, that's where things went south. They said they needed to touch my torso. I refused. I told them they could search the area that alarmed, but nowhere else. They had two screeners and a supervisor there – they told me later that they were the ones that had locked me out of the kiosk. Two screeners and a supervisor. Would I please let them touch me? It would only be like "this." No. I was wearing a lycra-laced T-shirt, under which I wouldn't have been able to hide a Kleenex. No. We went around and around for over two hours, they trying to convince me to back down, me nicely, in so many words responding, "What about 'no' do you not understand?" They called my boss in Michigan. They called EDS Corporate. Over two hours of haggling. I never did get on that airplane. However, I had won over those three people. The manager let me use his office to make sure I could make arrangements for the three kids. He told me he respected me – called me a Rosa Parks. The two screeners asked me to please try and get the rules changed – they knew what they had to do was in most cases absolutely stupid. Those were their exact words. So I left the airport and went to a hotel in Arlington, where I sat for two days until I could grab a ride home on the corporate jet.

On day three a limo came to get me, taking me to Plano headquarters. I sat around in a conference room until 5 or so, when someone came to fetch me so I could get on the corporate helicopter that would take us to the private jet. I was in the company of the CEO, the President… and Ken. Mr. VP Ken.

What I never will forget are the aircraft. The helicopter had powder blue leather seats for passengers. The jet had a smiling stewardess waiting at the foot of the gangway. The interior was arranged for work – leather lounge-like seats facing one another on either side of tables. Before we took off the stewardess took our dinner orders. Just like in the movies. And that's where I described my healthcare solution to Ken – across from him, over dinner. And that's where he told me to hold off until he could talk to his buddy at Wellpoint.

When we landed at what was at the time Detroit City Airport, we were met by two matching black limousines sitting out on the tarmac. One took me to my car at Detroit Metro; the other was for the executives. When I got back into the office I was told that the company "would think twice about ever putting me on a plane again." And that's exactly how the TSA – or more accurately, my refusal to be subjected to legal battery at worst, and sexual/physical harassment at best, every time I attempted to board an aircraft – eventually derailed my high-flying career. To this day I do not understand why anyone would think it is okay to have a strangers' hands all over another person's breasts and crotches as a condition of work. All for a threat smaller than the threat of being killed by a home appliance. At the hands of screeners with a tested 95% failure rate. Of course they can't – they are too busy feeling up the disabled to have the time to look for anything really dangerous.

I filed suit against the TSA a few months after my 8-trip debacle. It took a good eighteen months for the judge to decide that my case was filed in the wrong court – it should have gone straight to the Appellate Court. I could tell the judge was troubled – especially when I mentioned that Flying While Handicapped is the new Driving While Black. However, it was also clear to me that the judge had some significant political ambitions. So she stalled for eighteen months, trying to figure out what to do… and the answer was dismissed without prejudice, wrong court. At the time that was not known... and since complaints need to be filed timely, my grievance window had expired.

I was not in the least impressed with the Justice Department: instead of addressing the particulars of my complaint, they spent pages and pages on the timeline and passage of the Patriot Act. Nothing at all – at all – about the processes to which I had been subjected. I have seen the Justice Department in action in several of these TSA cases over the years, and I have totally lost respect for its integrity. DOJ attorneys lie, obfuscate, suppress evidence, delay and drag out everything – to hell with justice. With them it's win the case at whatever price. Sociopathic. If you are interested in reading about this behavior for yourself, you can find a wonderful example in the *Ibrahim* case.

To be subjected to the level and frequency of search that is exacted upon amputees is dehumanizing, degrading and humiliating. It is nothing but soul-crushing. Why not just have us sew a fancy little patch on our sleeves? Embroider a fancy red letter on our shirts? Flying While Handicapped truly *IS* the new Driving While Black. It is appallingly discriminatory, and it results in an alarmingly disparate impact. I will never board a commercial aircraft again until I can do so with assurances that my physical integrity will be respected. Period. Not for anything. The TSA can blather all it wants – it is impossible to honestly use the words "respect and dignity" in the context of the TSA.

Come 2005, I began to shuffle around the corporation doing this job and that – my highest and best use being blocked unless I frequently consented to embarrassingly personal searches with a 100% certainty. I did manage to make one family reunion, and I also managed to fly to and from Europe, though – I took off my leg in the security line, put it up on the conveyor belt and hopped through the metal detector. There were screeners that were discomfited, and there were screeners that took it in stride. Funny thing: take it off, my body is not checked. Keep it on, and I end up with blue gloves all over me. That is one serious flaw in the current screening procedures: if anything, anywhere alarms, everything everywhere is checked, no matter what. I tried the AIT machine once – that was a joke. The word came over to check my right hip --- but the screener went right for my torso.

2006 was a significant year: Chris and Lena had left for college, Kevin was starting his senior year, Bill had been told his cancer had returned and this time it wasn't going away, and my father moved in. He had left California for Florida but wasn't there more than several months before he was diagnosed with cancer. I didn't know it at the time, but the doctors gave him only 2-4 months to live. He was going to try and drive himself some 40+ miles two and from the hospital for his chemo treatments, but I thought he wouldn't be in any shape to do that. I told him he needed to come live with me, because I wouldn't be able to take care of him 1,200 miles away. He thought about it and agreed, and was supposed to come after his first course of chemo. Well, he got impatient and left in the middle of his first course, packing up his car and driving straight through (except to pull off for a few hours to sleep in his car). I got a phone call to leave the door unlocked because he would be arriving around 3 in the morning. And could I arrange for his chemo for the next Monday? That's my dad.

I called the VA Hospital in Detroit, which partners with both Karmanos and Wayne State. I spoke to the head of Oncology, and I either was very convincing or absolutely pathetic, because I got the good Dr. Fontana to go from "No way" to "Bring him in Monday." So off we went.

My dad was using a walker at the time. He never told me of his grim diagnosis, so I had no idea. After about three weeks he didn't need his walker anymore, and after another several weeks he didn't even need his cane. My neighbor called my house Neverland. I think the key was nutrition. I tricked my dad into eating enough to keep his weight up: I would make him milkshakes but load them up with branch-chained amino acid proteins. I would make him porridge for breakfast but use flavored coffee creamer and maple syrup on it. Make homemade soups served with sourdough bread. He said he had no appetite, but he could not refuse my bacon and potato soup. And after several months he felt well enough to drive to Kansas or Missouri or somewhere Heartland to pick up a partially completed airplane, which he parked in the garage and worked on.

I was often working from home then, and he would come in my office in the morning, sit in my wing-back chair, and report on the flowers that were coming up around the house. I never knew he loved flowers so much. We would go to Starbucks for coffee every Sunday morning, sitting and chatting in the easy chairs by the window. And he would buy me flowers every week.

Those were good times – I finally got to meet my father, and he got to meet me. He was just so thoughtful: I had mentioned that the screening on one of the huge window well covers needed to be repaired, and one day when I got home from the office he proudly showed off his handiwork – he had repaired it beautifully. He had gone out, bought everything he needed, and replaced the screening. And those covers were heavy – they were made from composite and were eight feet long and five feet deep. I was so touched and incredibly pleased. I think he was incredibly pleased that it meant so much to me. I was not used to having anyone figure out what would please me, and then simply deliver on it.

I became an active participant in his healthcare. His was not a normal case, as evidenced by his remarkable improvement. He was one of those unusual cases where the cancer did not get used to the chemo – the therapy kept working for nearly two years, keeping the cancer at bay. Keeping the cancer at bay enough that my dad was to take a couple more vacations. But then he developed something else: something that the oncologist couldn't explain. So I took my dad to the University of Michigan, where he was seen by a charming US Navy Fellow. I really liked that guy. I can just imagine him up at three in the morning, looking at the symptoms and blood work and trying to figure out exactly what was going on... he was that kind of guy. And what was going on was, he guessed, some very rare condition called oncogenic osteomalacia. It was so rare that U of M could not definitively diagnose it – they had to send my dad's blood to Mayo and Harvard. At the time there were only 37 recorded cases in the US... and one in Japan. The case in Japan was a man who had both oncogenic osteomalacia and cancer, and who was in the same Prefecture as my dad when the bomb dropped, he being too young at the time to enlist. So I started digging. Come to find out, military records had my father in the hottest spot for fifty-three 24-hour days, broken up by trips to the infirmary, being that my father was quite ill from amoebic dysentery, malaria and pneumonia. At first he poo-pooed any connection, saying that he wasn't in Hiroshima until a couple of months after the bomb was dropped. I asked him, Mr. Physics Major, what the half-life was of Strontium 90, which is linked to bone cancer (which is where my dad's cancer ended up). The half-life is 28.8 years. He looked at me in wonderment and finally said, "Do you suppose that's what happened to you?" And that was the first logical explanation anyone had come up with, after all of these years.

When I was born, the cause of my bone abnormalities was "unknown." My condition is apparently congenital but not genetic, meaning that something happened to the way my cells were developing that is not inheritable. Radiation exposure has been linked to birth defects, but most of the studies have been done on mothers, not fathers. When I was having children my OB GYN asked about Thalidomide, but I was told that my mom didn't take it. My current hypothesis, which admittedly is circumstantial but undeniably credible, is that my father's exposure to radiation caused damage to the sperm that ended up being me. It makes perfect sense to me, and there has not been a competing theory offered except simple chance.

The oncogenic osteomalacia was more problematic for my dad than the cancer was. It made him weak, and made his phosphorus levels really low. If they got too low, he could go into a coma. Wanting to make sure the medications he was taking were working in the way intended, I took the vitals and blood work from his medical history, which was quickly filling up a 4" binder, and charted them against his medication and chemo schedules. Charted them using Excel, taking the results to Dr. Fontana. I became an adjunct member of my father's medical team – which caused my dad to start introducing me as, "This is my daughter, and she is never wrong." Whatever all of us were doing was working, though, because he was well past his prognosis.

Chris was away at college when my dad moved in. At the beginning my father didn't feel very well, and he told me he wanted to see Chris play football before he died. That, and see my sister's son Jonathan graduate. I would send him clippings from the newspapers about Chris – cute little quotes from the guys that covered the local high school sports scene, like, "But getting around #85 Thomas? Lahser by 12." He would hang them proudly in his hangar. So I wrote the coach and asked if he could find it in his heart to put my red-shirted son in, if only for one play, during the green-and-gold spring game. The coach said he would do better than that: he made arrangements for my dad to be an honorary coach, gave him sideline privileges, and allowed him to speak to the team in the locker room after the game. It was amazing. My sister and nephew flew in, because we all thought the end was near. My nephew, who had been out partying the night before and passed out in his car, missed the flight. My sister was livid. I got Jonathan on the phone and told him even Chris thought he was an idiot, that he needed to find a way, and that he should call me to tell me when to meet him at the airport. Jonathan did, and we all headed up to Marquette. Marquette is 422 miles away, and I attended every single home game – in all of those years I attended all but one. I would leave anywhere from 5:30 AM to 1 PM, depending on the time the game started, have dinner with Chris, spend the night in a hotel and drive back Sunday. My aunt Midge, uncle Ted and cousin Teddy would join us, if they were in town. 844-mile weekend drives. My aunt Midge was from the UP, and once a season Northern would host the local high school bands at half time. Midge used to play trombone for one of those schools, so I arranged for the band leader and a lead trombone player to come over and surprise her – they did. They brought her a corsage. It was a fantastic surprise for her. She was from Gladstone, and she knew the father of the band leader. Of course she did: Gladstone is a tiny, tiny berg, and everybody knows everybody.

Bill went to at least one game – maybe two, but for sure he and Diana went to one. He married Diana in 2002. When he was told his cancer was back he had outlived his 10-year prognosis by two years. In that last year he decided he wanted to stop working and travel with Diana – he was only 60. He called me and asked if he could stop child support for Kevin. I had previously told him he needed to contribute to college expenses. He at first said no, but then I told him that if he wouldn't do that voluntarily, I would go and ask for court-ordered support at current rates: I had never asked for an increase, thinking he would do the right thing all by himself. If he wasn't up for that, then the additional $900 a month or so I could get if I petitioned would be put aside for Kevin. He did start putting aside some money, but it certainly wasn't $900 a month. So when he asked to stop entirely, I said no. He had previously taken a buy-out from GM and turned right around and gotten hired by a supplier, so he was in effect getting a salary-and-a-half. He certainly could afford to support his son in his senior year, especially given the circumstances. Bill ended up being a 20% dad: he spent 20% of his time and contributed 20% of their non-living expenses (I covered all living expenses and 80% of everything else). I was the one at all of the games. Not Bill. It always broke my heart that I couldn't get Bill to be more involved in the boys' lives – I tried. Suggested he coach one of the high school teams: Bill was a 3-letter athlete in high school. Nope. Wasn't gonna do it. Before Chris was such a local sports star, I begged him to go to more games. Nope. Wasn't gonna do it. He saw that as me trying to control him. Silly man. I was trying to get him to be more involved in the boys' lives. Chris and Kevin did not learn about the cancer until 2006, when Diana took a one-year sabbatical from work and she and Bill took off for an extended trip.

~

In the fall of 2006, when Kevin was a blue-dress-shirt-and-varsity-sweater senior, he brought home a baby squirrel one day. While in class, he and the other students watched as a hawk latched on to a squirrel, and then the next day they saw two baby, orphaned squirrels. One of the science teachers took one and Kevin took the other. Named him Ron Burgundy. That baby squirrel and Kevin were inseparable. We bought some puppy formula, which we were advised we should feed him. I must admit, I have never seen anything so cute. That little guy thought Kevin was his mom, his tree, his playmate. And Kevin was totally smitten. One of those weekends I was up at one of Northern's games, and my dad was on one of his vacations. Bill and Diana were off somewhere – and Ron Burgundy went into convulsions. Kevin was frantic, but I was 422 miles away, it was a Saturday night, I had no good advice for him, and I knew no one I could call. Ron died that weekend, and Kevin was inconsolable. I felt so badly for him. I asked whether he wanted a puppy, but he said no. At first he said no, but after a while he said yes. So I started looking for an Irish Setter puppy. I couldn't tag one from an unborn litter – I needed one NOW. I found one in Minnesota. That was a weekend my father's blood levels were dangerously low, and his physician recommended if I was going to be gone, my dad should spend the weekend in the hospital. Well, that was never going to happen. But I couldn't let my dad stay alone, so I remember telling him he had three choices: he could go to the hospital, he could come with me, or he could risk waking up dead. He chose to come with me. I mapped out a timetable that had us close to a level 2 medical facility every night: Marquette General – the football game that was stop #1 on the tour: Mayo Clinic, 25 miles from the farm that had the puppy: Northwestern, coming through Chicago on the way home. So off the three of us went – first, the football game, then the drive through the UP, through upper Wisconsin, over the Mississippi to outside of Rochester, Minnesota, to the farm of Kevin Thomas Funk. To the litter of eight simply adorable puppies that stumbled clumsily out of the barn into the sunshine. I would have taken the sweet little girl that was hanging around my feet, but Kevin wanted the romping, curious male. He had already chosen the name Riley… and then we found out that the sire's name was also Riley. Riley the Menace. Oh boy. From the Kevin Thomas Funk farm – my son being Kevin William Thomas, my father being the son of Robert Funkie Sharp Thomson. So many naming coincidences that even my father was a bit freaked out. And that's how we brought Riley home, in a marathon road trip that took us from Marquette Michigan, over to Rochester, Minnesota and home via Chicago in one very, very long day.

Kevin graduated in 2007. He was very unsure where he wanted to go to college. I had sent him to lacrosse camp at the University of Virginia between junior and senior years, and as a result we kept getting letters from East Coast schools. One in particular – Roanoke College – sent us several letters. Neither of us had ever heard of it, but by the third letter I decided to look it up on the internet. Lo and behold, they were a D3 national lacrosse contender. So I told Kevin, and the next thing I knew, my dad, Kevin and I were in the car, driving the 686 miles to Salem, Virginia.

We all loved that school – even my father. Small, lovely... even the dining room, which used Fiestaware for their everyday dishes. Small class sizes, in the top 5% of business and economics schools – and the lacrosse! Kevin had a friend that was playing lacrosse at a men's college about an hour away, and we visited him. It was a done deal. Roanoke it was.

What we did not know about Roanoke is that it has a reputation for being a school of last resort for wealthy New Englanders who, despite all of their money, could not get their privately-schooled problem children into Harvard, Princeton, Brown or Yale. Roanoke would accept them (and the money that followed), but after six weeks of school, if grades were not up, the students would get a letter telling them that if within the next six weeks they could not bring their grades up, do not worry about returning in January. That actually happened to Charlie: Kevin's buddy Charlie did not bring his grades up, and he was dis-invited to return. His parents ended up sending him to an Outward Bound Program in Patagonia.

Roanoke was about three or four times more expensive than Northern, but I was making the big bucks, and Bill was contributing. So I drove Kevin down one hot August day, and we started piling his belongings into his dorm room. I made a Bed Bath and Beyond run to pick up a rug and some other things that neither I or Kevin's new roommate Connor had brought. It was really hot, I was starving, and I was so looking forward to that one last dinner with Kevin before I said good-bye. However, while I was shopping for him, he had made friends with a gaggle of lacrosse players, and when I called to tell him I was on the way back and where should we go to dinner, he said he was going with the guys instead. I broke down in tears. I really felt disregarded – I was so hot and tired, so hungry, I had spent the entire day making sure he had what he wanted... I stopped off at a convenience store and bought a milkshake or something similar and got to the dorm. I didn't even go in. We emptied the car right there in the parking lot, me sobbing uncontrollably, and I left for my hotel room. It was a really bad way to say good-bye.

I was under quite a bit of stress. My father was having more frequent marginal days, with only enough energy to play computer games. So I decided I needed to capture his story. I pulled out my video recorder, put it on its tripod, and started recording the two of us. We were at the kitchen counter. I asked him questions about his childhood – at first he had a difficult time remembering, but as we continued he remembered more and more. How he would go pick up horse droppings for his father's dahlia garden. How he made friends with the ice man, winning the privilege of sitting under the canvas tent covering the blocks of ice in the summer, traveling a few blocks with him. How his dad ended up being the baseball coach, being harder on my dad than the other boys because he didn't want even a hint of favoritism. How the family would go camping in the Irish Hills during summers. How he helped his dad build a house in Garden City – just my dad, my grandpa and my dad's uncle Jim. That was a two-year project: my dad's job was to take the nails out of the reclaimed lumber and chip the mortar off of the reclaimed brick, items my grandfather would scavenge from around the city. That was in the early thirties, a few years into the Great Depression. The house wasn't done by the first winter, so my grandfather sent my dad and grandma to live in Hamilton, Ontario, with my Gram's best friend, Jeannie Wilson. That was her maiden name, but that's how we knew her. Scottish vital records have always been kept in both maiden and married names, and that culture of name permanency pervaded the culture. That's why my father did both kindergarten and fourth grade in Canada, kindergarten in Ford City (Windsor) and fourth grade in Hamilton. In preparation for leaving, my dad and grandmother killed and canned all of the backyard chickens so my grandfather had meat through the winter.

My dad told of taking the ferry across the Detroit River on Sundays to visit with my grandfather's family, who had managed to settle near Clark Park before the immigration quota took effect. How his uncle Andrew, in his early twenties, had died in the parlor of their home in Windsor – 10 Francois Street. Andrew left behind a twenty-one-year-old, three-month pregnant widow. He told of shattering the dining room mirror with an errant BB from his BB gun. And how, as the Depression wore on, his heated bedroom was rented out, leaving him to sleep in the unheated attic. Then, how they rented that house out entirely, moving to an apartment over a bank in Dearborn which was part of the family's compensation for running the local movie theater: my grandfather keeping the equipment running, my grandmother doing the cleaning, and my dad being the usher. Six days a week. How they raised George the mean goose until Thanksgiving, George becoming the Thanksgiving Day main course.

And then he spoke of the war. How he was drafted at nineteen, a physics major sophomore at Wayne State at the time. How they sent him home from boot camp for three weeks because they had to have his boots specially made – they did not stock size 12-1/2 B. How he started in the Signal Corps, teaching radar to officers. How he had offers from Lt. Colonels to join their units in Europe, but how his CO would not let him go – too valuable. How he would get totally fed up with the stupid make-work, like painting rocks and digging holes just to fill them up, finally tossing his shovel high in the air and storming off. And then how, after he chose Army OCS and headed off to medical school, the Army changed its mind mid-stream and sent him to engineering and heavy artillery. How he made Captain and was sent to the Philippines: mission to march across the neck of the Bataan Peninsula to reclaim the island. And how his commanding general, so wanting to impress General MacArthur, did not listen to his scouts, did not listen to his aides, and sent the 34th into a slaughter. How my dad lost pretty much everybody under his command. How by the second day of fighting at Zig-Zag Pass, my dad was the battalion commander, because no other officers were left. How he was five miles behind enemy lines, no communications, wearing the same uniform for 59-1/2 days straight. In the jungle. How he had to take inventory. Inventory? In the heat of battle? And how he had to answer one poor mother, whose son lay in a field dead, my dad with strict orders not to retrieve. And having to read and answer letters from that poor mother; "Can you tell me of my son? Will you send his remains home to me?" And how that carnage has only been recorded in the records as "heavy losses were sustained." And how the replacement battalion, the 37th, I believe, was given all of the glory. And of how he absolutely, violently hated General MacArthur. General MacArthur, who made the Australian troops stop distributing matchbooks with the slogan "We will return" on them, in favor of "I will return." Egotistic bastard…that's what he was to my father. I ended up making a 20-minute or so long video, scrounging the internet for original clips with my dad's voice-over.

I found one of my dad's cousins in Niagara Falls, Ontario, via genealogy. I took him to meet her... I never knew how much he missed having his "own" relatives, even though my mother's brothers and their children were always extremely welcoming. We were introduced by my second cousin David, who lives in Dublin, Ireland. It was David that told us that my father had an older sister, Martha, who died back in Scotland, at four months old. My dad cried when he heard that...I think I was piecing together a life for my father that he didn't know how to do for himself, and it seemed to give him a better sense of wholeness.

I need to insert a quick side story here: Martha. I never knew why my grandmother was so very protective and fond of me – until Martha. Oh, I knew I looked like my grandmother and thought that maybe that was the reason. No, it was Martha. Martha was born on November 28 – I was born on November 29. I was the daughter my grandmother lost. I didn't know until I learned of Martha why my grandmother wanted me to come stay with her after Brittany died. I was living my grandmother's life, and she was living it all over again.

Both my dad and Bill were getting sicker and sicker. By Thanksgiving, my father had decided he needed to sell the partially-finished airplane, and by Thanksgiving my boys had to go and spend a couple of hours trying to get their father dressed for dinner – he was that weak. My dad had a good holiday meal, took several hours that Friday showing the woman that he had contracted to sell the airplane where everything was, and sat on the family room sofa Saturday finishing the pumpkin pie. He stayed in his room on Sunday, the doctor came Monday and told me he thought my dad had maybe a week to live. Tuesday my Dad couldn't get himself out of the bathroom, and I had to call paramedics to get him back to his hospital bed in the family room.

By Wednesday morning he was disoriented, by Wednesday evening he was in a coma, and by Saturday he was dead.

I had to make sure he had his morphine for those few days. I had to keep him sedated to keep my promises to him. I had promised him two things: that he would not be in pain, and that he would not die in a hospital. I take great comfort in knowing I was able to keep those promises. That final week, though, was brutal. I slept in my clothes, on the sofa right next to him, sleeping so very lightly, always aware if he made the slightest of movements. I never got more than maybe two hours of fitful sleep at a time. I had to learn how to change the sheets under a 238-pound man, and I had to do that so often that by the end he was sleeping on juvenile sailboat sheets – that's all I had left that was clean, since I didn't have time to wash, and I had to change the sheets that often. Hospice came and bathed and shaved him, so at least didn't have to worry about trying to shave somebody else. He lost his ability to swallow, so I was rubbing morphine on his gums, between his lower lip and teeth. The very last words he said to anyone else was that he had a lot of fun in his life, but the last words he said to me was that he was sorry.

The boys were home from university, but they were spending that time with their father, who was in at least as bad a shape. Thanksgiving was on the 22nd in 2007 – my birthday was exactly one week later, on the 29th. Chris had come over on my birthday to look through old pictures, getting ready for his dad's funeral, when the call came. It was about 5 PM, and we were in the basement storeroom. Diana called to tell Chris that his dad had passed. On my birthday. And my dad was upstairs in a coma at the time… he passed 36 hours later.

I had called my mother and sister when my dad went into a coma, and they arrived on Friday, the day after my birthday. One thing I had done: my dad absolutely loved his jazz. So I had jazz playing, every minute of every day – just in case he could hear it through his coma. Loud enough that it could be heard over conversation. That Friday night my sister told me I needed to go down the hall and get a decent night's sleep – she would take up the family room vigil. When I got up early the next morning and walked down the hall, though, the first thing I noticed was that the music was turned way, way down. She had turned it down to fall asleep. I walked in the family room and realized my father was dead. My very, very first and utterly dismayed thought was "Oh no... you turned down the music. Oh No!!! Oh no..... the day the music died."

That week was a horrible whirl. Two funerals, back to back. Bill had asked that I sing at his funeral, which I sensed did not sit very well with Diana. That, and she had to call me and ask about the details of what he wanted: where was the Pine Hill Cemetery? (right down the street from where we had lived). I think she wanted to be the one that knew that stuff... she wanted to be the one with that intimate knowledge. I met Amy in the parking lot, and Bill's oncologist, who had come to pay his respects. Amy introduced me as her step-mother, and then laughed at the doctor's confused look and explained that I had been SM #1. She mentioned that Bill always loved me, to which I replied that if that were true he had a funny way of showing it. I sang the Malotte's Our Father – I knew that's what he wanted: I had sung it at his brother's funeral, at his niece's wedding –I had to sing it a capella because the pianist was unfamiliar with that famous piece. I can't remember much else about Bill's service, because then it was over to the Kirk in the Hills to plan my father's funeral. Back to back funerals. My poor boys....

I couldn't bring myself to speak at my father's funeral. Just couldn't. My sons both did, though, and they did admirable jobs.

And for both services the military showed up and did the ceremonial flag presentation. The weather turned nasty for my father's, so the servicemen very solemnly unfolded and then refolded the flag, right there in the chapel, and with great dignity presented it to us. I have it in a display case in my family room.

The boys spent a lot of time over at their dad's house, for good reason, but that left me to deal with my father's death pretty much alone. Except for Diana's daughter Deb, whom I had never met, but who called me twice to ask if there was anything she could do for me. I will always be eternally grateful for her thoughtfulness. My mother and sister left right after the services. Come Friday, Chris was driving back up to Northern for finals, and Diana was supposed to take Kevin to the airport to fly back to Virginia. Except that, for reasons I cannot recall, I ended up taking him. Or, more accurately, we were on the way – but he said he was in a lot of pain. We were on Long Lake and Woodward – I asked him about what was going on. His stomach really, really hurt. I asked him if he wanted to go to the hospital – and he said yes. I suspected appendicitis... for my son to want to go to the hospital, something had to be spectacularly wrong. So quite literally, at the corner of Long Lake and Woodward, instead of turning right to head to the airport, I turned left to head to the hospital. And yes, Kevin did have appendicitis, and yes, he did have emergency surgery that night. They didn't have any room in the adult ward, so they put him in the pediatric ward and let me sleep there, right next to him. Amy came to sit with me that night – bless her. And the next morning, when Kevin awoke, I told him I was going to rush home to take care of the animals and come right back. Diana visited him while I was running my errand – she felt terribly guilty that she dismissed his complaints and asked me later how I knew. I just knew... I just knew.

How much can a person take in a week? Two funerals and an emergency appendectomy? I'm back at the beach, standing in the typhoon. I told the boys that after it was all over, when they had the time, we would go somewhere together to regroup. We ended up taking a cruise to the Caribbean: I took my dear friend Dana, Chris took his girlfriend Kelly, and Kevin took his roommate Connor.

~

I had not been doing a very good job taking care of myself during this time. I just couldn't get comfortable sitting – that's a bit of an understatement. It became impossible to sit comfortably, and upon rising, a pain would shoot through my right hip so searingly it took my breath away. I thought it might be my leg, so I went to my prosthetist. After over a year of no success – he kept on trying to fit me like a new amputee - I decided maybe I should try something different. I went to the University of Michigan, and that man put me into a new design that was meant to offer more ischial containment. Nope. That didn't work, either. Made it even worse. I went to a hip specialist in Chicago – at Rush Medical– thinking I needed a teaching hospital doctor that might not be confined to general thinking. I went twice, but what he was telling the medical student following him around somehow just didn't seem right. Over the course of a next couple of years I ended up going to four local orthopedic surgeons, only to be told by all four of them that they would not take my case. So I was back at my original prosthetist, looking for a new socket. Back in that same stupid box: so one day, in absolute, total desperation, sat at my home office desk armed with hard foam, electric tape and my Dremel. I took the rim down here and built it up over there, tried it on, readjusted, tried it on... I was at it for hours. I finally got a shape that was the least painful and took it back to the prosthetist, telling him, "Here. Make this."

This was actually just the tail end of the story. I had been in gradually increasing levels of pain for a good decade. It was never my preference to solve my bio-mechanical issues myself, but every single attempt at enlisting the medical profession's help was a total failure. So I went online and discovered that the procedure I had when I was a toddler is rare in the United States – more common in Switzerland. It's a total knee disarticulation named a modified Gritty Stokes. I found it in some arcane medical journal online. I also discovered, actually by accident, that I had been fit with legs that had been too short for my entire life. Reason? The crests of my hip bones are not perfectly horizontal to the ground. However, prosthetists place their hands on each hip bone to decide whether the leg is the right length – for lots of people, but not me. That approach left me wearing legs that were too short for decades. So now my lower spine is halfway between mid-center and my left side. The legs I had been wearing were designed for someone that had been walking "like a normal person" for at least most of their lives… but I don't walk that way. I engage my core muscles to walk, not my localized hip muscles. So they were putting in flexion in the knee, which messed me up. I know all of this is fairly technical, but the upshot was that an entire life of legs made by people who did not stop to figure out what I was and how I walked had resulted in permanent ancillary damage. I am the only expert on what I need. End of story. That's what happens when a person happens to fall far outside of the Bell Curve. Now, after over a decade of pain-driven discovery, I absolutely will not back down. Medical professionals are not comfortable with that – not comfortable with me walking in and telling them what scrip to write. But man, once again, it's a life on the line… and that life is mine. I give no quarter anymore. Just write down what I say, please.

Even with a more comfortable socket – even with the limb being the right length for the first time in recorded history – my hip still hurt. I had managed to alleviate my searing back pain, and I had managed to alleviate an excruciating ramus. Still had a hard time sitting, still had black-out level pain straightening up. I was two out of three.

I had been bouncing around at work from location to location, and at the time of two-out-of-three I was downtown at the Ren Cen. I tried chair after chair, but nothing was good. I finally asked if I could bring in a chair from home. At first they denied my request, but after they had exhausted every available chair they relented. I ended up bringing in my own chair the week they decided to transfer me to Pontiac.

As General Motors was relentlessly sliding downhill, so went the fortunes of the EDS GM account. Parts of the business had been competitively bid, and EDS lost chunks of business to others. The environment went from collegiality and camaraderie to a grim survival mode. Gone were summer company picnics at the pool or lake. Then, to make matters worse, Hewlett Packard bought EDS.

That was a horrible move for the people of the account. Rumor had it that EDS had made a bid for HP, but HP turned around and made a counter offer, which included millions and millions of dollars in bonuses for the EDS executives and board members responsible for making the decision. It felt like a bribe – a successful bribe. HP had tried more than once to get into the services business but had failed. Buying EDS, in their minds, would place HP on par with IBM. Looked good on paper, at least. However, HP had a manufacturing culture. They had no idea what it took to run a successful services business. There are all sorts of soft-touch dynamics that go into a services industry. Personalities matter. Flexibility and reason matter, up and down the line: a lowly server technician can make or break a customer service metric. It is a business approach that does not mesh well with an assembly-line/heavily capital-intensive manufacturing mentality. I knew there was trouble ahead after reading HP's declared policy towards employee benefits – there is was, right out there online for the employee world to see: it went something like this: "It is Hewlett Packard's policy to offer no benefits to employees except as mandated by law, or as driven by competitive pressures." Wow. Way to treat people like people.

Anyway, I had a team in Pontiac made up of great people. Hard-working, go-the-extra-mile people. And then HP came in and decided we all were overpaid. All of us. I took a $42,000 a year cut, but it was one of the women that worked for me that had it worse. She was pregnant with her second child, and she was given an over 20% knock in pay. HP so graciously said they would only take 20% the first year, and the rest the following. She came in sobbing. People were so, so angry that I heard comments like, "The minute I can get another job I'm out of here." "Not only will I never buy an HP product, I will advise anyone that asks me to steer away from HP products." Granted, this was 2008-2009, and the Great Recession had hit. That being said, the way the edict came down was at least as insulting as the massive and generally immediate pay cuts. And the disappearance of the small stuff that makes things a bit better: no funds for work anniversary lunches. I had my 30th work anniversary in 2009 (because of the way I bounced around during corporate purchases/divestments, all of my GM-ATK-EDS-HP years counted), and twelve or so people I worked with chipped in to buy me lunch.

Those were horrible times at work. I was assigned to run a team trying to make things right: HP had bid on a GM sector responsible for managing all of GM's leased computers and peripherals. They got the business by really low-balling their price, thinking they could manage with one manager and two part-time contractors. Horribly understaffed, HP approached the problem exactly like Lucille Ball approached not being able to keep up with the chocolate-covered cherries assembly line. They hid all of the records of equipment they couldn't get to in made-up locations. It was only when GM was hit with multi-million-dollar bills for equipment not returned timely that the issue came to light. Yes, GM was furious. And yes, they had every reason to be. What EDS would have done would be to bite the bullet and make it right, considering it a loss-leader to be made up elsewhere. Not HP. So I got put on that time-critical assignment late and realized the way that the existing team was trying to sift through the data would never meet the time deadlines. I wrote up an Excel spreadsheet that had if-then statements so I could dismiss as Not Applicable those pieces of equipment that were within their lease window. That really narrowed down the possible culprits. By the second or third week, my approach had been programmed into the records data dump so everyone could start using it.

Flushed with initial success, I was given the hardest GM sectors. Problem was, there were no more analysts available locally to put on my team – at least, no one during normal working hours. So besides a few people I had local and during normal working hours, I was given a handful of people that agreed to work overtime from 6AM – 8AM locally, I was given a couple of people in Australia, and I was given a team in Wuhan, China. Between them and my contacts in Costa Rica and Denver, I only had the hours of 2AM to 6AM free. I would have to go over everybody's work product every day because they were all new and in training, and either got things wrong or had questions that needed answering before they could continue. I was booking 110-hour weeks.

And then there was Don. Don was a financial guy that had aspirations, and this was his baby. A multi-million-dollar penalty was riding on it. I had worked with Don on and off for years, but I had never seen this side of him before. He was a manage-by-fear-and-insult kind a guy. He would storm in and threaten to take roll-call in the office – as if people were playing hooky. He never listened to challenges people might be facing. He never walked in and said things like, "What is slowing you down? What can I do to get obstacles out of your way?" Oh no – it was Simon Legree all the way. The beatings will continue until morale improves. I thought that behavior had gone the way of the dodo bird… apparently not.

And then there was the HP guy that was responsible for that sector. He never leveled with anyone in Detroit, and that was a big mistake. His baby, so we were dependent upon his records. And we would ask for inventory by location. We got inventory by location… but then we discovered secret "locations" where he was hiding records of overdue equipment. So we thought we had that part fixed, then GM came in and did an audit of one true location and found wrong records. Why? Because the records Pete was sending us had filtered out a whole bunch of equipment that was overdue. We never got those records, and we didn't know what we didn't know. But it wasn't Pete's fault… it was the team's fault. I have never worked in such a mess before in my life.

I was so burnt out. I was just so, so exhausted working in an environment where some accusatory manager would do a fly-by to insult and threaten a team on a regular basis, and the manager that had screwed things up so very badly believed he could continue hiding his fatally flawed approach from the very people sent to bail him out. I wrote an email to the responsible VP, telling him he might want to counsel Don on his management approach, and I went back to work.

Christmas 2009 was within this hellish time period, and then 2010 rolled around. GM wasn't getting any better, and HP wasn't getting better, and the layoffs began. Wave after wave – 6,400. 9,000. A total of around 25,000. I was called in on February 23... forced to retire. I could... I had far more years than necessary to retire, and I was going to reach the magic age of 59-1/2 on May 29. I was paid through April, retired on May 29, and started receiving pension payments on June 1. You know, I was okay with that. Better me than people with no alternate sources of income and families to support. That being said, I certainly had many curve balls thrown at me. For one, Bill had left everything to Diana, with no consideration for the two sons he still had in college. Everything... the boys had nothing. And Diana was not inclined share with the boys she called "family". So I had to pick up that slack. Then I took that $42,000 a year cut. Then I was unwillingly retired. Chris was not the problem: he was nearing the end. Kevin was a first-term freshman at an expensive private college. I wrote the school to tell them of our changed financial situation but did not get a favorable response. And with all of the emotional turmoil Kevin was enduring, his grades were terrible. By the end of the second term I sat him down and told him that if he was going to fail, he could fail at Western or some other state school. I made him take out loans for half of his tuition for every remaining term, and I told him that I would pay them off if he got at least a 3.5 GPA: anything between a 3.0 and 3.5, he was on the hook for half, and anything below a 3.0, that loan was his. He only missed 3.5 once – and he still owes me that money.

~

So there I was: retired. Able to retire – check. GM and EDS pensions, a substantial 401K and three annuities. Sons successfully out of college – check. I had met my two strategic goals. I was at a bit of a loss for a while, but I was reveling in the fact that I could go out and garden without worrying whether it was going to rain on Saturday. I could get up and have a leisurely cup of coffee in my bathrobe while I read the news. I was offered the opportunity to take a Mediterranean cruise – YES!! I jumped at the chance.

As luck would have it, we were to leave from Barcelona... the day after the Icelandic volcano eruption totally disrupted air traffic. I had asked Pam Johnson if she wanted to go – she was my cabin mate. Dana went with her friends the McLaughlin's. Dana and the McLaughlin's flew out of Florida, so they made it to the ship on time. Pam and I weren't so fortunate. We did finally make it to Barcelona, but we missed the ship's departure, even though the ship stayed in port an extra day. We booked to meet up with the ship in Florence, but we missed that flight because we were late getting in to Barcelona. We ended up flying to Rome instead, but our luggage was already booked to Florence and they wouldn't let us get it. We didn't see our luggage for about ten days – it caught up with us in Venice. I bought underwear in Sorrento and a dress onboard, and alternated between the two outfits for most of the entire trip.

That being said, it was a magical trip. Although we missed Marseilles and Florence, we managed Sorrento, Venice (again), San Marino, Dubrovnik and a few Greek islands before heading home. I had taken my dad's cane with me, and it came in useful in Venice, where we probably walked a good four or five miles back to the ship. I was in a great deal of discomfort.

I spent the rest of that summer working in the garden and generally decompressing from that last brutal work assignment... all except for trying to find someone that would fix my really, *really*, painful right hip. After the four local doctors turned me down, I made copies of my x-rays and wrote both the Mayo Clinic and the University of Michigan. I explained what I knew, but said that if they were going to turn me down, please do it before I made the trips. Mayo would not comment on the case unless I showed up in person: the University of Michigan surgeon, Dr. Miracle Worker, Dr. Brian Hallstrom, took the challenge.

What I hadn't known was that the ball of my right femur was totally gone. Ground down to nothing at all. Surgery entailed stretching my hip flexor and sciatic nerve ¾" over a new metal joint. I also didn't know that bone abnormalities were what was causing my inability to bend that joint past 90%, at best. I had very successful surgery in January of 2011. I bounced back wonderfully well... and then my wrist was bothering me enough that I had that examined.

I had separated my lunate and scaphoid and dislocated my wrist bone – all of the stress of lifting myself up around that impossible right hip had taken its toll. So, unexpectedly, I had my wrist repaired in April. That left me wearing a very thin black, heat-formed-to-my-arm, heavily zippered "fist of death" for four months. It was zippered so it could come off for therapy. Again, healing wonderfully, I was all set to go by August 1st. A friend from California was coming in at the end of August and invited me to go with him up to Mackinac Island. I hadn't been there since I was young, so I eagerly said yes. He is an athletic and active guy, and we cycled around the island twice. It was a really nice mini-vacation, even though my left hip started to twinge. I thought it was because I hadn't been on a bike for a very long time. However, after six weeks the pain didn't diminish, so I went back to Dr. Hallstrom. Yes, I had blown out my left hip. When I told him how, he just smiled and said, "What a way to go."

Another January, another hip replacement. However, this time was different: I didn't have an opposite leg upon which to rely. I had to use the operated side to go up any stairs. So instead of the three-day hospital stay and home therapy, I had in-hospital intensive therapy for eleven days, after which time I was able to go up an 8" stair on my operated side. I cannot say enough about the intensive therapy unit at the University of Michigan – they are nothing but amazing heroes. And "intense" is the perfect word: I would have 90 minutes of therapy in the morning and at least that in the afternoon. I would come back and sleep through lunch, I was so exhausted. But there I was, by day eleven walking the 1,100 steps back to my room and clambering [very slowly] up that first 8" tall step into my house – on my operated side.

There's not much more left to be fixed: oh, my knee is in shambles, and that's next. And if I don't get that fixed in a timely manner, I am sure I will blow out a shoulder or two. Hopefully I will tend to the knee before the shoulders happen. Maybe by the time I die I might have one little shred of natural bone or joint left… but at this rate all bets are off.

~

I saw my mother one last time – it was at my uncle's memorial service. I had gotten there before my sister, her foster son Latrelle and son Jon. When they arrived I was surrounded by the three of them. Mom was horrible, they said. Immature, they said. Impossible. My sister stated she wished Mom would die. Stating that when my father said the deal was I would take care of him/she would take care of mom, that she thought he liked her. I tried to keep my mother away from Tracy so Tracy could decompress, but I was having a difficult time getting through to her. So I finally let it out. I told my mother she was self-absorbed. That she was very difficult to be around. That she thought only of herself. She didn't listen – or so I thought. I guess it did sink in, because I heard later it made her cry.

Just before everyone was going to leave, my mother gave me her batting-her-eyes, very simpy, "But I love you," – that was the phrase she always said to evade hard questions or to change the subject. This time, I simply turned to her and said, "You don't know how." She looked at me very startled, and I looked at my sister and asked, "Should I stop now?" My sister said yes, and I said nothing more.

"You don't know how." Those were the last words I ever said to my mother.

EPILOGUE

I'm going to end my saga here. Oh, I got bored and became treasurer of a local non-profit. I did that for four years, and then I found a little one-day-a-week job for a very small manufacturing company for a couple of years. I am not the type to be content simply walking my dogs. Not yet. My one son has started a business, and I agreed to be his accounting manager until it gets big enough to need someone willing to work more hours. Four years into that, and it's going well. I also started a publishing company.

My next challenge will be refocusing myself to accept a future life that by necessity will be less productive. That being said, I can look back at what I have accomplished, cross my arms and nod my head once with a little satisfied grin – not bad. Not bad at all, for a disabled single mother.

~

My younger son asked me to include some of my life's lessons, so for those I have not yet covered, here goes.

(1) No matter what, the truth will generally, eventually come out. Hiding, obfuscating and/or hoping the issue will just go away is a poor strategy. Rotten fish do not improve with age.

(2) Don't be afraid of the hard stuff – in fact, don't be afraid of much at all. The only thing that becomes a crisis is something from which you cannot recover. And there is rarely an instance of not being able to recover.

(3) Face everything head-on, but be flexible enough to figure out another way if you hit a brick wall. Head-bashing is generally counter-productive.

(4) Balance is everything, especially balance in priorities. My example here would be money: yes, everybody needs money. Money is required for personal maintenance. But then, so is toothpaste, if you want to do a good job of it. Money should be considered just that: not more, not less. It's not crass or lowly to understand money is a requirement, but it also is not a good measure of who and what you are. Keep the emotion out of it: money is glorified toothpaste.

(5) Be strong enough to stand entirely on your own if need be. That's the only sure-fire way you can be strong enough for someone else, if that's required. Trust me on this one – I know there's a lot of literature out there that says the opposite. Poppycock. Be strong. Vulnerability is vastly over-rated.

(6) Understand that practically everything is a double-edged sword. If you understand the flip-side – if you can think through the unintended consequences - you will always make the best available choice. Most issues can be traced to unintended consequences. Single-mindedness might be good for the instant moment, but it's rarely good for the long-term.

(7) You should consider yourself successful at life if you can weather all that life throws at you and come out emotionally whole. The most tragic thing to witness is people breaking in the face of adversity – people that lose, or shut out, a part of themselves forever.

(8) Finally, some of my best advice: if you are going to be stubborn, you better be right.

And with that, gentle reader, I close.

ABOUT THE AUTHOR

Wendy Sura Thomson lives in Bloomfield Hills, Michigan, with her two beloved Irish Setters. She enjoys gardening, painting, knitting, writing, and remodeling her home. She has since re-joined Mensa, still sits on a non-profit organization's investment committee, occasionally sings around town, and has actually replaced that knee.

Made in the USA
Lexington, KY
10 December 2019